Śiva in the Forest of Pines

In memory of Victor Turner,
pioneer of the processual

Śiva in the Forest of Pines

An Essay on Sorcery and Self-Knowledge

Don Handelman
David Shulman

OXFORD
UNIVERSITY PRESS

OXFORD
UNIVERSITY PRESS

YMCA Library Building, Jai Singh Road, New Delhi 110 001

Oxford University Press is a department of the University of Oxford. It furthers the University's objective of excellence in research, scholarship, and education by publishing worldwide in

Oxford New York

Auckland Bangkok Buenos Aires Cape Town Chennai
Dar es Salaam Delhi Hong Kong Istanbul Karachi Kolkata
Kuala Lumpur Madrid Melbourne Mexico City Mumbai
Nairobi Sao Paulo Shanghai Taipei Tokyo Toronto

Published in India
by Oxford University Press, New Delhi

First published 2004

ISBN 0 19 566550 3

Typeset in Naurang
by Guru Typograph Technology, Dwarka, New Delhi 110 045
Printed by Sai printopack Pvt. Ltd, Delhi 110 032
Published by Manzar Khan, Oxford University Press
YMCA Library Building, Jai Singh Road, New Delhi 110 001

Contents

Acknowledgements

This book is a sequel or companion to our previous work, *God Inside Out: Śiva's Game of Dice*. It emerged directly out of the problems and perceptions that came into play in that volume but takes matters in a rather different direction. Like the earlier book, this one is rooted, at least implicitly, in ongoing fieldwork experiences in south India (Tirupati and more recently Vizianagaram) and, explicitly, in an ongoing conversation between the two authors. The story of the Dāruvana is the richest and most complex of all narratives about Śiva and, as such, provides scope for sustained interpretation nourished by many distinct vantage points and different strands of the tradition.

Initially we considered writing a book that would deal with the entire, vast corpus of texts relating to the Forest of Pines. We spent a year or two reading widely in the Sanskrit *purāṇic* texts and secondary literature and also taught a seminar together at the Hebrew University using fresh translations of classical Sanskrit as well as Tamil and Telugu versions. We want to thank the participants in that seminar for many lively and insightful discussions; in particular, we owe much to Carol Kidron, Melila Helner-Eshed, Dror Helner-Eshed, Nir Avieli, Dvora Amir, and Yohanan Grinshpon.

Eventually we came to feel that the Dāruvana narrative in itself has little integrity as a frame for coherent study—that the hundreds of texts that fit the narrative pattern come from periods and contexts too diverse to be lumped together as a single corpus. Structuralist selection and condensation à la Lévi-Strauss are inappropriate here. We therefore elected to concentrate on a much more delimited set of texts that do, arguably, have the integrity we sought—the long Tamil versions of the myth recorded at three major temple sites (Kancipuram, Cidambaram, and Tirunelveli) from a period after the mature crystallization of the

Śaiva Siddhânta system in the far south (fourteenth century). It is our contention that this central corpus of philosophical texts is clearly continuous with the narrative or 'mythic' texts about Śiva and helps us to understand the conceptual field within which the latter were articulated. We also argue for a new reading of the Tamil Śaiva Siddhānta system, one rather remote from earlier syntheses in this domain, which still bears the imprint of apologetic reformulations of major premises. We have also explored, to a more limited degree, still earlier Śaiva materials from the Tamil country insofar as they bear upon the texts or temples under discussion.

Each of the first three chapters takes one Tamil text, given in complete translation, as its base and proceeds to tease out its meaning. The reader who wants only the texts, literally rendered, is invited to dispense with our commentaries. A fourth chapter offers a comparative excursus from the northern reaches of the Tamil region and what is today southern Andhra Pradesh. Here we find a distinct, but not unrelated, version of what happened to Śiva in the Forest of Pines. We feel that this comparison offers a useful contrast and also links the broadly southern and north Indian strands of Śaiva myth. An appendix gives without comment a translation of one major Sanskrit version of the Dāruvana story, *Kūrma-purāṇa* 2.37, which some may find evocative by way of contrast and perhaps useful for future explorations.

We thank the various audiences who listened and responded to earlier versions of these chapters: at the University of Wisconsin, Madison; the University of Cologne; Department of Anthropology, Stockholm University, and Department of Anthropology, Uppsala University; Jangama Center, Bomballa, Australia; Mishkenot Shaananim in Jerusalem. Sascha Ebeling graciously provided us with Tamil material relating to Tirunelveli. We are grateful to the Museum für Indische Kunst, Berlin, and its then curator, Dr Lore Sander, for permission to reprint Plates 1 and 2. A special thanks to Anne Monius for lucid and encouraging responses. David Smith very graciously provided us with a copy of *Cidambara-māhātmya*, and John Loud generously offered a draft of his translation of Umāpati's *Koyiṟ-purāṇam*. Alexis Sanderson shared his vast knowledge of Śaiva texts and gave tantalizing hints of his understanding of the Cidambaram cult after a visit there in 1997. Velcheru Narayana Rao responded (as always) with original and provocative insights to our translation of the Tirunelveli text and to a lecture on the Dāruvana in 1997. Isabelle Nabokov discussed the story of Śiva's *brahmahatyā* with us over many happy occasions, usually near lakes and streams. Joyce B. Flueckiger read early versions of all the chapters and shared (or shaped) the early, formative moments in Tirupati. Nita Shechet pared away excess and listened with her perfect pitch. To these and other interlocutors and readers we humbly state our indebtedness; we hope they will recognize their impact on our thinking. Don Handelman completed his work on this volume during his appointment as a Senior Fellow at Collegium Budapest Institute for Advanced Study, 2001–2.

We are aware that the interpretations set forth here cut across much of the received wisdom about south Indian Śaiva religion. It is, of course, always possible to argue that the domains of ritual praxis, 'mythic' narrative, the cultic organization of individual temples, and abstract philosophical investigation are bounded off from one another, and that each follows a separate logic. It is even possible to conceive of such radical compartmentalization within a single person as he or she moves through different contexts. As already stated, the roles of mythographer, ritualist, and philosopher often merged in the great scholar-poets of the late-medieval Tamil *mutts*. We have read with care and attention the works of the outstanding modern scholars who have explored the southern Śaivâgama and its extensions and, as the notes will reveal, we are deeply indebted to them for many insights. We have, however, proceeded from a working hypothesis of a synthetic order—the sense that the above-listed domains actually reflect, replicate, and elaborate upon one another in regular patterns. Southern Śaiva 'myth' should not be allegorized or rationalized, for such modes are deeply foreign to its nature. Praxis, too, requires serious interpretation and extrapolation, beyond the literal statements of its canon. The changes Śiva undergoes in the Forest of Pines are very close to the daily discipline of the Śaiva ritualist. Indeed, the former may be, among other things, a vivid articulation of the latter; or the ritual could be seen as the practical and necessary consequence of a metaphysics embodied in Śiva's stories. Medieval metaphysicians have drawn in these linkages, but their transparency has often been lost in modern translations. For this reason as well, we have insisted on providing the reader with complete versions of the narrative texts, to be read (slowly) as richly textured wholes. Rereading also has its own rewards, and we have not hesitated to repeat textual segments through the chapters. These texts, including, of course, such philosophical masterpieces as Umāpati's *Tiruvaruṭpayaṉ* (with its sixteenth-century commentary by Nirampav aḻakiya Tecikar) and Śivâgrayogin's commentary on the *Śiva-jñāna-bodha*, resonate deeply with one another and often deliberately quote, paraphrase, imitate, engage with, or play upon one another. As in other musical events, it is worth attending to the ensemble.

Note on Pronunciation and Diacritics

Long vowels are double the length of short vowels. We mark the short Dravidian vowels *ĕ* and *ŏ*. Diphthongs (*e*, *o*, *ai*, *au*) are always long in Sanskrit and Sanskrit-derived words.

ṭ, *ṭh*, *ḍ*, *ḍh*, *ṇ*, and *ḷ* are retroflex, pronounced by slightly curling the tip of the tongue backwards as it touches the palate. Tamil *ḻ* is a retroflex liquid slightly resembling American pronunciation of *r* in *girl*.

Inter-vocalic plosives tend to become fricatives in Tamil: *c* is always pronounced like English *ch* in Sanskrit; in Tamil it is pronounced like *s* or *sh* when word-initial and like English *ch* when doubled. All geminate plosives are voiceless and double in length in Tamil. After a nasal, Tamil *k* becomes *g*, *c* becomes *j*, *ṭ* becomes *ḍ*, *t* becomes *d*, and *p* becomes *b*.

Aspirates (*kh*, *gh*, *ch*, *jh*, etc.) are pronounced with an audible puff of breath accompanying the plosive.

Modern place names are also without diacritic marking.

Illustrations

Into the Forest

A man walks off with a secret treasure.
Was the other sleeping
or not there?[1]

Introduction

Here are the events. A god wanders into a forest of Himalayan pine trees and becomes lost. Human beings of varying degrees of taste and discernment, as is generally the case with human beings, inhabit this forest and encounter this god. The meeting changes both parties. The human side, in its male aspect, begins to experience, through hate, something that could be called love, perhaps for the first time. The female aspect, freed from shame or restraint, turns fertile and generative. The god becomes more alive, which is to say, more full of self, more present, in deeper or more rapid movement. Deeper—since this is a process of involution and spin that takes the visible form of dance. This internal movement within the god and his cosmos is also, however, an exorcism, unlocking ensorcelled pieces of self.

In outline, we have here the story of Śiva's emergence as the dancer, Naṭarāja—the most salient of his forms in south India, and the most familiar to us from his iconography. No great Śaiva temple in the south is without this Dancer; but Cidambaram, the original site of the dance, has a special fame and prominence. A considerable theology strives to explicate this dance, which is known as the Ānanda-Tāṇḍava, the 'dance of rapture.'[2] Yet *tāṇḍava* has, from quite ancient times, unsettling connotations of wildness and destruction;[3] and surprisingly, the episode

[1] *Tiruvaruṭpayaṉ* of Umāpati civâcāriyar, 7.6.

[2] See Smith 1996; Gaston 1982; Coomaraswamy 1957; Zimmer 1972: 151–5.

[3] See, e.g., *Mudrā-rākṣasa* 1.2 (traditionally referred to the *tāṇḍava*); also

itself turns out to involve sorcery, exorcism, and black magic, the proper context for the dance. A rich medieval philosophical corpus, known in the Tamil area as Śaiva Siddhânta, 'the conclusive truth about Śiva,' works out a systemic understanding of the intuitions present in this story and other related texts.[4]

This essay seeks to illumine and interpret four classical south Indian texts that set out complementary versions of this most difficult philosophical narrative: the story of Śiva's adventures in the Dāruvana or Dārukāvana, Forest of Pines. There are no Himalayan pines in the southern deltas or in the rocky plateau of Rayalasima, to the north and west of the Tamil country, yet our texts insist on locating this story just here. We begin with the *Kanta-purāṇam* of Kacciyappa civâcāriyar—more precisely, with the compendium of Śaiva mythology in its sixth book, the *Takṣa-kāṇṭam*, which may be seen as a canonical statement of Śaiva narrative in Tamil. As such, its version of the forest tale serves as our base text. Kacciyappar belongs to the fifteenth or sixteenth century, according to our best guess on the basis of fairly insubstantial evidence,[5] and to the Kumarakkoṭṭam shrine in Kancipuram, in the north of the Tamil region.

We then turn to one of Kacciyappar's sources, the *Koyiṟ-purāṇam* of Umāpati civâcāriyar (early fourteenth century), on Cidambaram, the site that most strongly claims the story as its own. We read this text in the light of the Tamil Śaiva Siddhânta canon that was crystallizing at this time; Umāpati was a central figure in this process and the author of many important works, including the remarkable, laconic *Tiruvaruṭpayaṉ*, which we frequently cite (together with its eloquent commentary by Nirampav aḻakiya Tecikar of the sixteenth century). Taken together with the great Sanskrit commentaries by Śivâgrayogin on the *Śiva-jñāna-bodha* (mid-sixteenth century), these works of Umāpati civâcāriyar, Kacciyappa civācāriyar, and Nirampav aḻakiya Tecikar—the latter two possibly near-contemporaries—offer an internally resonant, well-integrated summary of southern Śaiva metaphysics in a particularly creative period, from the early fourteenth to the mid-sixteenth centuries. In this

---

Cilappatikāram 6.39–43, 28.67–75, for Śiva's dance in the cremation ground, known as *kōṭu kōṭṭiyāṭal*. See also Kaimal 1999: 402–4; Smith 1996: 3; Kulke 1970: 108.

[4] Strictly speaking, we should follow Sanderson and speak of 'Tamil Śaiva Siddhânta' as a corpus distinct from the more ancient Śaiva Siddhânta stream in Kashmir and elsewhere. See Gengnagel 1996: 13.

[5] See Shulman 1980: 331–2.

sense, our essay is focused on the interpretation of major themes occupying Śaiva poet-philosophers from the Tamil country during this period of some two hundred years.

By far the most elaborate version of the Dāruvana story, however, comes later and from much farther south than Cidambaram, from the ancient Śiva temple at Tirunelveli, where Nĕllaiyappap Piḷḷai composed his *Tirunĕlvelittalapurāṇam* in the early nineteenth century. His section on the Forest of Pines, studied in our third chapter, is an encyclopedic attempt to synthesize and make sense of the rich classical materials on this story available to him. We give complete, literal translations from Tamil of all these versions.

A concluding section extends the compass north to Andhra, the Telugu domain. Roughly contemporaneous with Kacciyappa civâcāriyar was the great Telugu poet Śrīnātha, who gives us a radical understanding of the Forest of Pines in his *Hara-vilāsamu* (*c.* 1400). The story is also, however, localized at Lepaksi in Rayalasima, one of the great Andhra temples. We explore this Telugu refashioning of the ancient story in the light of concerns proper to the context of medieval Andhra. In a purely geographical sense, our discussion thus moves from the plains of northern Tamil Nadu to the deltaic coast of the Tamil heartland, thence to the Tamraparni valley in the far south, and finally back north to Rayalasima and the rocky Andhra-Tamil border. Each of these ecological and historical contexts calls for explication.

More ancient sources for this story, mostly in Sanskrit, exist in some profusion, and we call upon them throughout this essay, but it is well to bear in mind that our primary focus is on a relatively cohesive, thematically integrated set of versions from the far south of the subcontinent, and from the later medieval period. It is the systemic character of this set of colourful tellings that allows us to generalize a latent conceptual context, susceptible to analysis by careful listening to the components of texture in its many forms. Phono-aesthetic, lexical, metrical, semantic, syntactic, figurative-poetic, iconic, and meta-communicative choices govern the expressivity we have called 'systemic;' and it is important to listen, as well, for the meanings that are embedded in silence. Our translations seek to reproduce and convey something of these mutually reinforcing dimensions.

Driving the analysis is a series of questions, some of which may be formulated as our introduction to the *Kanta-purāṇam* text. Thus: Can a god be ensorcelled, that is, blocked in self, inhabited by an alien persona or several such personae, and therefore 'appear' heteronomous, reduced, or, worse still, mad? What space does this god inhabit, in particular in relation to the surfaces in which he becomes visible or accessible to others, to us, or to himself? Is there a cost to his surfacing? Do pieces of godhead inhabit differentially situated or imagined depths? Does god move or, for that matter, rest? What does it mean for us to accelerate an intra-divine movement? More generally, is god restless? Empty? Full? Can he be exorcised—and if so, of whom? By whom? *For* whom?

These questions, like their potential answers, arise easily and naturally from our base text; indeed, to articulate them as one or the other—as metaphysical puzzle or intelligible conclusion—may be a matter of arbitrary choice. On another level, both formulations are possibly secondary to a kind of doing, for example in the Kanci temple where the poet first sang his narrative or at Cidambaram, where the ensorcelment actually takes place. A question, then, of a different order: What are we doing when we tell this story?

Kanta-purāṇam, *Takṣa-kāṇṭam*: 6.13.30–127

[The setting is Dakṣa's sacrifice, from which Śiva has been excluded. The sage Dadhīci arrives to protest this exclusion and to tell the tales of Śiva, including his visit to the Forest of Pines.]

Long ago, none of the sages in the Forest of Pines had any love for God. They performed endless rites, certain this was the way to freedom, with its delights. And they tortured their bodies for nothing: they were very determined. This went on a long time. Śiva, who breathes life into life itself, was sitting on Mount Kailāsa; he had the goddess Umā as half himself, which does away with all deficiency. But he knew everything there was to know about those sages and their ignorant ways. He wanted to do something about it. First he remembered Viṣṇu, the god who knows all; and Viṣṇu, sensing that he was being summoned, left the serpent on which he sleeps[6] and came straightaway to Kailāsa. Nandikeśvara, the gatekeeper, announced his arrival and ushered him into the palace, where

[6] Ādiśeṣa, the cosmic snake with a thousand heads, spread out like a bed on the ocean of milk.

he bowed at Śiva's feet. As he stood there, Śiva let him know, through signs, what he was thinking. Then, taking Viṣṇu's golden hand in his, Śiva, auspicious and good as he is, got up and left the mountain.

Looking at Viṣṇu, he said: 'You remember that femininity that once, long ago, you assumed so naturally? Do it again now.' So Viṣṇu instantly transformed his body, usually dark as the monsoon clouds, into that of a bewitchingly beautiful woman, who walked beside the god. Meanwhile, Śiva himself assumed a form of limitless beauty,[7] so marvellous that even Umā, the great mistress of illusion, would have grown faint had she but seen it. Is there anyone capable of articulating the real quality of form that our Father, the three-eyed god, takes on? That, in any case, is how they entered the forest. Viṣṇu was drinking in god's beauty with his eyes, painfully smitten with desire and confusion, weak with love—but somehow or other, that liquid love helped him to keep moving. Perhaps that was the day that they started to call him Māl (in Tamil)—the Bewildered.

So Śiva entered the Forest of Pines, where the sages were living. But first he took off the skin of the Man-Lion, that he wears.[8] He was completely naked, with three eyes, a trident, and a begging bowl in his hand. Viṣṇu the Bewildered clung to his side, and the whole world had reason to be amazed. No sooner were they in the forest than Śiva turned to Māl and said, 'Go to where the sages are clustered together, with no thought of us. Bewilder them. Disturb their vows and rituals. Then come back to me.'

Śiva walked on, but Māl, sent on his own mission, found his way to the clearing[9] where the sages gathered for their rites, since they believed[10] that two things alone—rituals and *tapas*—would produce freedom. 'He' was shooting coquettish glances as if the god of desire had multiplied himself infinitely and was shooting his intoxicating arrows, and, of course, when the sages saw 'him' they were overwhelmed with longing and at once quit their discipline and all ritual

[7] According to the commentator, the kind of beauty indicated by this word (*yāṇar*) becomes new and fresh with each act of embrace and union.

[8] Note this iconic idiosyncracy (Śiva draped in the skin of Viṣṇu-Narasiṃha, the Man-Lion).

[9] *avai* = *sabhā*.

[10] This belief (*kŏḷkai*) is identified by the commentary with Pūrva-mīmāṃsā.

activities. Drunk, seething, sweating, they stood there, as their inner feeling[11] melted away—like the wood-apple eaten by an elephant.[12] Through the goodness of our Father, Poison-Throat, they stared at the striking body that Viṣṇu had assumed; they threw off all rules and norms; like locusts drawn to a flame, they clustered around 'him.'

They were a bit incoherent. 'From this world?' they asked. 'From heaven? Brahmā's world? The paradise of desire? Viṣṇu's place? Where, that is, do you live? Are you the one—the ravishing Mohinī—who routed the demons and helped the gods? Is there anyone who can know you? Tell us a little.' And so on. They were really in distress, scorched like a garland of flower-buds fallen into fire—the fire of being separate. Those incomparable sages were more dead than alive.

Now let us follow Śiva's course. After sending off Viṣṇu, he took himself, with trident and begging bowl, to the street where the sages were living. He was singing the Veda, with its melodious tones, and he looked like a Beggar—though he is the breath of life itself, and the true knowledge that happens inside. When the wives of the sages heard that music, they wondered who had come there; their eyes longed to see him. 'Let's go, quickly,' they said, rushing in crowds into the street, where they caught sight of god.

And seeing him, they sank into desire. The true knowledge that happens inside was mingled with confusion.[13] Their breath trembled and grew faint. There is a very deep ocean that is called 'wanting god,' and they were drowning in it. Shall I tell you a little of what they did?

Some said, 'We see no ornaments on his body. No sooner did we hear his pure music than we fell into desire. This must mean his appearance is a game.'

'We know how the master acts. Stealing in here, begging for alms—none of this is real. The point is to drive women mad, despite their gentle nature.'

[11] *uṇarvu*—intuitive knowledge or feeling.

[12] The elephant is said to swallow the wood-apple whole and to excrete it whole, having digested its inner parts without changing the outer form.

[13] *māḻka*—the verb suggests loss and destruction, but also bewilderment, fascination, and the confusion/mingling of sexuality.

Some professed pity. 'It's all very well, but surely there must be some woman who would clothe this Beggar, give him food, and find unbroken delight—by marrying him.'

'But he has come here, to our flawless forest. It seems he wants no other village. Must be our good fortune, the fruit of early *tapas*.'

'He doesn't need anyone. That's the truth. But we would touch him, like those who worship his feet, in longing.'

Meanwhile, jewels, bracelets of gold, bracelets of conch, and all their fine clothes were slipping off their bodies, right in the middle of the street, as they stared at him. Embarrassed, afraid, they wrung their hands. They were bewildered, beautiful, disturbed. Desire was pricking every part of their bodies; their pores were flowing with juices, like milk pouring from the breast.

Some left slavery[14] behind. They knew they were seeing the ultimate state, and they performed acts of love, in passion: they let their sarees fall, and their bracelets, as they stared straight at the lord's penis,[15] and worshipped it.

Some gave him food—rice, milk, and curds, but their bracelets fell in as well—in their overwhelming hunger for our Father, who had come there, radiant with youth. 'Who could fault us,' they said, 'for serving him naked, when he himself came here naked (to say nothing of that third eye on his forehead)? If our sarees fall, let them fall.'

Others were saying, 'Shame has gone, and confusion come. Our heart is aflame. We have abandoned restraint, life itself is leaving, the body dying. Can he give us back our breath?'

Some decided he was begging for rice, so they approached him with some—but because they were burning with fierce desire, it turned to ashes in their hands, and they found themselves smeared with it—like Śiva himself.

Others tried to block the gift. 'He's only trying to inflame us with that maddening form. Even if we fall at his feet and beg him to take us, he will show no mercy. In fact, he'll soon be off. Don't give him alms.'

[14] *pācam* = *pāśa*, 'the noose'—the state of existential bondage, one of the three primary Śaiva categories (with *pati*, 'god,' and *paśu*, 'embodied beings').

[15] *kocam*, Skt *kośa*—literally 'sheath,' 'outer layer.'

They had lost their pearl necklaces, and the sandal paste on their skin was burnt off with all their body's juices. Prey to desire at every pore, they gave up all presence of mind and, indeed, all other burdens, starting with their gilded belts.

Some concluded: 'He has a trident; an eye of flames on his forehead; long matted hair; a red body; the crescent moon. He must be the god who once swallowed poison from the sea. A single drop spilled from within this huge sign, the *liṅga*, of our father, into the navel [of Viṣṇu] and became Brahmā, the Creator of the world.'

Bracelets, rings, banyan leaves, golden sarees—all washed away from these women, who were suddenly just like Viṣṇu in his ravishing female form that was wreaking havoc with the sages.[16] Their eyes were trapped in his lovely long hair, like a deer in a hunter's snare; they could not reclaim them. In their confusion they offered the rice they were bringing him in large ladles—to the empty air. Utterly confused, they failed to see through his visible form to the true form of Black-Throat, who bewilders the goose chasing the parrot.[17] So some brought the rice they had lovingly cooked to that external apparition that was really all light inside light. They saw god's body; they experienced desire; their clothes slipped away. In shame, they tried to cover the sign of their femininity; then they tried to cover their eyes—but their hands weren't enough: it was like trying to cover up space itself.

'You've come here as our guest,' they said. 'There are delicious things to eat, the stuff of immortality. Taste them, please: stay a moment. Then you can go. Put down your begging bowl and the trident. Come into our homes. There is always plenty of milk and butter and other food. Stay with us, for our sake. You are beautiful to the point of driving everyone who sees you, female or male, to distraction. What is this business of begging everywhere, with that maddening bowl?'

Some were sighing, breathing hard. 'Now that we have seen you, we are worn out by wanting you: it is our one passion. Our clothes

[16] This verse (63) breaks into *śleṣa*=paronomasia; *caṅku*=conch bracelets, and the ocean conch; *āḻi* = ring, and the ocean. The clothes and ornaments are washed away in waves, as consciousness divides into two superimposed linguistic registers.

[17] Brahmā chasing Tilottamā? [see commentary of Ci. Kaṇapatipiḷḷai]. Or Rati, riding the parrot?

have fallen off. This is it, the right moment, here: make love to us. The sages who live in this rich forest won't come back now. Don't worry about a thing. Here's the bed. Come in for just a minute.' And others added: 'You may be thinking that we are married women, that we belong to the sages. That's why you won't talk to us, or come close. But really: will any evil find you, as it might others? Come on, take us.'

And some went right up to him and whispered, 'Either give us back our clothes or satisfy our wishes. Even if you don't want to say anything, just come into us, love us. Show us your sign.'[18] They followed after him. 'This body of yours—is it for begging, or for killing all the women around? Tell us that. Even when we say to you straight, "*Please* fuck us," you don't comfort us in our turbulence, and you certainly don't bring us any pleasure. Everyone says you are known as Śaṅkara—"the one who makes everyone happy"—but this seems to be a misnomer.'

And there were some women—wild and good—who were scrutinizing his penis with a subtle intensity, as if they were devoting themselves to it, though they then bashfully rejoined the others, standing with bowed heads.

They thronged the streets. They had lost everything—sarees, bracelets, jewels, shame, womanly restraint; they could barely hold on to life itself as they followed him, in turmoil. He, meanwhile, was striding through the lanes, burning his golden feet. In one spot, he would play the vina; in another, he sang the Vedas; elsewhere he recited texts about Śiva. He would expose himself in one house, beg for alms at the next; occasionally, like one of his lovers, he would sing his own praises. The streets were flooded with flowers—those the women had flung at his feet, the wreaths that had fallen from their bodies, along with their bracelets and jewels, and the flower-arrows that the god of desire was shooting everywhere.

Life flows through bodies, and god lives in the feeling that flows through lives—and now god had put on that marvellous form and come begging for alms. If Viṣṇu the Bewildered, were even to think of him in that mode, he would grow faint with longing, so you can imagine what others might do. He, our king, churned the women,

[18] Or, taunting: what is that *linga* of yours for? *kuṟippu* = hint, intention, sign; cf. *kuṟi* = mark, *linga*.

delicate and beautiful as they were—dark eyes, red lips, glowing bodies—as if he were a thousand churning-rods ramming through their erstwhile modesty. And he had limitless forms, each one different and entirely magical. They loved him as he stood there, flawless, in the long street, and loving him they all became pregnant and without pangs or other sorrow gave birth to 48,000 worthy children. It all happened in the blink of an eye—the intense desire, then the birth of these children who immediately bowed at god's feet and praised him with a love informed by wisdom. 'Meditate on us,' he said to them, 'as you give yourselves to *tapas*, here.' And they listened to him, to the god with the moon on his brow and long, black matted locks; they offered homage, took their leave, and went off—all 48,000 of them—to a spot where they could engage in *tapas* with lucid hearts.

Śiva walked on—the god who had once received a thousand lotuses from Viṣṇu, and who had given the latter his discus.[19] Those born as his children were doing *tapas*, but the flood of mad women still flowed around him. Viṣṇu, now a soft woman himself, knew it was time, and rejoined him—like the dark Yamunā flowing into the white Ganges—bringing along all the great sages who had been following 'him.' They were stumbling along, falling, and because of their bad karma Black-Throat hid his own ancient form from them all and showed himself to them in some other form.

At that moment, when Viṣṇu, as a woman, reached the side of Black-Throat, those sages noticed their wives. 'They have been following someone, too, just like us,' they said. 'They have lost their clothes, and all sense of shame. They've gone beyond. What is more, it seems they saw this fellow—and fell in love with him.' They had been devoted to the way of silence, but now, as their infatuation with Viṣṇu lifted a little, and they observed the miserable state to which their well-bred wives had been reduced, they were troubled. Full of self-pity, wailing, but still ruled by pride, they stood helplessly, holding on as best they could to the life they still had within them.

'This singular woman—bracelets of gold, her sex draped with gold—came to us, ruined our discipline, and made us confused. And that singular man came, freed our wives of all restraint, and produced

[19] Viṣṇu offered Śiva a thousand lotus flowers each day. One day he was one flower short, so he offered one of his lotus-shaped eyes instead; for this gift, Śiva granted Viṣṇu the discus weapon.

a deep fascination.What weird game[20] is this?' Then they thought, and they knew: 'The one who shattered their self-control must be the three-eyed god who lives on Kailāsa; and the one who came as a woman to disengage us from *tapas* must be Viṣṇu the Bewildered, who devours the world at the end of time.[21] But Viṣṇu didn't come to us of his own accord: he was playing with us, at god's command. And what has he done, anyway? Our discipline has been overturned: so be it. We can make good what was lost. But is there any way to undo the stigma that attaches to Śiva? He came here to the Forest of Pines as if he were begging, holding a skull for a begging-bowl in his hands, and he has devastated the women's self-control. The whole world—sun, moon, space itself—is full of his shame. He put on a guise,[22] and he also sent Viṣṇu against us. It's all his doing. That's Three-Eyed Śiva for you, with his garland of sweet cassia flowers.' They were working themselves up into a fiery anger, the rage of arrogance.

Sparks flew from their eyes as they turned to the women, their breasts rising like golden hills. 'Just who do you think you're following? You've gone beyond all control. The best thing would be for you to die. But if you can't manage that, at least go home.' The women heard them and thought: 'Anyone who has seen Him here is now free and *cannot* die. As for the sages—they must be crazy.' Taking Śiva's luminous form into themselves, and moved by his unbroken goodness, they returned to their houses in the long street.

Similarly moved by that goodness, once they had gone home, Viṣṇu, who had become a woman, standing right next to Śiva the Pillar,[23] assumed a male form. All the gods, from Brahmā on down, came to see the transformation. As they arrived, the sages were studying Śiva—the first and endless god—with real hatred. 'Let's perform a violent sacrifice and kill him,' they said. In their innocence, their ignorance, they conspired together to produce an evil fire.[24] It was a shameful rite. From the midst of the flames leapt a cruel

[20] *māyam* [< *māyā*].

[21] Viṣṇu swallows up the universe during the *pralaya* destruction, and re-emits it at the time of creation.

[22] *veṭam* = *veṣa-*

[23] Sthāṇu.

[24] *tī makam*—usually defined, as in the commentary here, as a rite of sorcery (*abhicāra*).

tiger, unimaginably terrifying, with a thunderous growl, gaping mouth, eyes burning with rage, and sharp claws on its bright red paws. They worshipped this beast and ordered him: 'Go put an end to God.' Quickly it sprang at Śiva, the god with eyes of fire, and with a flick of his hand Śiva flayed it and draped himself in its skin, as suited him.

With the tiger gone, a lethal hatchet emerged from the fire, and the terrible sages sent it against Śiva—but as soon as it approached him, the god grabbed it in his hand, held it high, and said, 'Become our weapon.' Then a doe was born in the flames, and the sages incited it against Śiva; it jumped into the sky, crying a long harsh cry that threatened to destroy the world, until Śiva brought into play his compassionate gaze, to protect all living beings. His gaze included the doe, to whom he spoke: 'Come stay here, close to our ear, where you can give voice to your cry.' And gently he raised the doe high in his golden left hand.

Now there were snakes, innumerable, hissing with rage, that arose from the fire and were sent by the evil sages to attack Śiva. Elegantly he draped them around himself, joining them to the snakes that were already there, hiding from Viṣṇu's bird.[25] They suited him perfectly with their slippery sheen. From the midst of the fire, like streaks of lightning, a violent flood of ghoulish creatures came pouring out. 'Break the power of Black-Throat,' the sages ordered them, so off they went, roaring, rocking the cosmos—but Śiva just looked at them and said, 'You must never leave us. You are now my army.' He can, after all, do away with your bad karma, if you come to him. He is always there first.

So they bowed to him and stood beside him as his troops. By now the sages were even more furious. Out of their sacrificial flame there arose a white skull, laughing horribly, as if to swallow the world. They sent it at him, and again Three-Eyes gently kept the world alive: he took the skull in his delicate hand and lifted it into his deep red hair. 'Now do what you must do,' he said.

The sages were really perplexed. They stared at him, unstained as he was, with the skull on his head. They called up their trusted mantras, full of truth, and ordered them to put an end to all this.

[25] Garuḍa feeds on snakes.

And these mantras became a small drum pounding out a beat that could deafen the entire universe. 'Boom, boom . . .'—everyone and everything heard it, on earth and in heaven, and only by Śiva's grace did they all survive, though they were maddened by it, like serpents listening to thunder. The drum drew close to Śiva; he took it in another of his hands and said, 'Murmur in *my* ear.' As he held it up, the sages, for all their cleverness, were amazed—for there was no one who could do that.

They were still driven by a murderous rage. They didn't know that this wasn't right for Śiva, the only one who brings things to an end. Besides, the karma they had stored up from long ago was now ripening into visible reality. So they busied themselves again with the ritual, and now a certain Muyalakaṉ appeared in the midst of the flames. They addressed him politely, and, abandoning further ritual activity, they also spoke to the fire they had created: 'God made us lose our very selves, our natural state.[26] Finish him off.' What they had not lost, of course, was their confusion. Agni, the god of fire, would have been terrified by that fire, but Śiva, who is first of all beings, took it in his hand, while with a gentle kick he brought Muyalakaṉ down to the ground. Then, as the gods watched in wonder, Śiva pressed his foot into Muyalakaṉ's spine.

The evil sages watched, their eyes ablaze. 'God still lives, damn him,' they wailed. 'And all that we created with vast effort has died.' And now they uttered curses, without limit: 'May he who ends the world, end himself.' They had no doubts. And yet those curses never reached the god. They disappeared, like cotton put in the way of the fire that burns the universe at the end of time. And as the curses bore no fruit, anger left those men. Their strength waned. They stood there, doing nothing, weary, ashamed, shaking. Bearing all that endless evil and blame, they were a burden on the earth. What is there to say about their idiocy? They had no redeeming virtues. They performed a rite to destroy Śiva, the Pillar who has no end. They sent many weapons against him. They uttered curses. Is that any way to work transformation?[27] No wonder they lost their power.

With cassia flowers, the Ganges, snakes, and the crescent moon all high on his head, Śiva continued to press down on Muyalakaṉ

[26] *nan tam iyal akaṉṟ' iṭave cĕyta īcaṉai* . . . .

[27] *māṟṟ'iṭa vaṟṟo*: alternatively, 'Is that the way to wreak destruction?'

with his foot. And as the creature moved, slowly, gingerly lifting his head, Śiva took that as reason to dance—and danced, as if forever. It was at that moment, and that place, that the god of three eyes began his *tāṇḍava* dance, as the whole world shuddered, and the great mass of living beings trembled in fear. As for the cruel sages, with their karma cumulating through ritual performance—they collapsed. Brahmā and Viṣṇu watched Śiva's dance, and tears welled up in their eyes; they stood near him, their hearts alive with joy, while Indra and all the other gods fell at his feet in worship. Seeing their weakness, and the fear that had taken hold of the world, the god stopped his flowing dance. The gods stood up, hands folded in praise.

The sages who had scorned that god, who has the woman within him, now received wisdom.[28] They stood, they fell at his feet, they prayed: 'Forgive us, Lord, for the immense mistakes we made, for the terrible acts that brought sorrow. Forgive us.' He saw the mode they were in. 'Follow *our* good way,' he said, 'and no more violence. Now go back to your *tapas*.' He fixed them in place. Even enemies enjoy his grace.

After settling them in that spot and sending off Bewildered Viṣṇu and Brahmā and all the other gods, each to his world, Three-Eyes returned to the Silver Mountain, to live there together with golden Umā. Now you know how God acquired the tiger's skin he wears, and all those other attributes, and how he danced, that day, in the Forest of Pines—and other things, too. We have told it all here, at length. But there is still more to tell.

Self-glazing Cysts

What is the condition of Śiva at the outset of the *Kanta-purāṇam* text? We see him first as an androgynous being, male fused with female—a state of profound interiority and coherence, resonant for the entire cosmos.[29] He knows everything (as God should) about '*those sages and their ignorant ways*.' He is also moved to 'do something' about them. Why so? Something in these sages—in their ignorance and repetition—is, perhaps, an impediment to Śiva's own process of continuous

[28] *potam = bodha.*

[29] Handelman and Shulman 1997: 74–93.

internal movement, his flowing interconnectivity or self-interiorization. Something in this god crashes against something in the sages, and stops.

What is the nature of this challenge to a godhead that shimmers and moves, 'all light within light,' alive in the 'feeling that flows through lives?' Just who are these men? The Forest of Pines is a place of perfection, devoted to the self-transformation of the sages through their daily discipline and ritual. Yet no real change ever occurs there. The Forest is all surface, all stasis, a petrified space, as we will see from parallel versions of the story. It is not, however, foreign to, or wholly other than, this god. We might think of it as an extreme exteriorization and solidification of Śiva himself. The sages, too, are a fragment of Śiva (think of 'him,' for the moment, as a whole opening to all possibility)—a fragment that through the devolution of god has forgotten connectivity and has broken away, tearing a hole in cosmos. The flow of the possible is stunted. Śiva has become less than he was, and he will therefore pursue the Forest, the part that escapes him.

How 'distant' is this fragment from Śiva? The sages, paragons of ritual activity, perhaps even of a kind of virtue, know no possibility of being other than they are. Their selfhood no less than their praxis is locked into the blocked horizons of the forest. '*They believed that two things alone—rituals and tapas—would produce freedom.*' So petrified are these sages that they have forgotten they exist within Śiva and that he is their creator. Their connection to cosmos (and through this, to the possibilities of infinity) is shattered. Even worse, they have gone beyond indifference to god (that is, beyond indifference to undefined possibility) and now verge on actively disliking him ('. . . *none of the sages in the Forest of Pines had any love for god*'). At the outset they are on the cusp of hatred for god, seeing no linkage between their interminable rites and his modes of being, the being that he *is*. These sages are unreflexive, never asking why they make no progress towards liberation, incapable of perceiving their own stasis. From their own perspective they have gone 'beyond' god, beyond the pulsations of his process through entropy and regeneration, involution, and forgetting. Like them, the forest is empty of flow, an encysted solid hole in being; all that is visible to the sages living here is the sealed horizon of the hole into which they have fallen unawares.

Such holes are all surface, all exterior, in contrast to dense interconnectivity, to flow, which is all interior. Because the hole has no fluid filling, its very emptiness is defined by the solidity of its congealed surfaces. Then whatever encrusts and emerges does so on the 'inside' surface of the hole. The phenomenal cosmos is this encrustation,[30] a slowing down and constricting of possibility; time as we know it is this deceleration. Such holes—possibility encrusted and diminished—continue to solidify and petrify, becoming more and more empty of potential life. They naturally appear to be full—chunks of petrified solidity. The significant point is that these holes are empty of movement, empty of change, hence empty of all possibility. The interior of the forest may appear full though entirely empty.

The more possibility is emptied, the more reality becomes fixed and rigid, and the less it is open to inward movement. At the extremes of this process, parts of the cosmos—parts of god—break off and become externalized worlds unto themselves. In terms of their self-consciousness, their own sense of living existence, these fragments are no longer connected to the whole. God, Śiva, no less than other beings, is subject to this process of coming into consciousness through which the self creates otherness and then forgets its connectivity, thereby encysting itself in a self-glazing, cut-off, shut-in existence. In this way, Śiva, too, loses parts of himself and is diminished.

This point merits repetition, amplification, and emphasis. Adumbrating our discussion in later chapters, we can say, in a preliminary way: Śiva of the Tamil Dāruvana texts is neither static nor complete. Something—a certain lack or difficulty internal to his self-composition—impels him to go to the forest. Sometimes this impulse is glossed as play, unencumbered by utilitarian goals, autotelic. Sometimes, as in the *Takṣa-kāṇṭam*, he is eager 'to do something' about the loveless sages. But behind such assertions, and behind the sequence of wide-ranging transformations that Śiva undergoes in the forest, lies an experience of this god as subject to states or stages of differential intensity. He is, in a word, not always there, certainly not in a manner that is consistently 'integrated' or evenly aware. Southern Śaiva ritual regularly seeks to put him together—*saṃnidhāna*, the common term for the

[30] We note that Gengnagel aptly chooses 'Kruste' to translate *mala*, the existential stain or blockage affecting living beings in the evolving, or devolving, cosmos. 'Diese aus Smutz bestehende Kruste umgibt und verhüllt die Seele, die durch diese Verkrustung in ihrer Fähigket zu handeln und zu erkennen eingeschränkt ist.' Gengnagel 1996: 50, n. 34.

god's becoming present—in the sense of causing him to pay attention to what is happening to him, for example.[31] Such attention cannot be taken for granted. Indeed, we would do well to put aside, at least for the moment, all modern exegeses of the familiar Śaiva Siddhânta statements about Śiva as stable in being, unchanging, eternally pure, aware, and pervasive, by definition free and whole.[32] Perhaps there is, indeed, a level or dimension in which such statements can be understood literally; this is a possibility we will explore. We must, however, be prepared to enter, with an open mind, into the imaginative reality of the Tamil Dāruvana texts; and here, even at this early stage, we can sense that Śiva's being, playing, and knowing may have critical interactive, processual components and that, as a consequence, this god is neither self-contained nor fully autonomous. He operates, at a certain level, within a context of potential self-diminution, becoming much less than himself (and also other to himself). He comes, that is, to the surface, repeatedly suffering all that surface implies. He may also, it is true, move himself and his cosmos toward some form of tentative and restless completeness; but in doing so, he never acts alone.

Wood-apples Swallowed by Elephants

Śiva is drawn to the forest. It is an active choice: he calls Viṣṇu to him and asks him to take on the seductive, beautiful female shape of Mohinī. In a Śaiva world such as that of the *Kanta-purāṇam*, Viṣṇu is also a part of Śiva, the left-hand, female half of god.[33] This female part of the god appears, *prima facie*, to be less stable (perhaps more susceptible to transformation) than the male part. Or perhaps these two aspects are in ongoing movement, impinging upon one another or, better, opening to one another, reflecting back at one another. Śiva himself takes on a form of 'limitless beauty.' Naked, with trident and begging bowl (the skull of Brahmā that sticks to Śiva's hand after he cuts off

[31] See discussion of the Śaivâgama materials (and the notion of attention) by Brunner 1986: 95.

[32] See the classic exposition of such themes by Schomerus 1912, *passim.* Such somewhat slanted, even apologetic readings of the Tamil Śaiva Siddhântin canon have also entrenched themselves in modern Tamil commentaries—at least since the days of the great nineteenth-century Jaffna scholar, Āṟumuka Nāvalar. See the essays collected in Āṟumuka Nāvalar 1954.

[33] Cf. *Tiruvāppaṉūrppurāṇam* of Tiruppuvaṉam Kantacāmippulavar, *kāppu.*

one of Brahmā's heads), Śiva and Mohinī/Viṣṇu enter the Forest of Pines. Carrying his begging bowl, Śiva is Bhikṣâṭana, the wandering Beggar. Bhikṣâṭana belongs in the Forest of Pines, where he begs primarily from the wives of the sages.[34] The Beggar hardly speaks except to say, '*Feed me*' (*bhavati bhikṣāṃ dehi*). His nakedness tells us something about god in this state, in which visible surface is somehow true, thus deeper than surface—though not everyone can see this.

Emptying through consciousness, possibilities petrifying, the Beggar is always hungry, never sated. He seems initially incapable of filling himself from within. One may say that there is emptiness within his being that he strives to fill with stuff from the rim or surface—stuff that is no longer conscious of being within him and has therefore hardened, broken off, and fragmented; that is, therefore, apart from him, within him but no longer conscious of this and that, therefore, empties him. Śiva seems to strive to enter the solid tear in his fluid self, to stuff the unselfconscious, encrusted exteriority that is this hole (and that he misses from his inside) back into his flowing conscious self, his interiority. He might thus fill himself again with the consciousness that is continually leaking away, eroded through existence. In this regard, it is significant that the foodstuffs he receives from the women are usually soft and flowing: milk, ghee, milk rice. These foods seem to indicate how the petrification of exteriority begins to soften in the Beggar's presence.

Śiva tells Mohinī, '*Go to where the sages are clustered together, with no thought of us. Bewilder them. Disturb their vows and rituals.*' Mohinī finds the super-ritualist (Pūrva-Mīmāṃsaka) sages at their rites. On seeing her they turn liquid with desire. '*Drunk, seething, sweating, they stood there, as their inner feelings melted away.*' Their petrified innerness, empty solidity, melts and flows out of them. There is no longer any pretence of disciplined form. Deflated holes, the sages collapse within themselves. They are 'more dead than alive.'

Naked Śiva, singing the Veda, takes himself to the sages' street. (Naked, begging the surface into himself, he has begun, as it were, to remove the outermost layer of his own exterior.) The sages' wives rush out, see god, and sink into confusion, loss, fascination: '*There is a very deep ocean that is called "wanting god," and they were drowning*

[34] Smith 1996: 166.

in it.' Melting, drowning—the crucial point is that these women are so immersed in fluidity that they no longer differentiate between their own surface and the interior of god. Their insides are beginning to be sucked into god (in contrast to their husbands who are sucked-out shells, made still more empty by Mohinī). The women are utterly bewildered, full of desire for the Beggar who takes in everything around him.

As they gaze at him, wondering who he might be or why he has come, '*. . . jewels, bracelets of gold, bracelets of conch, and all their fine clothes were slipping off their bodies, right in the middle of the street. . . . Desire was pricking every part of their bodies; their pores were flowing with juices, like milk pouring from the breast . . .*'. The surfaces of the women turn slippery. Their exterior ornaments and garments become frictionless and slide off their bodies. They feed the Beggar soft foods—rice, milk, and curds—while their sarees slip down their thighs into the dust. They are filling him from the outside, working change upon him, edging him toward movement, even as they themselves are swept along in an accelerating fusion of surface and interior, anticipating and conditioning the direction he will loop and turn.

'*Some decided he was begging for rice, so they approached him with some, but because they were burning with fierce desire, it turned to ashes in their hands.*' The wives are aflame, their interiors so hot that anything on the surface either slips off or burns to ash. The street is awash with the fallen surfaces of these women. So, too, with their emotions: their insides are exposed, their feelings naked, without shame, full of hunger and filling with love, their hearts and bodies naked, opening to the Beggar. They seem to be at once expanding and interiorizing. They are unable even to cover their eyes: '*Their hands weren't enough: it was like trying to cover up space itself.*'

By contrast, the heavily encrusted sages lose their exteriors to Mohinī's beauty, yet this only reveals their empty (non-existent?) insides. Their rites and disciplines are shown to be congealed facades that achieve nothing, since existentially these men are hollow beings. They exist on their own empty surfaces that mask their absence of interiority (the danger from which god is in the process of saving himself). Mohinī herself is a transform, perhaps illusory to a degree. Mohinī is something of a mask that pretends to femaleness, and that resonates with the sages' state: they are unaware that they are wearing their rites and discipline on the surface, as a mask that merely pretends to interiority, and that unselfconsciously hides its absence from itself. Mohinī is the seductive mask of Viṣṇu, the deeper female; and *she* does not reveal *himself*, although this mask seems integral to the possibility of further transformation. Unlike the sages, Mohinī knows that 'she' is a transform, hence rather impermanent. Because the rites and discipline of the sages are 'mask,' they are vulnerable to seduction by Mohinī. As mask melts mask, we see the sages' selves atrophied and disconnected from others. As the text says, the sages are like the wood-apple swallowed by the elephant—excreted whole with its exterior, its appearance, its apparentness, but hollow inside.

Śiva melts the exteriors of the wives, yet despite their confusion and fear, these women are focused in experience. The women are made fluid—a veritable flood. True, Śiva-Bhikṣâṭana is the Beggar, continually asking to be filled and sucking everything around deep into himself. Doing this, he fills the women with his own flow. Mohinī, by contrast, is seductive surface, opening up the emptiness of the men. The surfaces between Bhikṣâṭana and the women evaporate. They are hungry to be filled with Śiva: this is expressed as love, desire, longing, but also as liquid movement. '*Life flows through bodies, and God lives in the feeling that flows through lives.*' As he fills himself with their melting interiors, he flows through them. Flow is connectedness and mutuality, one being within another, other becoming self.

Śiva 'churns' the women, '*as if he were a thousand churning-rods ramming through their erstwhile modesty.*' The allusion is sexual, but more significantly, ontological: the crucial point is that his dynamic movement, his fluidity, enters them. Indeed, as they look at him and love him, the women are filled—they become pregnant, but in a way that seems to flow from foetus to foetus, each generating another until, without pain, the women give birth to 48,000 children. And, in keeping with the dense flow of connectedness, this happens with near simultaneity—'in the blink of an eye.' Surface appearances notwithstanding, the story of the Dāruvana is less about sexuality per se than about the composition or recomposition of god in terms of his uneven presence in human lives, or in his own awareness.

As their petrified solidity melts, the women fill with flowing love for Śiva and they discover a deeper, fluid innerness within themselves (unlike their excreted wood-apple husbands). Now pregnant with possibility, the women give birth. They are becoming processual, interconnected beings—all that their husbands are not. Indeed, from birth their children are deeply interiorized beings, born with a lucid consciousness, capable of immediately knowing God; and he sends them to do their discipline (*tapas*) with the purpose of meditating on him (of discovering him within themselves), the very gift the sages lack. Thus these offspring of innerness at once rejoin Śiva, sucked into the interiority of god. Their mothers continue to move in relation to the interior—'*the flood of mad women still flowed around him.*' As he sucks in broken-off parts of the petrified forest, the Beggar softens them so that they fill once again with possibility. They return to him, flow into him, and his own petrification melts further, as infinity fills.

Sorcery, Epilepsy, Dance

One vector of the narrative has reached its culmination: female generativity is activated and fulfilled by contact with the apparition of a naked, hungry god. A second, male vector requires further development in the direction of sorcery or black magic (*abhicāra*)—an intensification of the difficulty that afflicts the sages from the beginning.[35] On one level, this is a story about sorcery and exorcism or, put differently, about the fragile emergence of an unencumbered self. On another level, we have the conditions that drive God into spinning movement.

Viṣṇu/Mohinī, trailed by the bedraggled, stumbling sages—emptied of their solidity yet still vacant—rejoins Śiva. The sages naturally perceive only the loss of their wives' exteriors (self-control devastated, clothes gone, shame absent). They tell their wives: '*The best thing would be for you to die. But if you can't manage that, at least go home.*' The women, existing now in a sense within Śiva, fluidly full of his movement, his love, think to themselves: '*Anyone who has seen Him here is now free and cannot die. As for the sages—they must be crazy.*'

The sages decide that Śiva and Viṣṇu were playing with them, for no discernible reason. So just what had they lost? Merely the mechanics of their discipline, which they could re-establish easily enough. But what god had done to their wives was unforgivable: '. . . *Is there any*

[35] On sorcery in south India, see the analytical model proposed by Nabokov 2000: 44–69, arguing that 'in Tamilnadu sorcery is first and foremost a *psychological* expression' (48); counter-sorcery is thus therapeutic and regenerative. While we recognize these latter functions, sorcery cannot be reduced to social relations; in the Śaiva materials we are concerned with the 'cosmic,' i.e. cultural dimensions of sorcery are paramount.

way to undo the stigma that attached to Śiva. . . . The whole world—sun, moon, space itself—is full of his shame. . . . It's all his doing. That's Three-Eyed Śiva for you, with his garland of sweet cassia flowers.' Empty of innerness, of possibility, these men see only surface. Their emotions continue to resonate with the previous condition of the forest—emotions that petrify, separate, and disconnect beings from one another. So, too, they believe themselves autonomous of God, who exists only as another dislocated being, an evil trickster who does not belong to the forest, a guileful passerby who happened upon the forest, and despoiled its perfection. Śiva is stigmatized by his shameful deeds and should be punished. For the sages there is no greater being, no forest that fills and flows with possibility.

Their lack of love for God now turns into real hatred:

'Let's perform a violent sacrifice and kill him,' they said. In their innocence, their ignorance, they conspired together to produce an evil fire. It was a shameful rite. From the midst of the flames leapt a cruel tiger, unimaginably terrifying, with a thunderous growl, gaping mouth, eyes burning with rage, and sharp claws on its bright red paws. They worshipped this beast and ordered him: 'Go put an end to god.' Quickly it sprang at Śiva, the god with eyes of fire, and with a flick of his hand Śiva flayed it and draped himself in its skin, as suited him.

First the tiger, then a hatchet, a doe, raging snakes, ghouls, a skull—the entire iconographic array proper to this god. All emerge from the flames and are drawn into the god's orbit as characteristic pieces, tools, ornaments of his complete self. The sages persist in their destructive obsession, sending fail-proof mantras against Śiva; and these mantras become his drum, the medium of his aural connection to the world and the starting point for his creation. As a final effort, the sages produce from the fire yet another strange creature, named Muyalakaṉ—the demon of epilepsy (Sanskrit Apasmāra).[36] Śiva perches himself on the spine of Muyalakaṉ and draws the remnants of the sacrificial fire to his hand. The sages' despairing curses cannot touch him; they trail off into space, like the doe's heart-wrenching howl, like the horrible laugh of the white skull, the thunderous mantras. A cacophonous chorus,

[36] See discussion in Smith 1996: 225; Dorai Rangaswamy 1958: 1: 530.

so reminiscent of this god's own eerie voices—such as the wordless scream that gives him his ancient name, Rudra[37]—is silenced as Śiva slowly begins to turn and spin.

> *. . . Śiva continued to press down on Muyalakan̲ with his foot. And as the creature moved, slowly, gingerly lifting his head, Śiva took that as reason to dance—and danced, as if forever. It was at that moment, and that place, that the god of three eyes began his* tāṇḍava *dance, as the whole world shuddered. . . .*

Each weapon generated from the fire threatens the existence of the cosmos, the existence of Śiva; each is an attribute, a part, that is integral to the god's self. Perhaps Śiva has lost these attributes (through his own petrifying process of existing), or possibly the sages have turned his own attributes against him. In either instance, they are now reabsorbed into his fuller self. It is as autonomous, displaced fragments that these attributes are dangerous to the integrity of the cosmos. Up to this point in the story, Śiva the Beggar has been melting this petrified cosmos and filling himself with its fluid contents. Now he pacifies these wayward attributes, resuming them within his being. The recomposition of the god is part of the more general process of recapturing the forest, turning it from the self-perception of brittle autonomy, from interior-as-surface, back into that of a deeper interiority. In this respect, 'sorcery' is of special significance.

Muyalakan̲ is the most evocative and dangerous force that emerges from the fire of sorcery. The sages tell him that, '*God made us lose our very selves, our natural state.*' They are convinced that their empty selves, flattened on the surface of the petrified forest, belong to the natural condition of cosmos, within which Śiva is a strangely destructive intruder. As they state earlier in the text, they should have no difficulty reconstituting their own selves through rite.

But who is Muyalakan̲? As epilepsy, he may signify loss of consciousness, spasmodic (rather than fluid) movement, movement without meaning, the swallowing of the tongue as the loss of speech and the encapsulation of (autistic) being within itself, utterly cut off from others. As the force of forgetting, Apasmāra, he presumably makes beings forget that which is perceived or known. To forget is to become fragmented or, worse, erased, since the self depends on memory to know

[37] On the god's names, see *Kauṣītaki-Brāhmaṇa* 6.1.3.9, 17–24.

itself and others. Forgetting is the greatest diminishment of the consciousness of self. Remembering generates connectivity; forgetting destroys it, fragmenting beings into parts that lose one another in the empty gaps of time, space, and language. With connectivity gone, the fluidity of possibility leaks out of these beings, and they congeal into extreme petrification, lacking agency and volition. Muyalakan̲ may be the most extreme exteriorization of innerness—as a being constituted of forgetting, a force that utterly nullifies consciousness, Muyalakan̲ may never be able to develop a self. He is, that is, iconic of sorcery itself.

In this version of the Dāruvana story, Śiva enters the forest as Bhikṣâṭana, a beggar, hungry to be filled. God, it seems, has externalized himself (at least to a degree) and is also in the process of emptying the possibilities of infinity. He begins to be filled, destroying the surfaces of the sages, sucking in their wives and then his own attributes, nullifying and destroying sorcery, dismantling, as it were, the forest as a separated, autonomous entity. As he fills up, his being alters—he becomes more complete, more continuous, stronger, changing from Bhikṣâṭana to Naṭarāja, the Dancing Śiva, crushing his opposite, Muyalakan̲, forgetfulness, underfoot. As he dances, whirling around and through himself—the vortex creating the flowing Pillar (Śiva as Sthāṇu, without top or bottom)—he threatens to suck the entire cosmos into himself. Drawn into the vortex, opening to infinity, the cosmos and perhaps God himself would cease to exist. This is the perennial danger of the *tāṇḍava* dance; seeing the fear of gods and people alike, Śiva stops. Yet this dance, the climax of the process described in linear terms in our story, is by far the most powerful mode of moving from exterior to interior, closing the holes in god (the cosmos) and the holes in infinity (god). Drawn inwards, even the sages acquire an unexpected wisdom. 'Even enemies enjoy his grace.'

Seeing Space

This is one direction, a possible reading. It assumes a staggered presence in the god who undergoes this course of changes; parts of him are broken off, separated, solidified, objectified. There is good reason to make this assumption, which certainly suits the axiology of the temple context in Kancipuram where Kacciyappar was working. Tamil Śaivism, in its various strands, tends to recognize a fuller or subtler level of godhead, always unmanifest, and diminished levels that are defined as *upâdāna*—the phenomenal substrate, normally identified as evolutes of Śiva's feminine energy.[38] Transitions between this more objectified level and that of the godhead's potential existence are a matter of considerable debate in the Śaiva Siddhânta philosophical sources, which are committed to a notion of god's unchangeability *(nirvikāratva)*. This would seem to make Śiva's experiences in the Forest of Pines a matter of playful illusion, replete with intentionality—a lesson that, almost by definition, fails to affect the god's composition; or, in terms familiar to us from over a century of modern explication of the Śaiva sources, a complex allegory meant to drive home certain didactic truths about ontology. Yet there is more to this problem than can be solved by a simple notion of hierarchized modes of being. The unchanging god is also said to be the world, in the sense that he is 'not two and not one.'[39] If he were two, the world could be utterly distinct from him (as the authentically dualistic Śaivas maintained)—and it is not. If he were one, the autonomy of phenomenal reality would be completely lost—and the Śaiva Siddhantins, in general, refuse to take this step. It seems, then, that the philosophers, too, may have to find place for a god who inhabits some (possibly uncomfortable and largely unstable) middle space.

A logical difficulty quickly makes itself felt. The very terms we are using—'depth' and 'surface,' for example, or 'periphery' and 'middle,' or (for that matter) 'inner' and 'outer'[40]—may have no referents in a Moebius-like world where surface twists and loops, so that surface *is* depth: witness the Dancing God.[41] Yet to no small extent we are following the chosen idioms of the Śaiva authors themselves. If we are to escape a too-easy resort to paradox, we will have to define, analytically and empirically, these spatial constructs.

[38] See *Śivâdvaita-nirṇaya* of Appayadīkṣita 3.18352 (p. 50).

[39] Cf. *Tiruvaruṭpayaṉ* 8.5 (on *iṟaivaṉ*, god, and *uyir*, living being), with remarks by Nirampav aḻakiya Tecikar.

[40] See Devasenapathi 1974: 86.

[41] See Curtis 1983: 93 on Śaiva Siddhânta notions of space, in particular the relations of Śiva as manifest to Śiva unmanifest: 'the unmanifest triangle folds back against the manifest.' Curtis offers a persuasive analytic description of Śiva's emergence onto a surface; note the expressive language of 'folding.'

Perhaps a visual excursus will help. A pair of carved wooden figures from somewhere in Tanjavur district (nineteenth century) show us the two complementary focal points of the story (Figures 1 and 2). Look first at Bhikṣâṭana, the beggar (Figure 1).[42] The god is naked, standing on wooden sandals. A snake coils around his waist. His two upper arms hold drum and trident, respectively, the latter delineating an angular vector behind him. His lower left hand carries a container—perhaps a betel-bowl,[43] from which he has drawn a leaf that he is feeding, with his right hand, to the leaping deer to the left. The dwarf Pot-Belly (Kuṇḍodara) stands beside him with a plate of sweets on his head. On the far left, one of the sages' wives is offering alms, her dress slithering toward her knees. The god appears relatively peaceful; he is, perhaps, filling up with himself, and at the same time coming out of the curvature that enfolds him. In a sense, this curvature tells the real story. The woman is still deeply part of it, almost a bas-relief of the curve itself, a flexed space out of which the male is emerging. Śiva's trident shows the depth of his separation: he can now move back and forth, inwards or outwards, losing or finding himself as he works his magic on the forest. He is, we might say, unfreezing, as he watches a world awakening around him.

He is also, as we might expect, poised off-centre, his legs pointed in one direction, torso and head in another. He is in movement, bountiful; his stance, highly relational, creates depth. In the foreground, the hand that feeds draws our eyes: this is the dynamic focus of this tableau, the locus of giving, of relational transaction and connection. The woman's arm is also converging on this same spot. The deer twists its head backwards, its horns slightly entangled in the falling saree, a strong statement of discarded surface. The deer is alive, hungry, feeding. Food dominates each of the margins, but these, too, are in motion: Kuṇḍodara seems to be withdrawing into the curve, even as the woman comes forward with her offering.

[42] This iconic form is to be distinguished from its two closely related *mūrti*s, Bhairava and Kaṅkāla-mūrti. See Adiceam 1965 for a detailed discussion. *Dīptāgama* 47.2 distinguishes two forms of Bhikṣâṭana, one carrying Brahmā's skull and the other the skeleton [of Viṣvaksena, Viṣṇu's gatekeeper]: ibid., 84. Often, Kaṅkāla-mūrti and Bhikṣâṭana can be distinguished only by the fact that the former is clothed, the latter nude, as in the case of our woodcut. See further discussion below. We thank the Museum für Indische Kunst, Berlin, and Dr Lore Sander for making photographs available.

[43] Thus Wibke Lobo in Härtel et al. 1980: 74.

Figure 1. Bhikṣâṭana in the Forest of Pines. Nineteenth-century woodcut, Tanjavur district.
Reproduced with the kind permission of Staatliche Museen zu Berlin—Preussischer Kulturbesitz, Museum für Indische Kunst.

One side—the left—is coming alive, waking to feeling, and Śiva's head and eyes are engaged in this direction. Filling with love, feeding the animal at his feet, he is becoming more and more present. Those around him, closely bound up in this process, fuel it with the means at their disposal. The woman is rapt with the moment's richness, apparently unaware of, or indifferent to, her dishabille.

Figure 2. Mohinī in the Forest of Pines. Nineteenth-century woodcut, Tanjavur district.
Reproduced with the kind permission of Staatliche Museen zu Berlin—Preussischer Kulturbesitz, Museum für Indische Kunst.

Were we to accelerate the implicit movement, the god would begin his dance. This unbalanced stance, between the dwarf who is a part of him and the woman who is still outside him, is the first step. Forward and backward vectors draw him toward a spin, or a loop, that can twirl through curving space, opening up *more* space. As the dancer, Naṭarāja, Śiva seems to curve space *around himself* (centripetally) rather than being flung (centrifugally) away from himself. In any case, the dance is generated precisely here, in the fulcrum of woman, hand, deer, the point of contact with a replenished being who is visible, naked, alluring, unmasked. This fulcrum reveals a high degree of reciprocal action and emotion, the secret of generativity—at base, a matter of generous giving and its implications. More precisely, this is the point at which two complex processes intersect: on the one hand, a bringing forth or giving out (offering, feeding, emerging outwards), on the other hand, a taking in or taking away.[44]

Turn now to Mohinī, his partner in seduction (Figure 2). Unlike Śiva, she is centred, balanced, at home within the curve. If he creates depth by movement, she is immersed in pre-existing depth. She leans on a pillar, legs crossed, a parrot in her hand. Inside, only the pillar is linear; all the rest—her own body, the vegetal luxuriance around her—is curved, lithe, supple. These are haptic curves, heavy with texture. At the edges, symmetrically planted on either side but entirely outside this bending universe, stand two lumpy, awkward sages—exiled in straight lines. They are pot-bellied and aroused yet somehow lifeless and blind, capable, at most, of mimicking her mode. There is no way they can reach her. She dwarfs them, and they—powerful images of failure—will next move into sorcery, as we know. Yet in this same poignant failure, that attests to incipient awareness of another potentiality, these sages, too, have been drawn out of their initial stasis. They, too, will be changed.

The contrast sustains, in its very starkness, the perception of two complementary responses. Śiva attracts the women of the forest, who very readily slip away from surface, moving toward a space that, as it opens, sucks up everything alive. The dancer himself is swirling deeper into this space as it turns on itself, filling as he is filled through reciprocal feeding. Arid surface has come alive and begun to move; the god has unstuck himself from the petrified, outer limit of his being. The sages, on the other hand, are condemned to peripherality and repetition; they repeat the attitudes of perfection that have constituted this strangely lifeless forest, that has nonetheless, unaccountably, broken open to reveal a living apparition at its heart. The apparition, however unsettling, still embodies a certain balance, unlike the emergent god beside it. The Tamil wood-carvers have captured unerringly an early stage in the narrative; captured something of its ambiguity as well as

[44] These themes are discussed in detail below, pp. 206, 217 ff.

the distinctiveness of its two operative modes. 'Depth' here appears to be a derivative of movement.

Liṅga: Latent Transformer

We speak of movement not as datum but as direction—a problem to be resolved. Insofar as god remains unmoved, even in the smallest part of self, he needs the forest. Like human beings, like the sages, he is in danger of slowing into stasis, or, stated differently, of moving from middle to centre or middle to periphery. The dance restores him to the middle in active collaboration with his human witnesses. If we can define this middleness, we may be able to formulate the logic that drives the Dāruvana texts.

One way to begin is to study what is visible. The Beggar appears in the forest as a naked, ithyphallic, unsettling apparition. In the middle of his body there is the erect *liṅga*, carefully noted by the storyteller. What is this *liṅga*? We have already said that the Dāruvana story is less about sexuality per se than about internal processes unfolding within this very unevenly present god. But the wives of the sages, at least some of them, apparently focus on Śiva's penis, which they refer to as *kuṟi*, 'the sign,' or as *kocam*, 'the outer layer.' Here is what they have to say.

> *ĕntaiyār tamm irun kuṟiyiṉ kaṇe*
> *cintukiṉṟa tivalaiy ŏṉṟ' allavov*
> *unti mel vant' ulak' aṉaittun tarum*
> *anta nāṉmukaṉ āṉat' ĕṉpar cilar* (62)

He has a trident; an eye of flames on his forehead; long matted hair; a red body; the crescent moon. He must be the god who once swallowed poison from the sea. A single drop spilled from within this huge sign, the liṅga, *of our father into the navel* [*of Viṣṇu*] *and became Brahmā, the Creator of the world.*

They have identified the naked Beggar as Śiva, and they therefore know something of his cosmogonic role; the world itself, as they know it, has emerged out of this god. But the drop (*tivalai*) that became the Creator is actually said to be pouring *within* the great mark (*kuṟi*) that belongs to Śiva. Perhaps, then, the created world is not entirely external to him; we will return to a notion of strong mutual interweaving of being affecting both Śiva, *pati*, and other living creatures, *paśu*. But what of this single, middle point that so interests the sages' wives and that seems to them to have originated the connection between them and Śiva?

Kur̲i is a standard Tamil term for Śiva's *liṅga* and, like the Sanskrit term, suggests a primary sense of 'signing' or 'marking.' From *kur̲i* there is a short and not uncommon step to *kur̲ippu*, 'intention,' 'hint,' as we see in verse 74:

āṭai tārum at' an̲r̲' ĕn̲ir̲ kŏṇṭat' or
veṭai tirum viḷampukilir ĕn̲ir̲
kūṭa vāruṅ kur̲ipp' umakk' ĕn̲ ĕn̲n̲ap
pāṭu cerntu pakarnt'iṭuvār cilar

And some went right up to him and whispered, 'Either give us back our clothes or satisfy our wishes. Even if you don't want to say anything, just come into us, love us. Show us your sign (kur̲ippu).'

Śiva's 'intention' is somehow implicit in his sign. Other Tamil Śaiva poets go further with linguistic play of this sort:

Your devotees may come together,
but *you* still have no character,
give no sign [*kur̲ippu*].[45]

Śiva is 'signless' as in *Śvetâśvatara Upaniṣad* 6.9 (*naiva ca tasya liṅgaṁ*), although in the Tamil verse the missing sign is, or should be, pregnant with awareness. *Kur̲i* lends itself to such hints, combining by implication a notion of memory or recognition—usually, in Dravidian, a matter of making or seeing a mark[46]—with both the physical sign of gender identity and the volitional field of intentionality. Yet, as with the Sanskrit term *liṅga*, we err by rushing to an overly concrete identification.

Kur̲i is by no means a common term for genitals. Even less common in this sense is *kocam*, which appears twice in our version of the Dāruvana:

[45] Cuntaramūrtti *Tevāram* 77.10 [790]: *kuṇam ŏn̲r̲' illīr kur̲ipp' illīr*. Cf. Shulman 1986.

[46] Discussion in Ramanujan 1993; Shulman 2001: 201–5.

pāca' nīṅkip para-patam īt' ĕṉav
ācaiyoṭu kaṇṭ' aṉpu cĕyvār ĕṉa
vāca' nīṅki vaḷaiy ukutt' aiyar taṅ
koca' nokkiṉar kumpiṭuvār cilar (54)

Some left slavery behind. They knew they were seeing the ultimate state, and they performed acts of love, in passion: they let their sarees fall, and their bracelets, as they stared straight at the lord's penis [*kocam*] *and worshipped it.*

aṇaṅkiṉ nallavar aṇṇa' ṟaṉ koca' mel
[n]uṇaṅku māloṭu nokki ataṟku muṉ
vaṇaṅkumāṟ' ĕṉa maṟṟ' avar nāṇupu
kaṇaṅkaḷoṭu kaviḻntu cĕṉṟār cilar (77)

And there were some women—wild and good—who were scrutinizing his penis [kocam] *with a subtle intensity, as if they were devoting themselves to it, although they then bashfully rejoined the others, standing with bowed heads.*

There is no doubt as to what these women are staring at, and yet the word itself is surprising. Its long prehistory—Skt *kośa* is well known to us from the Upaniṣadic discussions of the five 'sheathes' or 'layers' enveloping the hidden self[47]—leads us to expect a notion of an outer container meant to be peeled away as one proceeds inwards toward something more real. Tamil *kocam*, in fact, can also mean the womb.[48] The 'sheath' seems to become an external surface only in the course of being exposed, as if a deeper, fuller reality were assuming visible, layered form. We might, then, be justified in asking: what is it that Śiva's penis contains?

The question is particularly salient because our southern versions of the Dāruvana story have effectively substituted the entire sequence of black-magical rite and Śiva's dance—the culmination of the dramatic narrative—for an older pattern in which Śiva loses his *liṅga* in the Forest of Pines.[49] Usually the sages, very angry at the Beggar's seductive spell over their wives, curse his *liṅga* to fall, and the god deliberately

[47] *Taittirīya Upaniṣad* 3.1–10; *Paiṅgala Upaniṣad* 2.5.
[48] Thus Villiputtūrār *Pāratam* 1.227 (the *kocam* of flesh that Gāndhārī carries and gives birth to). Cf. Skt *garbha*, womb, foetus.
[49] As noted by Doniger [O'Flaherty] 1980: 139–40.

lets this happen.[50] Such is the perceived origin of *liṅga*-worship, that is, of Śiva's presence in our visible world in the form of the stone *liṅgas* at the heart of his shrines; what happened in the Dāruvana explains this important 'fact.' The episode looks rather like a castration, however we wish to understand this; yet neither an overly semiotic nor a literal or physical reading of the *liṅga*'s fate in these materials is likely to be correct. *Liṅga*, like *kuṟi* or *kocam*, is neither just a sign nor a part of god's body. Something else is being said in these texts.

As stated at the outset, our essay focuses on the south Indian variants of this story, which we see as inextricably bound up with notions of sorcery and exorcism. Still, we need to look, however briefly, at the more ancient materials relating to the loss of the *liṅga*, for there is—as the verses just cited would suggest—a strong line of continuity between these materials and the prominent southern themes of black sacrifice and dance. We can phrase this as a series of questions: What is it that leads from the (lost) *liṅga* to the dance? Do these two facets of god's existence share some affinity? Are they in some sense interchangeable? Just what does *liṅga* mean for this god?

Observe, then, the earliest Sanskrit version of this part of the story—the *Mahābhārata*'s myth about Rudra-Śiva as Sthāṇu, the lonely Pillar. This excursus into another level of narration takes place at the darkest moment in this dark text. Aśvatthāman, the cruel, unscrupulous Brahmin warrior, has just murdered in their sleep most of the sons and cousins of the Pāṇḍava heroes. Yudhiṣṭhira, the grieving father, asks Kṛṣṇa—that is, god—to explain to him how, or why, this happened. Here is Kṛṣṇa's answer:

Aśvatthāman had placed his hopes in the unchanging lord of all the gods; that is how he killed so many all by himself. Mahādeva, the great god, can give immortality when he is pleased with someone. Or he, Giriśa, might give vigour enough to destroy Indra himself. I know about Mahādeva, as he really is; and I know his many ancient and varied deeds. He is the beginning of living beings, and their middle, and their end. This entire world moves through his activity.

[50] A considerable secondary literature documents this stratum of the Sanskrit sources. See the foundational study by Jahn 1915, 1916, 1917; Kulke 1970; Doniger [O'Flaherty] 1973; Kramrisch 1981; Reich 1987. We offer one annotated version of this type in Appendix 1 [*Kūrmapurāṇa* 2.37].

*At first, when the Grandfather [Brahmā] wished to emit living beings, he saw him and said to him: 'Emit living creatures at once.' Lordly Śiva with his brilliant hair (*hari-keśa*) agreed; but since he could see far into the future, he heated himself for a long time while immersed in water. The Grandfather waited for him for a very long time, but finally he externalized, mentally, another creator of all living beings.*

This latter creator, noticing his brother, Giriśa, asleep in the water, announced: 'If I have no other, elder brother, then, and only then, will I create beings.' The Grandfather reassured him: 'There is *no male other than you, or born before you. This Pillar (*sthāṇu*) is quiescent, immersed in water. Go ahead and make creatures.' So Dakṣa, the Prajāpati, swiftly emitted all living beings in their four developmental classes. And no sooner were they emitted than all of them ran, famished, toward Prajāpati in order to devour him. Already being eaten up, fighting for his life, Prajāpati rushed back to the Grandfather: 'Save me from these! Ordain some form of sustenance for them.'*

The Grandfather gave them food—plants, fixed in place, and also the weaker, moving creatures that serve as food for the strong. With their food appointed in this way, these beings were satisfied and went off wherever they went. From then on they multiplied pleasantly, in their various wombs.

Once this whole mass of beings had multiplied and the gods and anti-gods had come out, the First-Born emerged from the water and saw all these creatures in their many forms, fully externalized, fully grown—through his radiant vitality. He was very angry. Seeing them, he struck his liṅga, hurling it against the earth, where it impacted and stood firm. Imperishable Brahmā spoke to him, as if seeking to calm him with words: 'What, Śarva, were you doing for so long in the water? And why did you make this happen—causing your liṅga to penetrate into the earth?'

The master of the worlds, very agitated, answered the guru: 'These creatures were produced by someone else, so what will I do with this [liṅga]? It was by my heating myself that food was obtained for creatures, Grandfather; that is how plants are growing, and how creatures continuously increase.'

And after saying this, still angry, hostile, depressed, Bhava, that person of great inner discipline, went away to Mount Muñjavant to heat himself further.[51]

[51] *Mahābhārata* 10. 17.6–26.

This, then, is the beginning—the first time we hear of Śiva's angry attack on his own self or body, which is divested of that part that seems to define this god and that, as such, as either the indicator or generator of his creative force, makes its violent way to the earth. It happens, it seems, because Śiva is furiously jealous, angry at having been preempted by his younger brother; but also perhaps because he sees, as only he can see, the terribly flawed nature of a creation that is as hungry, lacking, rapacious, needy, and driven by desire as Dakṣa's was destined to be. Śiva, from the start, is *dīrgha-darśin*—one who can see far into the future. He knew what sort of creation might emerge if it were not preceded by long *tapas* and the deep processes of internal fusion that accompany this discipline. Dakṣa's hungry and sexually self-reproducing creatures are the predictable result of hasty externalization, and Śiva's rage at this state of affairs is entirely of a piece with his ancient protest against imperfection.[52] On the other hand, this same protest, or the energy bound up in it, seems to be what sustains and nourishes the now existing, imperfect world.

This is the apparent paradox at the core of much classical Śaiva myth: a violent negation effectively nourishes and affirms. Creation itself seems to proceed, in such a cosmos, in the sudden twists and involutions of generative rejection, or of an emphatic 'no' that gives life.[53] The very energy that moves this cosmos through its constant turns is somehow produced out of the act that denies its wholeness, or that, negating, empties out its partial or superficial forms. More precisely, 'no' takes away, opening space that can now become full (of god). Hence, perhaps—through the force of the paradox that binds together two seemingly antithetical vectors—the twisted or braided quality of the Śaiva universe, which never unfolds or develops in straight lines. And yet this god himself is, in the text just quoted, a vertical Pillar, Sthāṇu—uncharacteristically stable and fixed in place for long periods. Only upon emerging into visible presence is he overcome with rage and depression to the point that he mutilates his previously intact, previously withdrawn and heated self. His *liṅga* comes crashing down to earth where, breaking through its surface, it comes again to stand firm (*pratyatiṣṭhata*)—in shrine after shrine. And still we ask: what is this *liṅga* that Śiva hurls at the earth? What part of him has come unstuck or been torn away?

[52] See further discussion and examples in Shulman 1986.

[53] See below, pp. 104–5.

Or let us ask differently. When the *liṅga* is present on earth, Śiva himself goes far away, out of sorts (*vimanas*), still hostile. Who is leaving whom behind? Perhaps the *liṅga*, now autonomous and active, has shed the partial and bewildered presence that previously appeared to contain it. In the major *purāṇic* versions of the Dāruvana story, the *liṅga*'s fall to earth is by no means the end of the sequence.

'It all happened in a flash. The liṅga, from Śiva's remarkable body, was like fire; it burnt everything in its path, wherever it went, moving across the entire earth and then to the Nether World and to Heaven as well. In no place was it steady and firm. So all the worlds were in turmoil, and the sages were suffering, too. Neither they nor the gods could find respite anywhere.'[54]

Ritual remedies may eventually fix the *liṅga* in place in some detached, less threatening form, but its inner dynamism and spin are no incidental accretions. In some sense, as the Sthāṇu text and its *purāṇic* successors suggest, this *liṅga* is the most active part of god. His iconography, his names, even his rather capricious and changeable emotions—all these are close to the perceptible surface with its natural tendency to deform, to crystallize or congeal, to mask. The *liṅga* is not a mask.

It is, in fact, probably resistant to any form of ruled or defined existence. Lacking contours, lacking directionality, it moves, as the Dancer moves, whirling around its own axis. In all likelihood, it moves continuously through itself, twisting as it spins, so that what is outside is discovered inside—if these terms retain any meaning. This is not a matter of marking as we conventionally understand it but rather of breaking through to a surface which is fashioned in the shape of the mark.[55] But we might do better to avoid this issue of signs and marks altogether, at least for the moment. Think instead of one of the most resonant meanings of *liṅga* in classical texts such as *Śvetâśvatara Upaniṣad* 1.13:

> *vahner yathā yoni-gatasya mūrtir na dṛśyate naiva ca liṅga-nāśaḥ/*
> *sa bhūya evendhana-yoni-gṛhyas tad vobhayaṃ vai praṇavena dehe//*

'As the form of fire within its source is not seen, while its potentiality (*liṅga*) is not lost, so it can be grasped again in the firewood source—

[54] *Śiva-purāṇa* 4 (*Koṭi-rudra-saṃhitā*), 12–13.
[55] See Narayana Rao and Shulman 2002: 187–96.

in this way both [levels] are in the body, [to be grasped] by the syllable Om.'

Fire pre-exists its emergence as flame. It lies latent, a fiery potential, in the wood.[56] Despite the views of modern commentators,[57] this potential does not seem to be a matter of 'essence.' Indeed, if anything it is highly anti-essentialist, a potentiality that has, it is true, certain given features that govern its breaking out into external or concrete space but that is in another sense unpredictable, awaiting the mark.

We suggest that we begin to think of *liṅga* not as an identity (gender) marker, and not as an anatomical feature of the formed and bounded male body, and not as subtle substance within the outer casing (*kośa*) of psychosexual being—although all of these identifications are possible and sometimes present in Śaiva texts—but as a processual core of being, spinning god through his transforms, replenishing god and world through the potentiality that fuels this core, sustaining or nourishing those pieces of god that have broken through into brittle surface, as Sthāṇu tells us in the text above. As potential being, the *liṅga* is restless, turning, revolving, twisting toward surface. It is generative and never still, never more lively in movement than when present in the pillar-like stone. Presence, indeed, is its playful telos if we study it from a human vantage point, but also possibly from within its own auto-telic process. We could also speak of *liṅga* as made of light, as the Śaiva authors often say.[58] The *liṅga*, in short, is the core of this god at home in our world: an ontology of pure potentiality is present

[56] Cf. Mallinātha ad *Raghuvaṃśa* 3.9. Precisely the same image is used in *Kāmikâgama*, *pūrva-bhāga* 4.352, for the way mantra makes Śiva, already potentially present, fully manifest: see below; Brunner 1986: 94.

[57] Kramrisch 1981: 167: '*Linga*, "sign," not only signifies the existence of perceptible things, but also denotes the imperceptible essence of a thing even before the thing in its concrete shape has come to exist. Thus the form of fire, which exists in the kindling stick in a latent form, may not be seen, yet its *linga* is not destroyed but may be seized again by another kindling stick (*Śvetāśvatara Upaniṣad*. 1.13).' Kramrisch (ibid., 166) distinguishes three meanings of *linga*: sign, phallus, and 'cosmic substance (*prakṛti* or *pradhāna*), which is the subtle body (*liṅga śarīra*) of Śiva, who is the absolute reality.' She is not far from our reading, if only one deletes the misleading 'absolute' and avoids hidden essences. Compare Olivelle 1996: 254 for the above verse: 'When a fire is contained within its womb, one cannot see its visible form and yet its essential character is not extinguished. . . .'

[58] See below, pp. 79–84.

here. Such an ontology has little in common with a universe of present objects, sharp contours, linear sequence.

We will return to these themes, which are central to all attempts to describe Śiva's travails in the Forest of Pines. The *liṅga*, it could be said, drives him there and is sometimes left behind, or leaves him behind. Two further conundra become salient at this point. First, while the full potentiality of existence seems to be located, by the end of the story, in the world we normally inhabit, god 'himself' is elsewhere, on Mount Muñjavat, for example. The deeper meaning of this division remains unclear. We observe, however, that the Śaiva deity is literally moved—set into motion—by strong feeling (anger, frustration, hunger), sometimes intense enough to tear him apart. Feeling is movement. Second, for all this to happen, Śiva seems to need to be literally filled up from the outside. The plenitude of the *liṅga* is actualized, and movement intensified, by feeding, by strong feeling that empties the outer domain into the god or that melts it into a liquidity that is continuous with god. And whether his *liṅga* is torn away from him or a rite of sorcery is practised against him, trauma of one type or another appears to be integral to the process he undergoes.

We are not alone in thinking there is something here of paradox or riddle. That which is itself unbroken light, spinning movement, inexhaustible fullness, neither male nor female or at once both male and female, ever moving subtly through one to the other, appears to us, much as it does to the sages, as needy, hungry, and incomplete. Replace the irritating 'Absolute' in the following poem with something closer to what we have been describing, something more like the shifting, dancing Śaiva god of unconfined potential, and we have the paradox of the Bhikṣâṭana-Beggar in all its fierceness:

Show me
that walking without feet,
touching without hands,
tasting without a tongue,

show me how that Other, that Absolute,
begs, with all Feeling for a begging bowl,
begs 'Give me now that Absolute.'

Show me that, O Lord of Caves.[59]

[59] Allama Prabhu, translated by Ramanujan 1996: 184.

Finding the Middle

God begs. This is the first fact of the forest. He undergoes change within himself, within the terms of his inner composition. This is the second fact. The first leads directly to the second and, in all versions of the Dāruvana, there is a logic to the progression. It is this logic we are seeking to unravel.

Certain issues have by now emerged and will require much closer attention. There is the strange matter of god's unstable velocities, his habit of slowing toward frozen stasis and, in the other direction, of accelerating into total movement. These differences appear to be linked to notions of filling and emptying, which in turn suggest images of an interior waiting to be filled. But if Śiva is, at times, such an interior, what are we to make of the persistent generativity of his *liṅga*-self, seemingly so full of potential presence? And if Śiva is endowed with the *liṅga*—attached to it, emerging out of it, extruding self into cosmos—why the harsh movement of break or attack, with its persistent aouth Indian themes of black magic, epilepsy, possession? Why exorcise a god—and of whom?

Surely not by chance, we find ourselves repeatedly speaking about 'presence.' There is a sense in which this notion, which speaks to the modes of god's awareness and accessibility to others and to self, is the fundamental problem motivating the others we have mentioned. In the world of south Indian Śaiva ritual, based on the *Śaivâgama*s, Śiva's coming into presence, that is consciousness, is a primary, quotidian goal.[60] It is not a simple matter; tremendous opposition, in the form of various opacities and obstructions (*mala*), has to be overcome through ritual and meditative means.[61] Once again we find ourselves in the domain of the Dāruvana sages; once again we might ask where they went wrong. The easy answer is that they were not, after all, intent on making Śiva present; they were, on the contrary, arid Mīmāṃsakas, performing ritual for its own sake in an automatic, even atheistic mode.[62] They were thus, in the most devastating sense of all, entirely dependent, non-free.[63] Notice this question of freedom in its relation to Śiva and to

[60] Davis 1991: 108, 112–36; Brunner 1986: 95.

[61] See below, pp. 88–95. On *mala*, see Gengnagel 1996: 50–2; above, n. 30.

[62] Thus the great nineteenth-century Śaiva thinker from Sri Lanka, Āṟumuka Nāvalar, in his commentary on *Koyiṟpurāṇam* 2. 44.

[63] Ibid. [*para-tantirar*].

those illusionary forces that block his coming into being. Śaiva Siddhânta aims at a deep reality of freedom, its final raison d'être; and this freedom, which is clearly known to the Siddhântin authors from experience, is unmistakably linked to the process of making the Śaiva god present (*saṃnihita*) in that particularly enhanced form of being (*visiṣṭa-saṃnidhāna*) which reveals him visibly in the *liṅga* (*āvir-bhāva*), 'facing' (*abhimukha*) his devotee.[64] Freedom could, in fact, be said *to be* this presence. Perhaps not surprisingly, the same Upaniṣadic simile that we cited earlier, with reference to the *liṅga*, turns up in this context as well: 'Just as fire is made to arise in wood by rubbing it and so on, Śiva is manifested through the power of mantras and through devotion.'[65] The god's presence, that is, is a matter of actualizing a potential, even perhaps of entering into the potential space of the *liṅga* and thus knowing what it is to be free.

Both affective and cognitive aspects accompany this experience. *Saṃnidhāna* (also *saṃnidhi*, Tam. *caṉṉiti*), 'presence,' is literally a kind of integration, the bringing together of discrete or discontinuous parts.[66] This may indeed be a form of knowing. And there are also the extreme forms of loving and feeling that, as we saw from the case of the sages' wives, induce change in god from brittle (empty) surface to an open-ended and subtle nearness—*aruḷ*, in the language of the Tamil Śaiva texts. There is an unfortunate tendency to translate this critical term, in nearly every context, as 'grace,' with its heavy Christian connotations. *Aruḷ* can, it is true, correspond in Śaiva texts to Sanskrit *anugraha*, the god's compassionate giving to his servants. More often, however, it approximates a notion of coming into being or freely becoming present, close, alive.[67] In village ritual contexts, *aruḷ* may mean simply 'possession'—a presence intensified beyond bearing—or the experience of the deity's 'true' (*nija*, *aghora*) form.[68] From here there is but a short step to a positive notion of self-possession; *aruḷ*, in this sense,

[64] Davis 1991: 119.

[65] Ibid., citing *Kāmikâgama*, *pūrvabhāga*, 4. 352; see above, n. 56. Davis notes the potential conflict between this notion of manifestation and the principle of Śiva's all-pervasiveness; the problem is solved by postulating two levels of Śiva's presence, very much in the manner of the Dāruvana narrative.

[66] Cf. the discussion of *caṉṉiti* in relation to *uyir* in *Civañāṉacittiyār*, *cupakkam*, 4.2.3 (197).

[67] Shulman, in press (2).

[68] See discussion in Macilamani-Meyer, 1984: 221.

is the true opposite of empty encrustration, self-diminution, and be-witchment. The Dāruvana is, quite simply, set up as a site for doing or producing *aruḷ*.

We tend, wrongly, to think of the Śaiva Siddhanta theology as a step removed from this practical world of manifesting presence, with all the dangers and difficulties this entails. In fact, the philosophers have, for the most part, reformulated, with only slight abstraction, the intuitive metaphysics that drive both narrative 'myth' and rituals of possession or exorcism. *Aruḷ*, for the Siddhântins, is a *śakti*—an active and female aspect of Śiva. Not 'grace' but 'emergent presence.' It, or she, is dynamic and oriented toward freedom, in the sense stated earlier—an experiential process of *full*, unconstricted potentiality.[69] The precise relations between this *aruḷ-śakti* (or *cit-śakti*) and the ultimacy of Śiva as independent lord, *pati*, are a matter of profound concern. *Aruḷ* has a place within Śiva's selfhood as, in iconography, she occupies the left half of his visible body. She may, unpredictably, 'fall' upon the person who is ripening into readiness for initiation (*śakti-nipāta*), thereby transforming this person in the direction of the awaited free-dom.[70] In the forest, this function has devolved upon Viṣṇu-Mohinī, the active seductress of the sages who is also identified as the female half of Śiva's own self.[71]

The god becomes present through a modality seen as female, active, affectively powerful; also perhaps full or filling. She, however, stands off-centre in the internal economy of divine being—somewhere to the left. Off to another side, it appears, is one more critical *śakti* of Śiva's, that known as *māyā*, 'artifice,' or *tiro-dhāna*, 'veiling.' This other female piece of god is all that *aruḷ* is not—dependent, thus non-free, unaware, substantial. Still, as Śivaraman observes, 'Admission of *māyā* as *śakti* of God amounts to a rejection of metaphysical dualism.'[72] 'Veiling' is one of god's primary activities. In the context of his dance in the

[69] *DED* 190 identifies Tamil *aruḷ* (*aruḷu*) as a root meaning 'to be gracious to, favour, speak graciously, command, grant, bestow'; cf. Telugu cognate *arulu*, 'tenderness, affection, fondness.' Tamil *ārvam*, 'affection,' (*DED* 323) is suggested as possibly related. One is tempted to link both roots to *DED* 313, Ta. *ār*, 'to become full, spread out, be satisfied, eat drink; n. fullness, completeness,' despite loss of long vowel.

[70] See Davis 1991. 92.

[71] See n. 33 above.

[72] Śivaraman 1973: 206.

forest, or at Cidambaram, it is perceptible in Śiva's foot resting on the epileptic dwarf Muyalakan̲. As Śiva dances, swirling into total movement, he hides reality from our eyes; the dance could even be said to be rooted in, or balanced upon, this ongoing action. It is never good to underestimate the necessity of the veil. Creation, in the forms it takes in the spiraling Śaiva universe, is wholly permeated by this process. So we might be tempted to set up a facile opposition between these two female powers, which are really vectors, signalling direction: veiling moves toward a world of objects and dependence, presence galvanizes the contrary movement toward freedom. This neat contrast will not, however, survive a closer scrutiny.

They are not, in fact, in any way balanced or equal. The magnetic pull of *aruḷ* is actually much stronger. For example, a rather tantalizing discussion by the fourteenth-century philosopher Umāpati of the powers of the great Śaiva mantra, *namaccivāya* (Skt *namaḥ śivāya)*—'Homage to Śiva'—removes the living being (*uyir*)[73] from the middle space between *aruḷ* and *tiro-dhāna*. Each syllable in the mantra belongs to one ontic category: *na*=*māyā*; *ma*=*malam*, 'dross'; *ci*=Śiva, god; *vā*= *aruḷ*; *ya* = *uyir* or *āvi*, breath. The normal linear order of reciting the mantra is set aside; it is better, the text tells us, to begin by reciting the syllable *ci*—that is, Śiva—whose position in the middle of the linear sequence actually suggests the 'first' or 'highest' point. Similarly, *ya*, the 'living breath' at the end, is actually to be placed between *na* + *ma*, that is *māyā*- impurity, and *ci* + *vā*, that is Śiva + his *aruḷ*-presence.[74] One would thus recite *civāya nama* instead of *namaccivāya*; and the original end (*ya*) gravitates to the linear middle. But in 'reality'—and since this middle position suddenly seems to be of exceptional importance—this living being, *ya*, *cannot* stand anywhere between *māyā* (*na*) and *aruḷ* (*vā*); rather, this living entity—the subject of the entire Śaiva

[73] Following Nirampav a̲lakiya Tecikar's sixteenth-century commentary.

[74] *Tiruvaruṭpayan̲* 9.3. *ūn̲a naṭan̲am ŏru pāl ŏru pāl ā/ ñān̲a naṭan tā'n̲aṭuve nāṭu.* 'The dance of the body on one side, the dance of wisdom on the other—and [reality] itself in between.' Each side of this equation is a dance, *naṭan̲am/naṭam*. Nirampav a̲lakiya Tecikar explains: *pir̲appin̲ai viḷaikku' nakāra-makāraṅkaḷ ākiya kūtt' ŏru maruṅkākavum vīṭṭinaiy utavuñ cikāra-vakāraṅkal ākiya ŏru maruṅkākavum yakāram ākiya ān̲mā ivviru vakaikkum naṭuppaṭṭat' ŏn̲r̲ākavum vicāritt' ar̲ivāyāka ĕn̲ka*, 'Think of it as follows: on one side, the dance of *na* and *ma* that produces creation; on the other side, the dance of *ci* and *va* that offers release; the living soul that is *ya* is the one force between these two.'

ritual-philosophic system—is ultimately to be positioned in the middle (*iṭai*) of *aruḷ* (*vā*) and god (*ci*), that is, the two syllables that precede it in the original linear pattern.[75] What is alive, that is to say, occupies a middle space between god and presence.

The technical play with syllables is not, needless to say, the point, although it is interesting in its own right, especially when the end-point keeps slipping into one form or another of middleness. What does matter is precisely this question of the middle in relation to the whole, to freedom, to truth. Middleness, the property of the semi-vowel *y*(+ *a*), is the natural condition of the *paśu*, those living beings who are not yet god but who, with the active assistance of *aruḷ*, may yet come to know themselves as god or to make god over as themselves. God is *not*, we would imagine, normally situated between presence and god. Yet in the process of becoming present—to others as to himself—he does move into and through this middle space of whatever lives (*uyir*) or breathes (*āvi*).[76] This is where we find him in the forest, moving toward the middle, toward the dance poised on the back of Muyalakaṉ, incorporating the dwarf's dark quality of veiling. Hiding, a middle quality, is an integral part of god.

As we said earlier, middle is not centre. Indeed, the Śaiva middle is distinctly *off*-centre. A noticeable asymmetry is at work throughout this cosmology and is particularly evident in the Dāruvana materials. In music, too, Śiva sometimes inhabits this off-centre middle; he is *ma*, the middle (*madhyama*) note of the *mūrchana*-scale of Bhairav rāga, a fulcrum of instability and further movement, resting below the fixed perfect (and central) fifth, *pa*.[77] As singers know, this middle note holds the key to the rich unfolding of the rāga's particular presence and its creative elaboration. *Ma* is restless, precipitating movement. Asymmetry, impelling the recurrent loops-within-spin as the god unfolds, speaks to the restlessness of middle space. This is where living happens, where subtle distinctions obtain. The world is not not-god: it is not-

[75] *Tiruvaruṭpayaṉ* 9. 9. *āci'na vā nāppaṇ aṭaiyāt' aruḷiṉāl/ vā ciy iṭai niṟkai vaḻakku*. Nirampav aḻakiya Tecikar: . . . *yakāram ākiyav uyir avvakārattiṟkuñ civam ākiya cikārattiṟkum naṭuppaṭṭu niṟpatu muṟaimai ĕṉka*.

[76] For an Āgamic variation on this theme of the 'middle level' of Śiva's being and coming to be, see Brunner 1968: 446 (Sadāśiva poised between *niṣkala* and *sakala*, or *avyakta* and *vyakta*, modes).

[77] Cf. Danielou 1980: 26. Bhairav is, of course, closely connected to Śiva in his Bhairava guise: see below, 2.2. We thank Osnat al-Kabir, citing Ritvik Sanyal.

two, never-two, yet at the same time not-one.[78] God and *uyir*, the living being, are not one and not two (*ŏn̲r' an̲r' iranṭum il*).[79] Yet god appears to move within himself from one to two, although he may not be aware of this progression. To be aware, and to move through two back to one again, or to more than one, he needs the sages, their wives, an entire forest.

There is no room in this cosmos for severe dualism of any kind.[80] The non-dual god is the world, and he never changes—which is to say, all changes are included within him. The middle precludes the dual. By the same token, middle space is the only locus for interaction—again, the forest as we know it, where Śiva meets others. Something happens there to the god's innerness and sense of self: he fills up, he reaches the middle, begins to dance himself into presence. He is standing on the cusp of a curve, the twist that turns surface, Moebius-like, into its opposite, and his dance thus shares the strange inside-out quality of the *liṅga*, another middle point or space. From the middle, only from the middle, one can move in any direction. But none of this is given—certainly not presence, not 'being,' not movement toward or into being.[81] It has to be made where potential exists—interactively at that, in the space between.

[78] Śivaraman 1973: 143: Śaiva Siddhanta affirms 'the secondlessness of the second.'

[79] *Tiruvaruṭpayan̲* 8.5. See above at n. 39; also Devasenapathi 1974: 110 (on *Civañān̲acittiyār, cupakkam* 90).

[80] This despite the common description of the *Śaivâgama* as 'dualistic' in relation to other Śaiva materials. One can, at most, speak of a cosmos in which distinctions in existential levels can be asserted, and in which the individual living being (*paśu*, also Tamil *uyir*) is not fully merged in with the god. We take up this theme at length in the following chapters.

[81] Cf. Sivaraman 1973: 529.

Cidambaram
Making Space

> None can approach him who bears this burden now
> except him who is already so close.[1]

On Breath

If you say simply *koyil*, 'temple,' in Tamil, in a Śaiva context, you mean Cidambaram, in South Arcot district, south of Madras, where the Dancing Śiva, Naṭarāja, lives in the inner chamber known today as the *cit-sabhā*, 'the room of (or for) awareness.' There are, of course, historical reasons for this pre-eminence of the Cidambaram shrine; here, as so often, history follows a logic internal to the culture. Cidambaram is also where the analytical and experiential features proper to the Forest of Pines first crystallized in the Tamil pattern familiar from the text quoted in Chapter 1. Or we could say that Cidambaram forged the link between the forest and Śiva's dance, a link that became canonical in Tamil Śaiva works. As we have seen, the Beggar Bhikṣâṭana *becomes* the Dancer, and this progression has a particular set of meanings within the south Indian Dāruvana texts. This chapter explores these meanings, largely in relation to the themes of sorcery and exorcism that lie at the heart of the Cidambaram tradition. We also suggest that the progression just mentioned is, in fact, part of a larger and more fundamental sequence that, in its fuller form, illuminates these intra-divine developments. Our argument includes a historical hypothesis on the early

[1] *Tiruvaruṭpayan̲* of Umāpati civâcāriyar 7.5: *kiṭaikka takume nar keṇmaiyārkk' allāl/ ĕṭuttuc cumappān̲aiy in̲ru*. One could also translate: 'None can oppose/ encounter him who bears this burden now except him who is already so close.' *kiṭaikka*—'to approach, join, merge, come close;' also 'to encounter, oppose.'

(that is pre-Chola) history of Cidambaram and its cult. At the same time, we continue to consult the somewhat later Tamil Śaiva Siddhânta works for the light they throw on the Forest in its local forms.

The prehistory of the Cidambaram temple has been studied in some detail by Kulke, who argues for the antiquity of the so-called *mūlasthānam*, the 'original [*liṅga*-] shrine' which survives today in the second *prākāra* enclosure, to the north of Naṭarāja.[2] In Kulke's view, the Dancing Śiva is a younger, 'more dynamic' element of the Cidambaram cult; only in Chola times did it come to dominate the entire Cidambaram tradition *at the expense* of the *liṅga* shrine. This view has much to commend it. We know through Chola-period painting and epigraphy of the enormous popularity that the Cidambaram Naṭarāja came to enjoy as, in effect, the family deity of the royal dynasty.[3] There is good reason to agree with Kulke's reading of an eleventh-century institutional transition at Cidambaram, with Naṭarāja standing at the nexus of royal patronage and the fixing of the ritual order, under the control of the Dīkṣitar Brahmins, more or less in its present form.

Still, it is clear from the Tamil *Tevāram* poems, from an earlier point in the evolution of the tradition (seventh to ninth centuries), that the *ci<u>rr</u>'ambalam*—the 'little chamber' that, we may assume, eventually became the *cit-sabhā*—was a powerful focus of devotional attention, and already connected to the Dancer, long before Chola times. For Appar in the seventh century, for example, the god at Cidambaram was

kaṇ ni<u>r</u>ainta kaṭi pŏ<u>l</u>il ampalatt'/
uḷ ni<u>r</u>aintu ni<u>nr</u>' āṭum ŏruva<u>n</u>e//

the one who stands, dancing,
filling the space
inside the *ambalam* chamber
[surrounded by] groves filled with
honeyed fragrance. . . . [5.1.8]

Here the [*ci<u>rr</u>'*] *ambalam* apparently encloses the Dance in some inner, structured space; but he, for his part, fills and thus no doubt contains

[2] See Kulke 1970: 41–4, 215–20; also discussion by Smith 1996: 50–1.

[3] See in particular the tenth-century painting of the Cidambaram *cit-sabhā* largely as we know it today, on the walls of the Bṛhadīśvara temple in Tanjavur. See also Śivaramamurti 1955.

this same space, perhaps by the dance that he performs while, in effect, standing still. Or the two spaces may well pervade and contain one another, each being, in a sense, interior to the other. Cidambaram is, first of all, a site of spaciousness and undiminished movement opening up within a deeply inner space, and such seems to have been the case already in the time of Appar. Conceptually speaking, the temple is built around such space, which expands to include or encompass the apparently enclosing structure; or which, in another sense, actually produces this structure as a first, outward movement toward encrusted surface—as we shall see. The interior space is presumably unrestricted or infinite (if one prefers this latter term).[4] We have to keep this fact in mind when we try to think about the forest in relation to this site.

Being unrestricted, this same inner space is readily identified with the spacious awareness—a kind of breathing—that classical Vedic-Upaniṣadic texts have defined as a stable correlate of infinity as they understand it. Thus in the medieval, self-consciously Sanskritic sources from Cidambaram, the *cir̲r̲'ambalam* has become *cid-ambaram*, 'expanse of awareness.' Hence the common name for this temple-site, a synonym and synecdoche for the more specific inner 'chamber of awareness,' the *cit-sabhā*. Kulke has traced the Upaniṣadic borrowings very precisely; the *ambalam* 'chamber' has become an *ambaram* 'expanse' which, following the Upaniṣadic identifications, exists as infinite space within each individual's heart (the *dahara-veśman,* that is, the tiny dwelling in the microcosmic organism that is filled with *ākāśa*, ether/space) where awareness comes into being.[5] The *cir̲r̲'ambalam/cit-sabhā* is the site of the invisible and subtle *liṅga* made of space, *ākāśa*. But this is not only a matter of inventive Sanskritization of the type common throughout the Tamil country, in shrine after shrine, in the medieval period. For the same idea, without the Upaniṣadic terminology, turns up in the Appar *Tevāram* with reference to this same 'little chamber' at Tiger Town (Pĕrumpar̲r̲appuliyūr), the old name for Cidambaram:

ūn̲il āvi uyirkkum pŏl̲ut' ĕlām
nān̲ nilāviy iruppan̲ ĕn̲n̲ātan̲ait
ten̲ nilāviya cir̲r̲'ambalavan̲ār
vān̲ nilāviy irukkavum vaippare

[4] On culture-specific definitions of infinity, see Mimica 1988; below, p. 219.
[5] Kulke 1970: 136–45. Cf. *Chāndogya Upaniṣad* 8.1.1.

Whenever breath comes alive in flesh,
I meditate on my lord.
The Lord of the Little Chamber,
filled with honey,
will fill me with sky
and make me be. [5.1.5]

We could also divide the first two words of the verse differently, as *ūṉ* + *nilāvi*, and translate: 'Whenever flesh is filled and quickened [with breath] . . .'. *Nilāvu* [non-finite *nilāvi*], the central verb of this verse, means 'to exist' in the sense of 'to fill, spread, pervade, emit light'—hence, also, 'to think or meditate upon,' since meditation, as entering into the spaciousness inside self, is a matter of filling, pervading, illuminating, coming alive. What breathes has attributes of spaciousness, aliveness, fullness, luminosity, and awareness: these semantic domains overlap to a remarkable degree in Tamil (as in Sanskrit).[6] We may assume, from our earlier discussion, that spaciousness of this kind is also a version of middleness, situated 'between god and presence.' And we will see that the awareness that belongs here is a rather special kind of knowing, powerfully connected to the question of the god's self-knowledge as he undergoes apparent change.

For present purposes, the critical connection is between the *ciṟṟ'ambalam*, or the god present there, and the filling up or thinking or knowing that open space implies. It is this matter of space that the Cidambaram tradition has, from relatively ancient times, located at its core. So the more significant tension may thus be between the two forms of *liṅga*—one visible, stony (at least on its surface) and fixed in place in the *mūla-sthānam*, the other hidden from our eyes, ethereal, but present in an infinitely tiny or inner, hence infinitely open, setting. A field of force exists between the two *liṅga*s; both may be necessary forms of this deity, and both must 'breathe' and act upon his more external parts as process-oriented transformers at the core of his existence.[7] The history of the temple cult at Cidambaram, as Kulke implies, is largely the history of the relations between these distinct *liṅga* modes. But, as already noted, the *cit-sabhā* contains other essential elements apart from the *ākāśa-liṅga*, and these, too, have a part in the temple's story.

[6] As is well known, verbs of illumination often serve as copulas in South Asian languages. Existence implies luminosity and, apparently, space that is in movement.

[7] See discussion above, pp. 36–8.

Let us name them now, following the insightful and detailed presentation by David Smith.[8] First of all, there is Naṭarāja (in bronze)—probably another form of the ethereal *liṅga*, as we shall see. Beside him stands the goddess, his local wife, Śiva-kāma-sundarī, 'the one who longs for Śiva.' On the wall to the right is a curtain, red inside, black outside, that hides what is known as the Cidambaram *rahasya*, the 'secret'—a *yantra* cosmogram, apparently a variant of the so-called *Śrī-cakra*. The secret is a real one, and many modern voices insist that behind the curtain there is, again, only 'open space,' the 'nothing' that is full of being.[9] To the other side of Naṭarāja and the goddess, one finds a head-*liṅga* (*mukha-liṅga*) that is the head of Brahmā, whom Śiva/Bhairava decapitated. A distinctive, full-fledged Bhairava form—Svarṇâkarṣaṇa-Bhairava, 'who attracts gold'—is also here, as are Śiva's sandals, an image known as Bali-nāyaka, 'lord of offerings,'[10] and the small Ruby Naṭarāja (*ratna-sabhā-pati*) and a crystal *liṅga* that, together, receive the main ritual attention of the Dīkṣitar priests in daily worship.

Were we to classify these components, ignoring sequence of any sort for the moment, we might say that the Dancer, in male and female segments, exists beside Bhairava and Bhairava's victim, on the one hand, and the Beggar's sandals, on the other. This triad constitutes a primary set, as the Cidambaram *purāṇa*s clearly show us. In addition, the invisible *liṅga* is condensed into a crystal miniature, just as the Dancer exists in the modular form of Ruby Naṭarāja, and both these Śaiva icons are joined to the 'lord of offerings,' that is, Śiva crowned by the moon. Still more abstractly, the triad Bhairava-Bhikṣâṭana-Naṭarāja stands in distinctive relation to the spacious and transformative openness that is the god's depth (the hidden *liṅga* of space) and to the no less spacious and hidden Secret, with its feminine aspect (*Śrī-cakra*). Three is the number best suited to this space—Bhairava-Bhikṣâṭana–Naṭarāja are a single, compounded element in the higher-order triplet with *liṅga* and Secret, and these combined sets extrude the miniature triplet of ruby, crystal, and moon-soaked lord of offerings. We might also posit a more specific, intimate link between the invisible space-*liṅga* and the

[8] Smith 1996: 89.

[9] See Natarajan 1994: 222–3. Natarajan adds a somewhat tantalizing, unfortunately anonymous exegesis: 'A great saint has been heard to say that the superimposition of *Sri cakra* over *Pancakshara cakra* produces the configuration of Naṭarāja.' Ibid., 222.

[10] A Candra-śekhara image: Śiva with the crescent moon on his crest.

normally invisible Secret, as if together they comprised a subtle and mutually generative *liṅga-yoni* pair, each emerging out of the other and flowing back into or through the other. In this case, the basic, male-dominated triad (Bhairava-Bhikṣâṭana-Naṭarāja) would be the limited projection onto a differentiated surface of a deeper level of divine existence in which *liṅga* and *yoni* are continually weaving themselves together through the fullness of inner space. Both Beggar and Dancer, that is, are shadows cast on the sheer surface of the empty chamber—like the painted, perhaps superimposed cosmogram itself—out of an inner restlessness that belongs deeply to what is called god. Or perhaps god is just this restless movement as it emerges into visibility and then vanishes. The *liṅga* extrudes the faces of Beggar and Dancer, usually in this order, as it moves through or into the Secret, while the latter maps these regularly emergent forms. These shadows or projections have volume, contours, definite features, and, above all, clear direction of movement. All that remains is to tease out the logic of the latent sequence.

Bhairava: Taking Away

To situate the dance from the Forest of Pines at Cidambaram, as the local cultic and *purāṇic* traditions have done since Chola times, at the latest, is to suggest that Śiva undergoes certain characteristic processes in relation to self and cosmos at this temple. Stated in the barest schematic outline, the Beggar's trajectory of filling up, confronting the sorcerer-sages, and accelerating into the total movement of the dance is implicitly, and continuously, re-enacted here. Cidambaram, as we will see, is said to have an existential advantage over the 'original' forest: the Tamil shrine is capable of containing and sustaining the god's dance without pause, whereas the forest was in danger of being sucked up into it and consumed. Cidambaram offers a secure and accessible space for the dance. At the same time, the local tradition adds certain key elements to the Forest of Pines template, thereby enlarging our perspective. Most salient of these is the role of Bhikṣâṭana's precursor and model, the violent Brahminicide Bhairava.

Within the inner 'room of awareness,' we find a Bhairava who 'attracts' gold, like a magnet, drawing precious substance toward himself just as Bhikṣâṭana draws to himself the women's rice and curry as well as their awakening feeling and generative power. But Bhairava is the god who beheaded the five-headed creator, Brahmā—perhaps the most aggressive and consequential of Śiva's mythic deeds, and as such a catastrophe of sorts within the internal economy of this deity—and this act, too, has left its traces in the *cit-sabhā* in the form of the severed head that has become a *liṅga*. What, we need to ask, is Bhairava doing there? How does this rather gruesome but fundamental, and also strangely seductive, presence connect with the dance that is, so its name insists, all rapture (*ānanda*)? Or, stated more generally: what is the secret of Bhairava's attraction, which he seems to share with the Beggar?

It is one thing, and no longer such a mystery, to attach Śiva's begging to his dance, or vice versa—as we saw in the *Kanta-purāṇam* text. Already in the ninth century, Māṇikkavācakar, one of the great Tamil Śaiva poets, does this naturally:

ambalatte kūttāṭi amuta cĕyap pali tiriyum/
nampaṉaiyum tevaṉ ĕṉṟu naṇṇumat' eṉ eṭi//

The Dancer in the *ambalam* chamber
wanders as a Beggar in search of food.
How can we approach such a god
as God?[11]

In the poet's mind, at least, these two forms of Śiva at Cidambaram have an intrinsic affinity, which comes through later, in the fourteenth century, in the local *purāṇic* text we cite in section 3. Still, the composite image as a whole seems paradoxical, even somewhat forbidding. How is one to approach such a god (as God)? This question has a no less paradoxical, but entirely persuasive, answer in the second half of the verse, spoken by a woman engaged in this exchange of riddles: 'That is his nature, and he is the one I love [*because* of this very nature?—*nampaṉaiyum ām ā keḷ*];' besides, the four Vedas, that cannot know

[11] *Tiruvācakam* 12.17 (*tiruccāḻal*). Commentators sometimes understand this question as directed by a sceptical female companion to the heroine (*talaivi*) who has fallen in love with Śiva; so the question would then be, 'How can you take such a man for your husband/lord?' (Thus Ka. Cu. Navanīta Kiruṣṇa Pāratiyār on this verse, 1954: 637). The *cāḻal* form is a playful dialogue between women—challenge and response. The Śaiva tradition, however, puts the challenge in the mouth of the Buddhist teacher with whom Māṇikkavācakar debated at Cidambaram, and the affirming answer is that of the hitherto dumb daughter of the Lankan king: *Tiruvātavūraṭikaḷ purāṇam* of Kaṭavuḷ māmuṉivar (fifteenth century?), 498–9.

him, say he is God. So the enigmatic texts know without knowing, and the pilgrim or lover approaches what is unapproachable but necessarily fused, Dancer and Beggar somehow becoming a single being, to be taken and worshipped as such. A deeper, more compelling affinity seems to be hinted at here.

The god's composite identity is entirely explicit in the Cidambaram sources. We have already noted Bhairava's presence beside the Dancer and the strong suggestion, arising from the iconographic and ritual order of the *cit-sabhā*, of a deep relation between Bhairava and the Cidambaram Bhikṣâṭana. Of course, on one level Bhairava and Bhikṣâṭana are versions of one another, as we have seen in Chapter 1; more precisely, Bhikṣâṭana, like the Skeleton (Kaṅkāla-mūrti) with Viṣvaksena's bones on his trident, is a particular crystallization of the Bhairava mode, or a phase in Bhairava's mythic biography. These three—Bhairava, Bhikṣâṭana, and Kaṅkāla—belong together in classical south Indian iconology.[12] But this hardly explains the meaning of the association. To go a little deeper, we need to examine at least one canonical south Indian Bhairava text that can stand beside the Bhikṣâṭana of *Kanta-purāṇam* and the Cidambaram parallel to the latter version in Umāpati's *Koyiṟ-purāṇam*. Once again, our base-text provides a point of departure. Here, then, is the *Kanta-purāṇam*'s portrait of Bhairava, an entirely normative south Indian account (from the Kumarakkoṭṭam shrine at Kancipuram, c. fifteenth-sixteenth century):

Kanta-purāṇam, *Takṣa-kāṇṭam*, 13.154-97

One day, long ago, numberless sages and gods came to see Māl[13] *and Lotus-Dwelling Brahmā on a golden peak of the Golden Mountain. Bowing to them, they asked, respectfully, 'One of the three great gods is the First. He has no beginning, no middle, no end. He is wealthy enough to give everything. He is the highest of all, the breath of life that breathes through, and within, imperishable worlds. Who is he? Both of you should tell us now.'*

*That is how they put it, and Brahmā, who was trapped in the magical net woven by God, said at once, 'I am that first and total god (*ya<u>n</u>

[12] See above, p. 25; Adiceam 1965.
[13] Viṣṇu.

attalaimaiy ām piramam ākum*), as you should know very well.' But Nārāyaṇa protested: 'It was I who gave birth to you! I am that high, total god.'*

And with that they started arguing—a violent, cussed argument that went on for many days, replete with sterile, hair-splitting logic and much heat and rage. The gods and sages, without exception, went away, feeling that they had caused this quite terrifying state of affairs. The quarrel just went on and on. Eventually the Veda itself and the single syllable Om *took various other forms and went there to put an end to it. 'It is Śiva,' they said, 'who is the breath breathing in all that breathes, the father of everyone, the true ultimate. Stop arguing.' But the two contenders brushed aside these words and went on fighting.*

Śiva, powerfully present to everyone and anyone he marks, saw this and felt compassion. He wanted to end this harsh conflict. So he, who has no limit, above or below, appeared in the middle of the sky as pure light. But neither Nārāyaṇa nor Brahmā recognized him as Śiva. They were unable to extricate themselves from the tangled skein of māyā*. Still, they wondered what this light could be.*

Śiva, seeing how matters stood, came a little closer, in the middle of that light, but in the active form that he has when he sits in state on Kailāsa, merged with the goddess Umā—the form that comes to possess us. Now Viṣṇu, dark as a rain cloud, recognized him as Śiva and quickly rose and bowed. Brahmā, on the other hand, didn't budge one iota from within the net of māyā*; unlike Viṣṇu, he showed no love for the father who had appeared, and would not bow to him. What is worse, he opened the foul mouth in his head—well, actually, there are five mouths and five heads—and started to abuse Śiva, who had just emerged before his eyes. Still, the ultimate lord, who is an ocean of compassion, did not get angry. If he were to be even a little angry, could any of the galaxies and the living and breathing beings within them survive?*

Rather, to do away with Brahmā's error, to transform the egoism of the other gods, and to remove the sages' arrogant excess, the Lord of the Veda joyfully and compassionately created from inside himself the god Bhairava—his body emitting a dark blue light, anklets on his feet, a fiery, poisonous snake around his waist, millions and millions of skulls bouncing in garlands on his chest, his hands holding a trident, an axe, a noose, and a drum. He had three eyes; sharp teeth white as the moon; long matted hair, red as sunset; the kind of smile that means fierce anger. All in all, it was a fierce apparition[14] *that stood before god, our Father Black-Neck. Śiva looked at this Bhairava and said to him, to outline his task: 'The head of Brahmā, our little son on the lotus, has insulted us. There it is, right on top of his body, the highest of his heads.*[15] *I want you to snap it off with your hand, immediately. Then give him back his life and, holding the head, go from city to city of the sages and gods who sing their own praises; beg alms of blood from them, from their putrid bodies. And as you take their alms, give back an excess of life to those who die. Transform the selfishness they have acquired by all their study and thinking. Then find a place to stay at the highest point in the cosmos. That site at the zenith was set aside for you long ago. From there, you must protect all the living world and the assembly of the gods, so that they are free of sorrow.'*

*Śiva, our King, is a veritable ocean of love. He gave Bhairava the full force of his loving presence and merged into immaculate light. That light, with the First God within it, emerged unseen by those who were there. Māyoṉ-Viṣṇu, understanding it all, thought it would be unnatural to remain there, so he bowed to Three-Eyed Śiva and went off to his own world. No sooner had he gone than Black Bhairava (*kāri*), filling with fury, plucked off Brahmā's top head with his fingernail and held it in his hand while blood flooded the world. Brahmā fell down dead. The river of blood washed around great Mount Meru at the centre of the cosmos. Bhairava turned his fiery forehead eye on the flood and dried it up. He then restored sweet breath to Brahmā, who arose, awake and aware, as if from sleep. His ancient wisdom restored, Brahmā bowed, with natural love, at the feet of Bhairava and said, 'The mistakes I made in opposing Śiva, the Unstained, are beyond counting. Hence the terrible disgrace I have suffered. Please, from this moment on, remove anger from your heart. Bhairava, you who can make an entire universe into nothing in the blink of an eye, through your compassion I have attained the ancient wisdom. Bear with the meanness that was mine. And to purify this miserable, mean head of mine, so that confusion will disappear whenever I see it, I ask you in all humility to keep it in your hand, as if it were the great trident that you carry.'*

The Lord looked at Brahmā, who still had four heads, and said, 'So be it.' He then left the golden mountain. With his perfect blue body, he

[14] *ukkira vaṭivu kŏṇṭu* [Skt *ugra (mūrti)*].

[15] Of Brahmā's five heads, this one perhaps towers over the others.

created an army of ghouls to accompany him—Wind-Speed, Fire-Head, Gentle Somaka, Death-by-Poison, and innumerable others. With them our Lord hurried off to every forest retreat on earth where flawed ascetics lived and to all the various heavens of the gods. Everywhere he went he took as alms the thick blood flowing from their bodies; then he gave them back the breath of life and purified their inner spaces. He is an ocean of deep feeling.

Bhairava rapidly finished with all the worlds of the gods and moved on to the city that is home to Viṣṇu, whose pride was still intact. His immortal ghouls preceded him. But the doorkeeper and commander of the army, Viṣvaksena, who looks just like Viṣṇu himself—with conch and discus—barred their way. Wind-Speed and the other gaṇas *began to fight with him, until Bhairava himself arrived and speared Viṣvaksena on his trident. With the body raised aloft, Bhairava continued on to the place where Viṣṇu rests on the many-headed serpent, with Earth and Lakṣmī on either side of him. Viṣṇu rose, with his two wives, to greet Bhairava with his long spear, the corpse dangling at the tip of the trident. 'Why, father, have you come here?' he asked.*

'We have come to beg alms,' said the three-eyed god. 'Give us blood from the head that sits so properly on your body.'

'With pleasure,' said Viṣṇu, and tore open a vein in his forehead with his fingernail. Blood gushed out toward Bhairava, into the skull he held in his hand. It flowed for ten thousand years until it was exhausted. At this point another kind of confusion took over. The skull was not yet even half full. Viṣṇu lost his strength and fainted. Earth and Lakṣmī, seeing their husband's condition, began to plead.

'Don't be afraid,' Bhairava said to them as they fell at his feet. He cleared confusion from Viṣṇu's heart and gave him breath. Then he left that place. But Viṣṇu followed after him, begging him to stay, praying to him to have mercy—as was only right—on Viṣvaksena, impaled on his trident. So Bhairava, with the skull still in his hand, released the Commander and restored his breath.

In that same form, Bhairava left Viṣṇu's world together with his gaṇas *and went to the zenith of the cosmos, where he lives day by day, watching over many universes. At the time the cosmos comes to an end, by Śiva's command, he demolishes the heads of the gods, from Brahmā on down; he transforms all that breathes; he makes the worlds into dust. He wanders through the cremation ground where all sensate, living beings, and all the worlds come to an end and are destroyed. He bears the Veda in the form of a dog on his banner, and what he feels is an extraordinary joy.*[16]

Now you know how Śiva, with the river flowing through his hair, made the Pure God emerge to receive alms of blood from Brahmā and the other gods. We have described how he wandered inside every part of the earth and the sky, the hostile head in his outstretched hand. All this awful begging is the story of Śiva's punishing kindness.

Bhairava guards Kancipuram[17] as he guards other Śaiva temples, including Cidambaram and—as the text tells us—the entire cosmos. His true place is at the outer edge or at the zenith, the highest point in created space. Perhaps these two spaces coincide.[18] But his act of watching or guarding is apparently of a piece with his role in destroying, chopping off heads, and restoring them to their owners. It is in this role that Bhairava wanders constantly inside each part of earth and sky. He is inside all space only insofar as he is *above* space, outside or beyond. In this guise he begs and receives blood as alms, filling up the head that earlier refused to know him as god. The entire sequence or process is, moreover, glossed as kindness.

On one level, clearly recognized by classical Śaiva sources,[19] Bhairava's lethal act against Brahmā is an attempt to transform a consciousness absorbed in egoism and self-delusion. If, like Brahmā, you are lucky, Bhairava will eventually cut away your head and replace it with a wiser one. There may be no other effective path to growth or maturity. Note how the head, with its capacity to know, is clearly separated from the rest of Brahmā's being; it is the head, perhaps only the head, that fails to see reality and that insults Śiva, as the latter observes. Yet Bhairava's beheading of Brahmā is not without consequence for the active god himself, who remains tied, rather uncomfortably, to the head he has displaced. Moreover, this head is hungry—like Śiva himself in the

[16] The commentator tells us that this is what those who know the 'secret of destruction' (*caṅkāra irakaciyam*) say.

[17] The Bhairaveśvara shrine marks the western boundary: see *Kāñcippurāṇam* of Civañāṉacuvāmikaḷ, *Vayiravecap paṭalam*. Adjacent to the Bhairava shrine is a *linga* set up by Viṣvaksena, who is said to have danced a comic dance (*vikaṭakkūttu*) in order to force one of the skulls on Vīrabhadra's neck to laugh: ibid., *Viṭuvaccenecap paṭalam*, 19–22. Note the proximity of these two shrines to Dakṣeśa, linked to Dakṣa's sacrifice.

[18] See below, pp. 143–7 on the coincidence of middle and edge.

[19] See von Stietencron 1969.

unbalanced and seemingly empty mode in which he comes to the Forest of Pines. Brahmā's skull is, in fact, so hungry that it can never become full, though it consumes, sooner or later, the blood of all living beings, thus soaking up the entire created cosmos at the moment of its reabsorption into god. Note that this blood, classed as alms, invariably flows into the skull from the victim's head, as in the particularly impressive case of Viṣṇu in the text above. *All* heads finally flow into this one head in Bhairava's hand and in so doing inhabit what we might call the space of temporality, that form of linear sequence that repeatedly culminates in destruction on both an individual and a universal scale. '*At the time the cosmos comes to an end, by Śiva's command, he demolishes the heads of the gods, from Brahmā on down; he transforms all that breathes; he makes the worlds into dust. He wanders through the cremation ground where all sensate, living beings, and all the worlds come to aṇ end and are destroyed.*'

Time includes this moment in its rhythm, and Bhairava *is* this time—god in (or through) time. More simply, he creates or opens up time by repeated acts of cognitive violence. Each such moment of removing a head, any head, starts time off again on its devolving course. We will attempt a more precise formulation in a moment. Bhairava, we are told, wanders 'inside every part of the earth and the sky'—so this activity, so integral to god at the highest point in the cosmos, must be going on continuously, generating temporal space by extending, in demanding linear motion, the ever-unsatisfied skull. The god stretches out his hand—toward us, taking from us—and in this way makes room for us to live and die. This stark vision is also an ongoing movement within godhead in the direction of Śiva's dance, as the Cidambaram texts will reveal.

If we stay, however, within the confines of the passage just cited, we might say that Bhairava is that part of Śiva flung out into the world to redress or dissolve perception that has reified and crystallized as bounded-off selves, like the sages' notion of themselves when they first meet this god. Such crystallized selves are, to anticipate slightly, at least as mad as the voracious self that clings to Bhairava's hand—a mad, skeletal part-self of the god as Beggar evolving into the Dancer.[20] Bhairava is spinning on the surface that is whirling Śiva back into Śiva—in this respect he includes the Beggar Bhikṣâṭana within himself, to be

[20] See below, pp. 168–70 (a Bhairava myth from Mel Malaiyanur).

unfolded by a more detailed inspection of the form—though his relation to the zenith or apex, translated on earth into an outer boundary, actually points toward the middleness that we have identified as the more profound level of godhead. Bhairava, that is, is the creator of middleness within, for, and in relation to the god. In this respect, his characteristic combination of beheading and begging, the latter prefiguring the Bhikṣâṭana role in the forest, provides Bhairava with a rationale that can be articulated in metaphysical terms.

Bhairava's principal function is, as we have seen, to take something away (the confused head; the confused and unfocused life). But this act of taking away, which the Śaiva Siddhânta texts see as the most fundamental feature underlying god's freedom and mastery, means something more than the words alone might suggest. It is all too easy to gloss it, as generations of translators have, as a kind of destruction: Śiva, or Rudra, or Hara—the latter is literally the 'one who removes or takes away,' from the root *hṛ*—has for too long enjoyed the dubious status of Destroyer within a theoretically ordered Hindu pantheon. It is high time we did away with this nonsense. We would be much closer to the logic driving both philosophers and mythographers—they are anyway usually the same people in the medieval Tamil world—if we began to think of 'taking away' as, in fact, a way of 'filling up.'

To understand this equation, we need to enter a domain of sometimes unspecified axiology. Take, for example, the opening verse of the Sanskrit *Śiva-jñāna-bodha*, a series of twelve authoritative statements about Śiva which, in their Tamil form, became the core-text of the Śaiva Siddhânta scriptures:

strī-puṃ-napuṃsakāditvāj jagataḥ kārya-darśanād/
asti kartā sa hṛtvaitat sṛjaty asmāt prabhur haraḥ//

Because we observe the world as an effect, divided into feminine, masculine, and neuter,
the Creator [or active Subject] exists: taking it away, he emits it and is, therefore, the Lord, Hara.

As so often in the philosophical texts, a linguistic argument underlies the basic claim: as a sentence has an actor or subject, *kartṛ*, the world must have a creator; moreover, the material acted upon and active within this world must be divided into the three genders (or, in cosmogenesis, three modes of being), like nouns in speech. The result is a powerful and simple assertion of existence: [If language works,] god is (*asti*). But now the more descriptive part of the argument appears—for existence alone is not the issue. *How* does god exist? He externalizes (*sṛjati*) the world as effect—such is his manner of creation—but only after taking away (*hṛtvaitat*). Logically and existentially, taking away precedes emission. Moreover, this act of taking away is the guarantee of his unity, as the great commentator Śivâgrayogin tells us.[21] The same assumption about taking away underlies the serious claims about god's freedom—he is free, *svatantra*, just as the subject of the sentence is defined linguistically as essentially free (to act)[22]—and about his mastery or lordship (*svāmitva*).[23] There is, that is to say, an innate connection between notions of taking away as enabling or even defining creation and the related concepts of freedom and lordship as intrinsic, defining aspects of Śiva. We should also bear in mind that *saṃhāra*, this taking away in the sense of opening a space, also means 'completion,' as when one draws a full circle, for example.[24]

A complex but highly consistent discussion of 'otherness' and 'non-otherness' is woven into this argument. Remember that god is 'not two and not one,' and that he has a firm link to the middle space. Removing, he is non-other (*an-anya*), that is, whole in self and one with world: 'in his pervasiveness, that is, in the mode of initiation (*dīkṣā*), or through firm knowing, as the three chains (*pāśa*) disappear, he takes away in his visible self that is undivided [from the world], being thus non-other (*an-anya*).'[25] One might, that is, be tempted to imagine him as quite separate from his cosmos, insofar as he is free or released (*muktau*); but this is wrong because of the 'pervasiveness' that belongs to this

[21] *atra câstîty anena caikatvaṃ vivakṣitam*: 'in saying *asti* [He exists—in the context of taking away, *saṃhāra-śaktimataḥ eva siddhau*], his unity is intended.' *Laghu-ṭīkā* 1.

[22] Pāṇini 1.4.54.

[23] Śivâgrayogin, *loc. cit.*: *etena saṃhāra-kartur eva svāmitvam ity āha*, 'in this the mastery of the remover-creator is articulated.'

[24] *Saṃhāra* is sometimes replaced by *pratyavahāra*, 'withdrawing,' 'dissolving,' as befits this cosmology of breathing out and breathing in: see, e.g., *Raghuvaṃśa* 2.44.

[25] Ibid., ad *sūtra* 2: *vyāptitaḥ vyāptyā dīkṣayā dṛḍhatara-jñānena vā pāśa-trayâpagame sati svabhinna-sākṣātkāra-rūpayā 'n-anyo 'bhinnaḥ saṃhṛtiṃ karoti.* The *sūtra* itself, however, speaks of creation, *karoti samsṛtim;* Śivâgrayogin addresses this phrase earlier in the commentary in terms of the unevenness of karmic experience.

free deity, who is himself an open space. *Anyaḥ san vyāptito 'n-anyaḥ*, 'being other, he is non-other because he pervades,' as the second verse states. To pervade is to fill, as space fills an uncluttered 'void.' Śiva's apparent otherness is actually a function of the externalizing or creative mode, which is secondary to his taking away. In other words, god's pouring out of objects from within entails a self-displacement that might appear as otherness—a 'becoming' (*bhāva*) that, on some level, and certainly on the only level that allows us to know or perceive him (*bhāvaika-gamya*),[26] inserts an alien otherness into god.

This conclusion is important and should be restated as simply as possible. Śiva emerges in certain phases, faces, or aspects as not Śiva. He becomes other to himself and to any potential observer. Perception actually requires this otherness. Ritual means (*dīkṣā*) may be necessary to restore his completeness, to make him non-other, to fill him up as a pervasive and spacious god. It is in his visible (Bhairava) self, characteristically removing heads, that he achieves this (momentary) culmination, becoming fully himself again. Bhairava is thus god as he moves toward being or becoming god.

Thus Bhairava is the complete, non-other, entirely free aspect of god as that existence which, by existing, takes away or, by taking away, comes into existence. But we can go still further. In these sources, taking away is the first feature or moment of ultimacy, thus a strong ontic assertion—the proof of god's existence—but also a correlate of other important aspects of god such as his aliveness (*ajaḍatva*) and his playfulness (*līlā*). The latter notion is linked to notions of flexibility, lability, and pure potential. We will have occasion to return to these linkages and to suggest a more detailed, analytic profile. In the present context, the point is that *saṃhāra*—the business of removing or completing—serves as the metaphysical substratum that supports both story and temple ritual.[27] It is as if the very act of creating space by removing blocks, or stains (*mala*), or marks, or dead objects seen as part-selves, were what makes god into god; as if both in his world and within his own self the defining, existential necessity made for such an opening. As Śivâgrayogin's formulation suggests, as soon as the chains (or stains

[26] Śivâgrayogin ad *sūtra* 6.

[27] Cf. *Śaivâgama-paribhāṣā-mañjarī* 3.57–8, citing *Pauṣkarâgama*: Śiva's power of taking away (*hariṇī śakti*) is what frees the self stuck in the world and leads it to the highest realm. Ritual goals focus on this point.

or other impediments) disappear, this god, who is free and non-other, fills (*vyāpnoti*) the now open space.

In this system, taking away allows something new to come into being. Indeed, *only* in this way, it seems, can something new emerge. The Śaiva cosmos is in movement, renewing itself through removing. Such is the task of the Śaiva god who, antithetical to stasis, constantly moves the parts of the cosmos around, thus creating conditions for further movement, accelerating this movement, demanding and enabling the continuous emergence of something new. It happens moment by moment: what the temporal instant has produced always has to be cleared away. Indeed, one could argue that this description of process applies to the conceptual structure of time in a more general way, in one prevalent Indian mode.[28] Since Vedic times, the year (*samvatsara*) is a linear period of gestation—ten months long—leading up to the moment of birth or delivery that marks the onset of the monsoon; this is followed by two months of sequenceless 'monsoon time,' when the world reverts to water and cosmic domains intermingle. Probably all units of time, even the smallest, reveal a similar structure of linear sequence issuing into or otherwise containing a mixed, non-linear mode that does away with the prior sequence. There is a measurable emergence into surface that is cleared away before the next such pattern begins.[29] If one fails to open such a space by undoing the previous emergence, what remains is a clutter of days, years, objects—a suffocating and dying world. Put differently, in the perspective of Śaiva temple ritual, the day into which worshippers move in space, through time, will not fully come into existence unless the previous day is 'taken away.' Cosmos, in its temporal and spatial process, is recreated daily, the whole purpose of this renewed creation being to produce or ensure the potential for uncluttered, non-entropic, playful space. Hence the need for exorcism—for exorcising any overly solid entity, including the overly flat and solid parts of god himself. Linear sequence in and of itself has an oppressive and dangerous aspect; the longer it lasts and the more it unfolds, the more ramified it becomes and the less potential for movement and aliveness

[28] We thank Gautam Vajracharya for discussion of this question; see Vajracharya 1997.

[29] Among the almost endless exemplifications of this notion, we may cite the Virāṭa section of the Epic—the extra-temporal, non-linear moment of hiding, upheaval and transformation that complete the sequence of exile the Pāṇḍava heroes must undergo.

remains. Time saturates unless it is stopped and a space for transformation and renewal left open. By opening such a space, god allows it to fill up; this is the point of having a god.

In passing we may note the striking contrast with more familiar—say, Greek or Roman—notions of transformation as metamorphosis, one form issuing into another, often by or through a rupture. In the south Indian conceptual world we are exploring, there is, first, the act of removing, followed by a filling up; the gradual closure of linearity is stopped or reversed, and the space of potentiality momentarily comes into play.[30] This is *aruḷ*—god's coming into presence, a ritual effect. We could also describe the process by other topological metaphors such as looping or spinning, an initial 'as-if' linearity twisting around so that god continuously goes through himself, recreating himself moment by moment, stretching himself toward the cosmos in self-diminishing forms that are spun back into the potential completeness out of which they emerged. Here sequence destroys its own sequentiality. This may, in fact, be how Śiva gets from one moment to another.

A somewhat unexpected causality is implicit in this description. Effects are not latent in their causes.[31] Discontinuity of a certain type becomes essential if the cosmos is to breathe, although it is a discontinuity within the domain of obstructive and innately discontinuous forms. That is, what looks discontinuous to us is, under these conditions of god's playful intervention, reconnecting. Stated simply, something is removed, and then something else comes into being. Lines curve or twist. True forward movement proceeds by taking away, which allows filling up, or which actually *is* a filling up. Sequence aborts. Bhairava seems to proceed, initially, along a visible line or path—in the northern *purāṇa*s, he is walking toward Kāśī—but at Cidambaram, at any rate, he is replaced by the Beggar, also moving toward a geographical point, the forest. Once there, he begins to fill up, to bend and curve. The sages fling their fire-born weapons at him, in characteristically straight lines, but as he makes these weapons into parts of himself, they curve into him: the tiger's skin wraps around his waist, the deer stretches toward

[30] See Rajam 1985 on aspect-markers of unfinished process in the Tamil verbal system.

[31] In contrast to classical Sāṅkhya notions of *sat-kārya-vāda*: see Halbfass 1992: 55–8.

the sky that is swirling around him. A roundedness is coming into being. Note that this is the exact language of our texts, far from paraphrase: Śiva raises his foot, 'gracefully bent and poised,'[32] and begins to dance—standing on Muyalakan̲, the jerky, spasmodic spirit of epilepsy. To serve Śiva truly is to be 'enfolded' in the 'foot that is bent in dance' (*maṭitt' āṭum aṭimai*).[33] The curved foot, *kuñcitâṅghri*, is the visual focus of this dancing figure, hence a compelling subject for poets singing of Naṭarāja.[34] The arc it describes, repeated in the wider arc or nimbus of flames (*prabhā-maṇḍala*) that usually envelops the dancer,[35] is no incidental feature but rather shows us something essential to god moving in this mode: Naṭarāja is all continuity, a smooth spin that fills up space, each piece of him spinning on its own within the greater vortex[36] in which god flows through himself in all directions and times. By now there is only middleness, and no residual peripheries.

This pervasive, full mode of being is, Śivâgrayogin says, equivalent to *dīkṣā*—a ritual initiation, apparently something god also requires. It is also, somewhat more surprisingly, identified as a kind of 'firm knowing' (*dhṛḍhatara-jñāna*). This element remains to be studied. For now, we restate the major coordinates of this process as they appear at Cidambaram in the *cit-sabhā*. Śiva as Bhairava takes away (filling up Brahmā's skull with blood). He begs (filling self with rice and love). He dances, filling the subtle and pervasive innerness that is space itself, space as potential world. Insofar as the world, untransformed, survives outside this god, it is empty and ensorcelled; insofar as he is, or has become, this object-cluttered domain of apparent surfaces, he too is empty and bewitched. In reality, if we can use the word, nothing is ever finally outside him; but parts of him do become bound, mortgaged, frozen, or enslaved. When freedom reasserts itself, something is taken away: god

32 *Tirunĕlvelittalapurāṇam, tārukāvan̲accarukkam* 233 (*kun̲itta cĕṅkamalaccaraṇattāl*); see below, p. 134.

33 Cuntaramūrtti *Tevāram* 90.1 (913); see discussion in Shulman 1990: 573; Dorai Rangaswamy 1958: 2: 686.

34 Smith 1996 takes the *Kuñcitâṅghri-stava* as his point of departure.

35 See discussion by Guy, in press.

36 Note that in Kāraikkālammaiyār's early *Tiruvālaṅkāṭṭu mūtta tirupatikam* verse 8, the wilderness, the ocean, mountains, earth itself, and the heavens whirl and spin (*cul̲ala*) as Śiva performs his dance.

completes himself, and the cosmos comes alive again, becoming free or full. To get from point A to point B, one needs the forest.

Let us repeat, in a stark formulation: god, in this Śaiva world, is sometimes blocked. He includes within 'himself,' whatever such a word might mean, points of blockage, or clutter, or damage. In a certain sense, he, or some part of him, consistently and repeatedly crashes into these hard spots. They constitute a challenge to his fullest and most fluid level or existence—though existence of any kind is, in such a system, never a datum, always a mode of potentiality—and he is drawn inevitably to meet this challenge, to melt down the solid or encrusted hook or sharp angle that cuts through or hinders his movement. However, in another sense he is himself the author of these blockages, insofar as he breathes himself out into the world, creating surface. Creatures such as Brahmā or the sages of the forest are, one might say, cognitively and emotionally invested in such obstructions, which define them and their world; they cling for dear life to the crust. But we cannot understand this process as a whole unless we recognize, as they also come to do, that such obstructions and blockages are necessary components of the divine movement of spinning into and through cosmos and self. Indeed, we will argue that they constitute minimally necessary conditions for a certain type of self-knowledge that god seeks.

Iconographically, Bhairava thus moves into the Dancer—the Cidambaram progression that includes the Beggar in the Forest of Pines and that is present in the ritual organization of the *cit-sabhā*, as we have seen. A linear logic of evolution might outline three stages: First, Śiva bewitches himself by coming into presence within his cosmos; in so doing, he encrusts, fragments, and empties his 'self.' A mad self, insatiably hungry, turns up in concrete, visible form, for example, the voracious skull clinging to Bhairava's hand. Second, the fragments empty themselves even further by practising black magic against Śiva. Third, Śiva absorbs the fierce emptiness of the sages, filling himself with himself through the dance, the moment of presence that, in terms used earlier, creates middleness. The Cidambaram *purāṇas* show us very precisely how this happens. The *cit-sabhā* contains the detritus of this process—Brahmā's head turned *liṅga*, the sandals, the lord of offerings, the two condensed, crystalline and perhaps interchangeable forms of Dancer and *liṅga*. The Dancer, like the 'secret' emerging somewhere behind the curtain, has left footprints on his way toward total movement. Yet in the ritual perspective, these footprints effectively generate the foot—as is usually the case with footprints in India[37]—that is, they are useful implements capable of activating the dance, possibly by creating enough resistance to force the god to unblock himself at these points.[38] In short, they enable us, or him, to take enough away to become present. One begins to see why Bhairava is so important here.

But this sequential statement is also potentially rather misleading—a view from the encrusted surface, *as if* outside the god. Such a perspective, however natural to us, is, in the logic of these texts, fundamentally impossible. Fortunately, the Tamil Bhairava text we have cited offers another, perhaps more helpful language. Bhairava's constant preoccupation is with *uyir*—the breath that is life itself and also, as we have said, a kind of knowing. Situated at the zenith, hence somewhere within all forms of space or time, Bhairava 'transforms all that breathes' (*uyir mur̲r̲u' mār̲r̲i*, 194) by removing heads and pulverizing universes. His initial set of orders from Śiva, at the moment of Bhairava's externalization, includes giving back 'an excess of life [literally, "breath"] to those who die' (*vīntavar tamakku mīṭṭum viyan̲ uyir utavi,* 168). Bhairava is a master of breathing, very close to the notion of Śiva as a great Yogi.[39] Specifically, he embodies and also enables the in-breath, which creates space by taking away. Perhaps it is this dimension that is meant by our texts' emphasis on 'innerness.' A cosmos that breathes, to continue living, inevitably turns its life's breath inside out, outside in. In Śiva's cosmos, breathing out externalizes phenomenal realities, hardening the potentialities of cosmic evolution, cluttering phenomenal space, filling space with itself. Breathing in removes clutter, opening space that will then be filled by breathing out.[40]

The out-breath blocks, the in-breath unblocks. We could also say that the in-breath puts god into spinning movement, and that this movement continues with the out-breath, which continuously shapes itself as visible surface. Inward and outer vectors are both active in, indeed comprise, Śiva's dance. What moves inward takes away. The dance, therefore, is a process of taking away and giving out. In this, it is like all

[37] See Shulman, in press.

[38] See below, pp. 88 ff.

[39] See Biardeau 1972: 79–81.

[40] See Appar *Tevāram* 5.21.1: *ĕn̲n̲ uḷey uyirppāyp pur̲am pontu pukk' ĕn̲n̲ uḷe nir̲kum in̲n̲amparīcan̲e*, 'Śiva in In̲n̲ampar is what breathes within me, going out, entering in, remaining within'—a microcosmic and psychophysical formulation of the same conceptual pattern. The out-breath may be identified with the Vedas, blueprint for creation: Śrīnatha, *Bhīmeśvara-purāṇamu* 4.72.

other cosmic processes.[41] A strong notion of mutuality and interdependence—between this god and his worshippers and/or his apparent enemies, that is, all who exist somewhere or somehow within the out-breath—follows from this definition. Giving out and taking away are highly interactive processes. Even god can only take away *from someone*. The implication is that Śiva's dance is thus also interactive; he cannot and does not begin it alone.

In any case, three stages have reduced to two, breathing in and out—and still this is not quite correct. We might, for example, ask whether space still exists when phenomenal clutter is cleared away, or whether both space and time are continuously folded away, folded in, by breathing in, and unfolded or expanded through breathing out. Bhairava, master of breathing, is thus god as time, entering and dissolving time as time is breathed out and in. This is the deeper temporal rhythm hinted at above, a rhythm of generating time in the very movement that undoes it, or of exfoliating temporal sequence from a non-sequential and non-lineal dimension implicit in that apparent sequence. Time is breath. Breathed out, it hardens into knots at the extremity of lineal trajectory. Breathed in, the knot dissolves, loosens, curves flexibly through itself and thus unties itself. No temporal moment is devoid of either of these phases, though we probably experience time mostly, from a human perspective, as the periodic hardening or bunching up of uneven lumps and stubborn knots.

But what even this manner of speaking fails to capture is the literal simultaneity of the cosmic process. Even a sequence of two moments is a flattening out of the spinning curve that, at the deepest level, comprises this god. Logically, if Śiva breathes himself outward as cosmos, when he takes away from this cosmos he is taking away from himself; when he fills himself with cosmos, he fills cosmos as well. He fills himself as he empties himself; what momentarily disappears from one domain appears at that same instant in the complementary domain; both categories, the external and internal, belong ultimately to the same inseparable movement of surface into depth, or, better, of surface *as* depth. Being neither one nor two, this god moves simultaneously through himself in the interests of inhabiting and enhancing the middleness where awareness resides. Stated as apparent paradox, this god cannot empty himself without filling up at the same time; cannot breathe in without

[41] This point is discussed at length in our conclusion, below.

breathing out 'elsewhere,' though there exists nowhere else. We can stretch out this process of emptying and filling so that one follows the other; in this case, we get the series of Bhairava, Beggar, Dancer. These are stories god tells himself about himself, in various degrees and conditions of proximity to us, who sometimes overhear them—although we can understand them, as Umāpati's verse quoted at the beginning of this chapter suggests, only by virtue of a pre-existing proximity and intimacy with him, or by virtue of our resistance and opposition to him. 'None can approach him who bears this burden now except him who is already so close.' On another level, these stories tend to collapse into one another, as the *Kanta-purāṇam* folds Bhikṣâṭana into the Beggar, so that we get an accordion-like effect in the breath-filled god. Think of the breath the Yogi holds, motionless, inside his body, a timeless fullness. Think of the unthinkable simultaneity of Śiva's dance.

Fire-dipped Gold

The Cidambaram tradition has organized its vision of origins in several textual forms, including, most saliently, the Sanskrit *Cidambara-māhātmhya* [*CM*] and the Tamil *Koyiṟ-purāṇam* of Umāpati civâcāriyar (early fourteenth century). There is good reason to date the *CM* prior to Umāpati, who follows large sections of the Sanskrit text with transparent closeness. The *CM* is a much less clearly integrated work that *Koyiṟ-purāṇam* which, like most Tamil *sthala-purāṇa*s, is really a coherent lyrical poem (*kāvya*) with a recognizable poetic voice or tone. Kulke has argued for a relatively early date for *CM*,[42] which he thinks refers indirectly to the biography of the Chola king Kulottuṅga I (1070–1118). David Smith raises the possibility that Umāpati composed the *CM*, at least in its 'final redaction,' as well as its Tamil epitome.[43]

Purely intra-textual analysis is unlikely to resolve the still outstanding problems of historical development at Cidambaram. In particular, the place of Bhairava in relation to Bhikṣâṭana and Naṭarāja remains unclear in the Cidambaram *purāṇas*, although an implicit logic can, perhaps, be formulated in terms taken from the discussion above. What can be said with assurance is that by the beginning of the fourteenth century, at the latest, and probably some two centuries earlier, the story

[42] Kulke 1970: 192–213.

[43] Smith 1996: 45.

of the Dāruvana had been entirely absorbed by the Cidambaram cult as the mythic background to the now dominant Naṭarāja deity. We are now ready to see how Umāpati tells the story in its standard form:

Koyiṟ-purāṇam 2.1–78, 3.38, 41–52[44]

So Tiger-Feet[45] was serving god, hoping for freedom, begging for a vision of the unending Dance of Rapture. Let me tell you now how Patañjali came to him, how he was with him, and how he went away.

Once Viṣṇu rose from Ananta, the great serpent who is his bed, spread out on the vast ocean of milk. He was singing 'Hara! Śaṅkara!' with his hands folded in prayer above his head, his eyes pouring tears; he stood straight and unwavering as the flame of a painted jewelled lamp. Lakṣmī, who was afraid to approach him, was sad; others in his retinue trembled in fear—for he was immersed in an ultimate rapture. And then he put it aside and opened his eyes, like a double sunrise meant to dispel darkness that has enveloped the entire world. Sight opened up like flowers: he got off his couch, brought water for his worship, and took his seat on a golden throne beneath a canopy of pearls. The gods bowed before him. Something of the ecstasy that infused his sleep still lingered in his mind. He was thinking of god's dance and these thoughts, liquid and alive, swept him along like water that has broken through a dam, altering the constricting course of his deeds.

Somehow he managed to channel his thoughts, like rushing water held by a sluice. As his lucid mind awoke, Ananta bowed at his feet and begged him: 'Lord! You no longer rest on me or wake on me, as before. Please tell me, as truly as you can, the inner nature of this new mode.'

Viṣṇu laughed, alive to the need. 'Sit here,' he said to Ananta. He turned to the goddess, her hair filled with flowers: 'Sit here,' he said. 'If you want to hear of the great gift I received through the almost

[44] We wish to acknowledge with gratitude the illuminating work on the *CM* by David Smith, who often sheds light on Umāpati's interpretation, and an earlier translation of the entire *Koyiṟ-purāṇam* by John Loud, who kindly made this draft available to us. David Smith graciously provided us with a copy of the Sanskrit *CM*.

[45] Vyāghra-pāda, a devotee of Śiva at Cidambaram who had tiger claws to enable him to climb to the top of the trees in order to bring the god fresh flowers each day. See Graefe 1960.

unbearable compassion of god—the good god who possesses me—there is no way to contain it. It happened yesterday: I was offering worship to his healing presence on the splendid mountain of the north, Kailāsa, when he spoke directly to me, calling me to him with a smile. He pressed his own hand into mine and, rising, descended to the foot of the mountain, while conches roared on every side and the Vedas (so difficult to chant) were singing praises and his flawless *gaṇa*s and illustrious sages and the rank and file of the gods clustered around him. A sliver of a moon shone on his head.

He led me swiftly to a pavilion and commanded me: 'We are going to examine the innerness of the pure sages from the Forest of Pines. You are to assume the form of a woman and to remain in that form, which will harmonize with mine.' Then he, the noble lord (*nāyakan̲*), beautified his body: wooden sandals on his feet, his enticing waist visible above a white loin-cloth, triple thread, hairs curling right (above his navel), one auspicious line marking his breast, shoulders higher than mountains, a beggar's pouch, a drum (*tamarukam*), a bowl for alms. His neck was particularly splendid; a smile played on his bright red lips. He had long ears and a certain gleam in his eyes. Beads of sweat glistened on his forehead, just above his delicious eyebrows; his face was flushed like an open lotus. He had the dot on his forehead and tangled dark hair thick with honey and buzzing with bees. His entire body, in short, was more luminous than red coral, so beautiful that women who saw him would slide unconscious to the ground while their silk sarees slipped from their waists.

Fully a king, he stood before me. As for me, I covered myself with precious silk, the trail draped across my breasts with their gold chain (*karai*), and thence over my (left) shoulder; wove flowers into my hair, like stars dotting the black night; fixed the dot on my forehead. Jewelled anklets rang on my feet, and my arms were slender as flowering vines as I joined with god. He had once killed desire, but now he seemed overcome with desire himself as, stealing a glance at my ravishing eyes, he broke into a gentle smile.

Pārvatī, the Himalayan pea-hen, remained behind on the mountain as he, a moving red mountain, entered the Forest of Pines, where the Śaiva sages lived. He wanted those sages, untouched by untruth, to know him as a celebrated *yakṣa*, full of movement.[46] Now a

[46] *iyakkan̲* < Skt *yakṣa*; but also evoking *iyakkam*, 'movement.'

beautiful woman, I followed him there. When we reached the first cluster of houses in the village street, he went into the courtyard while beating his drum and turning on that radiant smile. Women with their dark curls pressed against him to offer alms, and he saw how beautiful they were. Standing there, he put on a vast show—countless millions of movements, gestures, acts—for the sake of those otherwise virtuous Brahmin wives with their melodious voices, who, clustering around him on all sides, let go their shyness, their innocence, their timorous delicacy and became as one. With one hand, they clutched at their braids that had come undone; with the other, they held up the sarees slipping from their waists. They were weeping torrents, ecstatic, bewildered: 'Look at those shining teeth he has!' 'Come. Now. Us . . . Take us. Want us. Please!' All in a rush, some took uncooked rice which they intended to give as alms; and the rice cooked and grew soft in their burning hands. Some poured it into his bowl. Others poured it on the ground. Some brought freshly picked, leafy flowers, cupped in their hands, and offered them as ripe curry-leaves to season the rice. They thought they were happy at last.

> This devotee of Śiva—maybe we saw him once before.
> The love-god, Rati's lover, is raining down arrows of flowers.
> We give him a handful of alms, and he gives us a heartful of craziness.
> Our bones are melting down with passion, and he doesn't care.

They cornered him. 'Stop. Give us back our bangles.' They embraced him: 'Just one word!' They showed off their bejewelled breasts and said, 'Here is home.' 'Actually, anywhere will do,' others cried, or 'Make love to me—no time like now!'

They were losing control, babbling, delirious. 'There's space for hesitation, but no space for us.' Or: 'Alms, yes; a place to put them, no.' Or: 'My waist is so small that you might doubt that it exists.'[47] And so on: they were getting more and more confused. What they meant was: 'It's no longer sure that my life still exists. Make love to me, and we'll find out.' Or, stuttering a little: 'The love-god, whom they call Bodiless, is disembodying us with his five arrows—or is it

[47] The waist of a beautiful woman should be small to the vanishing point, hence a suitable subject for cognitive doubt. The above three sentences are playfully superimposed possibilities for *aiyam uḷat' ilat' iṭai*. *aiyam* = 'alms' as well as 'doubt, hesitation.' *iṭai* = 'space, middle; waist.'

errors?—like Death cloned five times over. You could stop him just by looking at us. You could tell us not to be afraid.'

Some were dancing in positions never danced before. Some were running wild. Some were wondering if his begging bowl was a dead-man's skull. Some entered him, their long hair flying. Others were singing like flutes as they fell upon him. From young girls to mature matrons, they all went crazy in the street. It sounded like an ocean moaning or roaring to fill the sky. God stood there, laughing. Now let me tell you what was happening to me, right beside him.

No one who saw me could have mistaken me for one of those chaste housewives. In their eyes, I was a ravishing courtesan, splendid beyond words. My long eyes, a little red, were shooting looks, like piercing arrows, via the curved bows of my eyebrows, straight at the target—the sages' eyes. Those sages were masterful men, of unthinkable gifts, but now their tough hearts went astray, their tufts came undone, their clothes fell away—all except for the sacred threads, their one remaining sign[48]—and, out of control, they started making the most remarkable, indeed unspeakable, gestures. I was right next to god, and they wanted me.

He, meanwhile, whom no one, including me, can ever really approach, was visibly, quite naturally walking from home to perfect home, begging for the perfect gift. And they, though it was passion for Śiva[49] that they seemed to feel, kept staring at me in my woman's body as they slid from one terrible mistake to another. They were old men, and soon they were very angry. Banding together, they cried, 'What next? This man, carrying a skull, has come boldly into our ashram and ruined the faithfulness that should protect us.' Burning, wanting to burn him up, they spoke many unspeakable curses.

These curses dissolved without coming anywhere near him. The sages saw this and, anger still unresolved in their hearts, they dug a deep pit in front of him—as if to obstruct him; as if inviting him to dance. They kindled a steady fire, they chanted mantras, they packed the enclosure with all kinds of poisonous things and, aiming directly at the unstained god whom even the heart cannot imagine, they fearlessly, or thoughtlessly, embarked on a rite of black magic.

Their eyes were on fire, even more than their minds. In a flash,

[48] *kuṟi*.

[49] *civa-rākam* = *śiva-rāga*.

they produced from the fire a raging tiger and set him against our lord. He, however, smiled happily, picked the tiger up with his hand, and with a flick of his fingernail flayed its skin. He tied the skin around his waist, a bright silk robe. Now ghouls and demons emerged from the splendid pit—only to become attendants waiting, like Vedic sages, upon god. A jewel gleaming on its head, eyes smoldering, white teeth dripping dark poison, a great snake arose—to be wound swiftly around god's arm.

In this way he took shape before them—his hostile lovers—waving his two hands,[50] his black matted hair flashing light the way lightning dispels the dark. He had the poison that came, long ago, from the ocean, and the eye in the middle of his forehead. And the dance that he had mastered came and merged into his feet with the music.

As if the fire were spitting out the darkness it had swallowed earlier, a dwarf came roaring out of the flames—with fiery hair, eyes shooting sparks, gleaming teeth. Holding a hissing serpent, he rushed at Śiva, and the god leapt up, placed his foot on the dwarf, and crushed his back. The sages, confused, sent fire against him: God took it in his hand. The mantras they flung at him he fashioned into murmuring anklets for his feet. His demon *gaṇa*s were already dancing the wild *tuṇaṅkai* dance as he, too, long hair whirling, a garland [of cassia] around his shoulders, began to dance.

As for the sages, they were weary, thirsty, weak; their *tapas* had drained away because of their infatuation; they had lost their fire, lost their mantras. They were weaponless, adrift in sorrow. As god was drawn into the whirling movement of the dance, to a man they fell to the ground.

I, too, was afraid as the dance gained speed, and began to tremble. Gently he shielded me with his hand, with its bracelet fashioned from a snake. At that same moment, the goddess who lives in his left side arrived, riding the bull through the sky. He looked happily at her from the corner of his eye. As he embraced her, the gods poured flowers from above while Brahmā, Indra, and other gods worshipped him. I now put aside the self that gives such joy and resumed my old, tiresome body. I bowed to him, came close to him; I was still trembling, still shy. Pārvatī watched and was glad.

[50] The commentator asserts that this refers to the two more hidden arms as opposed to the two plainly visible in front. Normally Naṭarāja has four arms.

God, of the beautiful eyes, who joins and mingles, was whirling rapidly, his hair spreading in all directions, his hand swirling, full of fire, the drum thundering, filling all space. Many worshipped his feet, red as the red lotus. The goddess was filled with fear as he, our father, danced, entirely present now—and it was only the beginning.

He went through one step after another. One foot poised in the air, anklets ringing, hands alight, he blended into the snake-dance[51] which has no equal, which holds within it the long eyes of the goddess as they track his movement. He embraced it fully, offering it to the goddess, who was drinking it in, and to the splendid bull, as meanwhile he smiled a loving smile at me. I worshipped him; I was alive as never before, my mind melting. He gave me an eye with which to see.

Those great sages, in their weakness and longing, were now prostrate and clamouring before him: 'Keep us in your awareness, so that our fault goes away. Long live Śankara!' The Dancer ordered all their flaws to congeal as a single mass within dark Muyalakaṉ, while he stood upon him, crushing his back. Ancient blackness dissolved at the touch of god's feet. The innumerable sages watched with love, with terror; watched the dance that is rapture, while the tiny drops trickling from their eyes swelled to a cascading stream. Water-pots, *darbha* grass, walking-sticks—waving them all, shouting, they became wild in the dance.

The gods above folded their hands in worship and crowded around to watch. Tumburu and Nārada, practised musicians that they were, lost all their skill and stopped the song. Ghouls danced the *tuṇaṅkai*, and the god's wild retainers went through all the steps of his dance.

God said: 'Hari, Brahmā, Indra, sages, all of you—meditate on our delightful dance as if it were the *śiva-liṅga*. Serve it in love with fresh flowers.' Then, with the goddess on the bull, he vanished into the sky.

Everyone bowed in the direction he had gone. Then they left. Listen, Ananta: You, too, are focused on the knowledge that leads to victory. Yesterday, when I was lying on you, I was fully absorbed in the dance of the black-throated god, and I no longer needed the sadness we call sleep.'

[51] *puyaṅka' muyaṅkiṉaṉ* = *bhujaṅga,* presumably the *bhujaṅga-trasita* pose. See Kaimal 1999: 413.

That is what Viṣṇu said to the snake.

And Viṣṇu also observed that, when he mentioned god's dance, Ananta folded his hands in love above his heads, as if he, too, had seen it all. He saw that delicate tears were falling from the snake's eyes, as if he were melting into liquid. 'His real work,' thought the god, 'is the work of serving the feet of God, the handsome Beggar covered with bones. And my work is to free him from his ancient role as my bed.' He said this aloud, and the snake was grieved.

'I am no longer prepared to sleep on you,' said Viṣṇu. 'Teach this business to your son. You should be doing *tapas*.' Ananta was deeply moved. However sweet the thought of hurrying to worship the dancing god must have been, he could not bear the thought of leaving Viṣṇu. But Viṣṇu was happy. 'Go,' he said, 'to Kailāsa, in the far north, where god lives, and discipline yourself there. God, husband to the fish-eyed goddess, will come and grant you many gifts.' Ananta, flawless, beyond compare, bowed to flawless Viṣṇu and, taking leave, went to Kailāsa, which not just anyone can reach. The jewels in his thousand heads put sunlight to shame, and the heat he generated set off fires in every corner of space.

He held his breath. He swallowed nothing—not even the wind. Days went by without his notice. As if to turn his eyes—the eyes that would see god—into something godly, he focused them on the sun, melting them down from within. This went on for some time until God the Dancer came to measure his truth, as he had come to the sages of the forest. He took the form of Brahmā, riding a goose, and in this form was greeted by the snake.

'Enough of this painful discipline, angry snake,' God said. 'There must be one thing—pleasure, freedom, perfect knowledge, Yogic powers—that you want. Just tell us and we will give it to you.'

Though Ananta was overjoyed, he said, 'Actually, what I wanted was to summon Śiva.'

'But what difference does it make who gives you your wish?' asked Brahmā, a bit irritated, knowing the snake wanted nothing from the above list. 'Just tell me: what other logic is there for this total discipline you have adopted?'

Ananta replied, 'Freedom, pleasure without end, the eight Yogic powers, knowledge—what's the point? There is madness in me—a mad urge to see the Dance of Rapture that God danced *that* day in *that* luminous forest.'

Brahmā laughed. 'You really are crazy. You think you can make the impossible possible. God does only what he wants. Do you think somebody told him to dance that day in the forest? You're a fool.'

The snake answered. 'Isn't he dancing all the time? If you ask, in a loving way, for help from a generous person, will he suddenly refuse to give it?'

Brahmā sighed, still on his goose. 'After all this time, desire has not let go.'

'Endless time is only as long as my coiled and vulnerable body. *That* day can't be far off,' said the snake, looking at Brahmā in his apparent sorrow.

'And if you die, what good will that do you?' asked the god.

'You can see, can't you, the thought in my mind. Even if I die, I *will* see that dance.'

He heard the snake's determination. Suddenly the goose was a bull, the gods were raining down flowers, and there were tall, dark *gaṇa*s all around. Brahmā, who is without evil, turned into the god who is half Umā of the flower-filled hair, the bright dot on her forehead. Ananta saw him and began to tremble: 'I praise you, who are the cosmos, free, unstained, with the crescent moon on your crest. Forgive all that I, who am but a lowly dog, have said, black-necked Dancer who, out of your own free wish, came here to possess me!' He fell to the ground in worship, his brilliant mind melting. And the god with long matted hair urged his bull forward a little so he could embrace Ananta in a conspicuous show of compassion, placing his hands on his hoods.

'There is no way to know the truth of our delightful dance except by doing *tapas* as you have,' said the god of gods. 'On *that* day it will become clear. Put aside the grief that comes from exhaustion. Listen and learn, as we tell you about us, about our truth.[52] The cosmos emerges by way of *karma* out of *māyā*. Just as a pot will not take shape without a potter, so the cosmos requires a creator. If you ask how living beings can achieve real understanding (*uṇarvu*), the

[52] The *CM* (15.9) states: I [Śiva] will tell you the reality of my self/form (*yathârthaṃ mad-svarūpasya*).

answer is: that is why we exist in ourselves—in order to perform the five healing cosmic processes [creating, caring, taking away, hiding reality, and offering compassion]. Our body, which supports us, is both composed of visible parts and without parts. You may be wondering about this doubleness. One aspect is the form positioned opposite those who love us, with *śakti* as its substance (*upātāṉam* = Skt *upâdāna*); it is there to unchain the chain. The other aspect has no parts, no visible splitting, and exists as true understanding. Surpassing both these aspects is our natural mode of being (*iyalpu*), a self made of understanding that is light. We are what is alive (*uyir*) as rapture (*āṉantam* = *ānanda*). Our name is *para-pada*, the 'other, high place,' or *parama-jñāna*, 'ultimate knowing,' or *parāt-para*, 'other than other,' 'higher than high.' Non-being, saving, creating, wanting,[53] shading[54]—these are our dance.

'All the Vedas say that we dance continuously, but they cannot see or comprehend the reason for this dance, or its time, space, meaning, or place. That day that we danced the play in sight of Viṣṇu and others, making ourselves known in the splendid Forest of Pines, we noticed that the forest was shaken, since it could not bear this burden. So we soon brought the dance of victory to an end. This is also no place or time to show you the dance. There is, however, a certain space (*maṉṟu*) that can sustain it, so the cosmos can live on.'

Ananta burst out in praise. 'You have saved me—by mentioning this space unseen by gods or the Vedas. And since you have the thought of showing it to me in your endless, compassionate presence, coming into that forest, I can say I am now truly alive.'

The god with the axe and the deer in his hands—the god who took me, Viṣṇu, for his slave—spoke to the king of the snakes. 'Since the cosmos and the microcosmic body correspond, the *Iḍā* channel goes straight through Lanka, and the *Piṅgalā* channel goes through the Himâlaya.[55] The *Suṣumṇā* goes through the middle and reaches Tillai, rich in goodness. The Root Liṅga is there. To the south of it there is a space (*ampalam*) which the Vedas, positioned on all four sides,

[53] *iccai-cĕyti* = *tirodhāna*, hiding reality, in this list. *Tirodhāna* is, ultimately, the operation of *icchā-śakti*, the faculty of god's wanting.

[54] *niḻal*, apparently equivalent to *anugraha*, giving compassion.

[55] These two invisible channels of the subtle body are borrowed from Yogic physiology, as is the central *suṣumṇā*, here leading to Tillai/Cidambaram.

cannot see. That's where we dance continuously. Because it is real—it is the space of awareness (*citamparatta vāymaiyāl* < *cidambaram*)—it never decays along with everything that is bound up with the qualities of *māyā*. It's always there. If living beings cumulate limitless *tapas*, they win the enduring, almost unattainable eyes of understanding. Then they can see. Those who cannot see are born again.

'Anyone who sees you as you are, with your poison-filled mouth and fiery eyes and thousand hoods, will be alarmed. Meanwhile, the pure sage Atri and his wife Anasūyā have been cumulating *tapas* in order to have you as their son. Viṣṇu actually promised you to them, but you were afraid to be born. Now, however, you will come into Anasūyā's cupped hands (*añjali*) when she has bathed after her period. When she sees that you are a young, five-headed snake, she will drop you, in a mixture of love and fear. As a result, you will be called Patañjali—"Falling (*pat*) from the hands (*añjali*)." With that name, but with the consciousness, still, of Ananta, you must go to the world of the serpents. In the middle of that world there is a mountain, and to the south of it a long tunnel which leads directly to the Tillai forest. Emerging from the tunnel, if you turn north you will come to the Root Liṅga blossoming from the tip of that mountain in the cool shade of a banyan tree—a truly astonishing sight that even the gods find remarkable. Tiger-Foot, Vyāghra-pāda, worships that *liṅga* in the hope of seeing our dance. Join him. We will see to it that you see this luminous dance at noon on a Thursday at the time of the *Taipūcam* festival.'

Ananta, overcome by the god's loving presence, fell to the earth, bowed, rose, stood watching as the god of gods disappeared, together with dark-haired Umā, into the sky.

[In the form of Patañjali, a young five-headed snake, Ananta returned to the serpent world, where he found and worshipped the mountain that was mentioned by Śiva. He slithered up the endless tunnel, using the mantra *namaḥ śivāya* as his eyes, and came out in Cidambaram, where he introduced himself to Tiger-Foot and worshipped the Root Liṅga with him. Patañjali also set up his own *liṅga*, called Anantīśvaram, to the east of the pool there, along with Vyāghra-pāda's shrine, Pulīśvaram, and the Root Liṅga. For many days he and Tiger-Foot, joined by 3000 sages, worshipped Śiva and prayed to be allowed to witness his dance. On the promised day, at noon,

Śiva danced the Dance of Rapture before them, while Umā watched in the chamber (*manru*) that is unknowable, of ever-intensifying light. Their eyes could not contain this truth, this awareness, this space, this body; they cried out to god that they were still not full. Śiva offered each of them a wish, and Tiger-Foot asked only that his daily worship go on as before. Ananta-Patañjali, however, asked:]

'Let this dance never end. Dance on forever, present in compassion, with your loving wife, in the light of knowing that is this space, whenever those whose lives are but a flash of lightning connect their eyes to you.'

The Dancer said, 'Knowing is the space we inhabit. Awareness is not separate from us. What is real never leaves this world. We will stay here, as it were, just as the living breath (*uyir*) stays within the body. Enclose me here,' he ordered the gods.

They took in this ancient knowledge. They scattered flowers in worship, for they wished to know out of what they could fashion the enclosing wall. Naṭarāja said to them, 'In the First Book it says that the space of awareness is made of gold. So when people who live on earth see us, let this space be entirely golden.'

The gods bowed to this loving command. They brought gold, burnished in fire, with no thought to the expense; they fashioned that space in the golden image[56] fit for a great king. Like the golden mountain that turns everything that touches it to gold, or like the salt-flats that turn whatever grows there salty, the space of awareness, that holds the knowable but indescribable god, made the space fashioned by the gods into wisdom itself.[57]

From that day on, god danced continuously in that space, together with the goddess; the gods, Patañjali, Vyāghra-pāda, and other rarefied sages went there to worship, wherever they might live. As the dance went on without being concealed, the animals of the wilderness put aside their hostility and, together with the birds, grew drunk on the intoxicating chiming of Śiva's anklets; they lost themselves at the feet of the goddess.

So Patañjali got his wish. The *gaṇa*s, weeping, came to their leader, Nandin, with his four arms and three eyes, his short golden sword

[56] *patimāvā* < Skt *pratimā*.

[57] It appears that this verse seeks to explain the modelling of the present-day *kanaka-sabhā* after the prototype (*pramā*) of the *cit-sabhā*.

and cane. They knew he would be fair. 'What can we say,' they asked him, 'about this snake who, indifferent to god's pain, demanded that he stay in this state and this house forever? It's like a sick man who hears that a certain herb will cure him, so he pulls up the herb at the root and squeezes out every last drop.'

Nandin answered, 'That was Patañjali's wish—that the dance would be visible to whoever comes to Sthāṇu-Śiva. It is a request that continually intensifies, as granted by God. Who can question God's command, or understand it? As for us, our task from now on is to organize the times he can be seen.' He stationed them—the *gaṇa*s—to guard the innermost space (*akam*). *Bhūta* ghosts took up positions in the next circuit. Beyond them, in the middle space, furious *kūḷi* ghouls and Kālī stood watch. Outside he positioned a large group of guards.[58] All in all, the god was heavily protected. Next Nandin fixed the times for visiting: gods can come in early morning or at midday; other celestial beings come in the late afternoon; beautiful women from heaven, their eyes dark with kohl, come late at night. But human beings living on earth can come any time they want. The hours when no one visits are God's own private time, which he loves.

'This house is for *that*,' said Nandin, 'and so it will remain. But if you tell me that God is happy to enter the inner space and to stand there without stirring, is that not the final meaning the wise can reveal? Alas, when God puts himself together, everything is fused and confused.'[59]

A Self Made of Understanding that is Light

However we understand what happened to Śiva and the sages in the Dāruvana, it apparently repeats itself endlessly at Cidambaram. Indeed, the dance in the forest is seen as too threatening to the very existence of the cosmos to survive, or to be revived, in its original location; the Dāruvana could not truly contain it, whereas Cidambaram allows for its continual repetition and for universal access to viewing it. The Cidambaram temple is, as Śiva tells Patañjali and the gods, built primarily to 'enclose' this dance in an inner space—the *maṉṟu* or *sabhā*—that is equated to a full awareness of reality or a kind of knowing. Knowledge actually constitutes the space in which the god is moving; but since

[58] Bhairava and others, according to the commentator.
[59] *talaivaṉ muyakkañ cakala-mayakkan tāṉ ām.*

this space seems to require walls, a floor or stand, and various surrounding corridors and circuits, all guarded by members of Śiva's extended entourage of ghosts and ghouls and hungry goddesses, the special knowledge that activates and holds the dance is transmuted into its nearest tangible equivalent, fire-dipped gold. Moreover, this golden inner chamber is apparently shaped after an invisible prototype[60] that exists as consciousness itself—hence, if we are reading this passage correctly, we see today the golden *kanaka-sabhā* leading into the innermost space, the *cit-sabhā*, where god puts himself together (an endless process). Spectators, such as the Tiger-Foot sage who was there from the beginning, in ancient Tiger Town, as well as Ananta-Patañjali, who triggers the repeat performance of the dance, may be critical to the successful flow of this process.

Still, we should not assume too quickly that we know what this 'knowing' is all about. Who, in fact, knows what, or whom? As in the *Kanta-purāṇam* text studied earlier, Śiva seems to have his own compulsions driving him through the story and to Cidambaram. But in this case, the second segment of the narrative, localized in a recognizable temple at the northern reaches of the Kaveri delta, may shed light on the meaning of the god's adventures in the first segment, the Forest of Pines.

Formally, Śiva goes through the same stages here as he does in the *Kanta-purāṇam* version with which we began. He comes to the forest, elicits passion from the wives of the sages, fills up on their gifts, enters into violent confrontation with the sages themselves, and begins to dance. These adventures have, however, been reframed as a story narrated by Viṣṇu to the serpent Ananta-Ādiśeṣa, soon to become Patañjali, one of the two primary witnesses to the dance in the *cit-sabhā*. Indeed, the story of the forest is now the prelude to Śiva's far more stable and enduring dance at Cidambaram and to the story of the structures put in place to enable and contain it.

So on one level the *Koyiṟ-purāṇam*, like any Tamil *sthala-purāṇa* or compendium of local temple mythology, offers a rationale for the specific properties and blessings accessible at this one site. Yet in this case, perhaps more than any other in south India, the rationalizing of God's presence assumes a profoundly ambiguous perspective. For how can any space enclose space itself? How can golden walls contain a dimension obviously felt to contain them? And if god is continuously

[60] See the Vedic notions of *pra-mā* and *prati-mā*: Malamoud 1989: 255–6.

present, why must one circumscribe him with visiting hours, with guards and peons stationed at strategic points to protect these rules? What, in short, is the problem that this series of bounded and crystallized relations is meant to solve? Śiva himself, as we know, is the author of the series: '*Knowing is the space we inhabit. Awareness is not separate from us. What is real never leaves this world. We will stay here, as it were, just as the living breath (*uyir*) stays within the body. Enclose me here*.' Note the familiar analogy—Śiva inhabits the internal space of Cidambaram just as breath dwells in the body—and the significant subjunctive particle, 'as it were.' What is real never leaves the world, but not even Cidambaram can 'really' contain and delimit god.

Clearly, however, what is at stake here is a certain kind of knowing, as we have already remarked and as the verse just cited tells us. This knowing or awareness has dependable features: it is spacious and alive; it breathes; it embodies itself; it is a form of light. It is equated with Śiva's dance. It is not distinct from god himself. Śiva, at least insofar as he dances, *is* this awareness. An integrative aspect seems essential: the knowledge-space where Śiva dances is also the mode or domain in which Śiva puts himself together (*talaivaṉ muyakkam*), where everything is 'fused and confused.' More external spaces are fragmented, encrusted, clearly bounded. In a sense, then, the inner space in Cidambaram will actually have no true boundary: the walls are an illusion; gold is the nearest existential equivalent to the fluid fullness of god's becoming (as the First Book, the Veda, is said to have stated) or, put differently, to consciousness (transmuted into visibility); moreover, whatever comes anywhere near this spacious movement is dissolved and opened up, just as a salty strip of land makes everything growing there taste salty, or as the golden mountain turns whatever touches it to gold. Śiva at Cidambaram is the great melter and dissolver, uncluttering space, enabling a full, object-less awareness. Whatever might appear solid in his vicinity—including, one must assume, the famous image of Naṭarāja himself, to say nothing of the ritual detritus available within the *cit-sabhā* and the further structures surrounding the latter; including, that is, the temple itself—was actually long ago emptied out and allowed to revert to open space. As a further indication of this fundamental fact we have Bhairava in position, as usual, at what is ostensibly the outermost boundary of the enclosure where reality siphons off its false solidity, merges whatever is superficially bounded and fragmented, and reveals its innate luminosity and clarity. Thus this outer border is, seen from a more adequate perspective, as 'inner' as anything can be, indeed as inner as the inner chamber (*maṉṟu*) itself; and we know that the gold-attracting Bhairava rests in the *cit-sabhā* at the feet of Naṭarāja.

Yet a process is going on here, apparently without pause, and nothing that rests is actually devoid of movement. '*If you tell me*,' Nandin says, '*that God is happy to enter the inner space and to stand there without stirring, is that not the final meaning the wise can reveal*?' Total movement looks like standing still, as the Tamil Śaiva poets are fond of showing us.[61] Given this understanding, can we nonetheless define the primary features of Śiva's dance at Cidambaram in a way that makes sense of the process as a whole? We can pose two analytical questions aimed at illuminating the meaning of the dance, both drawn from its spatial and temporal periphery: first, once again, how does Śiva get from Bhairava to Bhikṣâṭana and then to Naṭarāja? How and why does the Beggar repeatedly become the Dancer? What is the meaning of this progression? Second, what is the logic of the sages' sacrifice, or of Brahmā's analogous hostility to Bhairava, and how does this logic relate to the awareness that the process liberates or reveals, the awareness embodied in the dance?

Perhaps the key clue to the first question is the statement Śiva makes to Viṣṇu, Brahmā, Indra, and the sages, while still in the forest: —'*Meditate on our delightful dance as if it were the* śiva-liṅga.' Here is an explicit equation that deserves to be taken seriously. North Indian texts of the Dāruvana story culminate in the fall of Śiva's *liṅga* to this world and its consequent worship in Śiva's temples; the structural replacement of this episode in Tamil Śaiva works is Naṭarāja's dance. But in what sense is the dance akin to the *liṅga*? We characterized the latter as a 'processual core of being, spinning god through his transforms.'[62] Both dance and *liṅga* exhibit an ontology of potentiality driving the emergence of crystallized forms. But the dance embodies and thereby reveals something of the processual innerness of the *liṅga*—something, that is, that is really happening, all the time, within this god. One could say that the dance is the *liṅga* made transparent so as to reveal what the inside of the *liṅga* consists of, or the processes going on continuously

[61] Thus Cuntaramūrtti *Tevāram* 6.7 (53): *niṉṟe . . . purintu naṭṭam puvaṉiy etta āṭa vallīr*, 'you stand and you dance, while the world sings praise.' The compound verb *niṉṟ'āṭu*, 'to dance while standing' (or 'to dance continuously') commonly characterizes Naṭarāja in the *Tevāram* and *Tiruvācakam*.

[62] Above, p. 37.

within it. The dance creates its own innerness by weaving around and through itself, shaping an axis that exists only through this movement, integrating itself solely from within. This whirling, Moebius-like process, potentially threatening to the stability of any bounded or solid state, is visible at Cidambaram, where we can follow the trajectories of the various curvatures that make up the dance and that also whirl through the *liṅga* at any given point. For that matter, the dance also allows us to recognize the holes or gaps in a cosmos that is simultaneously being taken apart (breathed in) and coming back together (breathed out). The Dancer both 'takes away' and 'flings out,' these processes unfolding in near simultaneity in a choreography of cosmic emergence and continuous re-immersion. Naṭarāja dances the possibilities of cosmos, synchronizing, calibrating, and coordinating them in forms of unbroken movement more completely and graphically imagined than in any other Hindu icon or story.

The *liṅga,* viewed in isolation and from the outside, gives a misleading impression of solidity. Perhaps the full simultaneity of its internal movement is what leads to this misperception. But even simultaneity has differential intensities, and we thus find a *liṅga* of wind (at Kalahasti), of fire (at Tiruvannamalai, or in the Bhairava myth), of earth (at Kancipuram), of water (at Tiruvanaikka), and of space itself (at Cidambaram). Movement within god fills the emergent gaps within god, as the dance demonstrates to those who can see it. There, too, one can confuse these levels or modes by taking a surface shape with fixed contours for something real, a curve for a straight line. To both those who see clearly and those who are blind, light and darkness appear uniform, as Umāpati says.[63] A person lacking awareness sees only darkness (that is, solid, non-translucent objects or states); an enlightened spectator sees only light, the actual reality of a spacious and luminous cosmos spinning ceaselessly through itself. Cidambaram is set up largely to facilitate this latter vision.

In the northern Forest of Pines, Śiva tends to disappear into his own *liṅga*: in topological terms, the exterior of the *liṅga* curves into its interior.[64] The seemingly monolithic, timeless solidity of the unmoving *liṅga* with neither beginning nor end, neither top nor bottom, becomes transparent in the dance: now we can see cosmos as a complex rounded movement in which this cosmos is always coming near itself or toward

[63] *Tiruvaruṭpayaṉ* 7. 4: *ŏḷiyum iruḷum ŏrumaittu paṉmai/ tĕḷivu tĕḷiyār cĕyal.*
[64] See Appendix (*Kūrma-purāṇa* 2.37).

itself from some space within itself, emerging through the intersections of the curves or loops, but at the same time distancing itself from itself, opening holes, forming crusts, fragmenting. Apparently there is something operating within this cosmos that keeps these rips and tears from expanding into still more lengthy linear trajectories, ever more distant from one another, to the point where the cosmos could disappear into its own gaps. There is, that is, a principle of restoring continuity or, put differently, of self-correction and self-purification.

We see the principle at work both in the forest and in Cidambaram: in both sites, something accelerates the god who has slowed into empty stasis back in the direction of total movement. All the south Indian texts of the Dāruvana focus on this rapid acceleration that takes place as Śiva begins to move, absorbing whatever the sages hurl at him from the fire, each attribute seemingly fuelling the spin further. Śiva is '*drawn into the whirling movement of the dance*' as if surrendering to a process that has overtaken him from within. This process has, as its culminating stage, a fullness of presence (*aruḷ, caṉṉiti*) seen as equivalent to rapid inner movement in which contours disappear and objects, or individual selves, fuse and merge:

> *God, of the beautiful eyes, who joins and mingles, was whirling rapidly, his hair spreading in all directions, his hand swirling, full of fire, the drum thundering, filling all space. Many worshipped his feet, red as the red lotus. The goddess was filled with fear as he, our father, danced, entirely present now—and it was only the beginning.*

Space itself, empty of obstruction, is now completely full, just as the god is becoming ever more full of himself, whorling and spinning around his own axis, binding the gaps that had opened in his inner being in the course of his breathing out the cosmos.

This direction of restorative movement—a ritual process enacted daily at Cidambaram—provides our story with a tentative teleology. The Beggar is moved along his turning axis toward becoming the complete Dancer, continuous in self. Or, more precisely: the Dancer locates himself somewhere in the middle space, between god and presence, or between self and self. In a sense, the Dancer is whirling between Śiva and Śiva, among many such spinning selves that together create selfness as an orbit—in which each twist creates a different relationship between

Śiva and Śiva and so, too, a different relationship between God and living beings. Perhaps only in this sense can we use a word like 'self' in relation to god, and only under conditions of potential, still incomplete emergence into a middle space in which he may become more present to himself and to others.

Yet such an understanding presupposes the possibility of forward movement within that flattened-out, linear stretch of cosmic process that we read or hear as the story. There is a fascinating problem relating to balance, at the end of this line, and to a directionality implicit in its beginning. Indeed, we can see this aspect entirely concretely in the icons of Bhikṣâṭana, such as the one discussed in Chapter 1.[65] Bhikṣâṭana normally has one foot in front of the other, as if shifting his body weight from one foot to the other, perhaps in forward movement. He is, we have said, creating depth by movement. In a sense, he is taking the first step in a curving arc that, as he fills up with the offerings of the sages' wives, will eventually swirl him into the dance. Such a progression has a linear aspect implicit in each narration of the Bhairava-Bhikṣâṭana themes, the latter expanding or fleshing out the coordinates set in place by the former. Iconically, this linearity is conspicuous in the Beggar's rigidly outstretched hand with the unbalanced skull (a hint of roundedness)[66] at its limit. Indeed, a certain asymmetry and lack of balance are evident in all these icons—Bhairava, Kaṅkāla-mūrti, Bhikṣâṭana—that precede Naṭarāja's emergence and reflect the inherent instability and fragility of the linear. Put abstractly, the always curving or spinning middle space attenuates itself when it is emptied into more narrow perspectives—although such narrowing is, in effect, the true evolutionary history of the cosmos, in which god is repeatedly forced to choose the direction in which he will move. Choice empties cosmos by driving a directionality that reduces potential movement. The Beggar shows us one such direction in several possible variant forms, all intimately linked to images of insatiability, relative emptiness, and a mode of deceleration bordering on stasis; each such image requires filling, rounding,

[65] See above, pp. 25–9.

[66] Note that whatever goes into this skull disappears, as if swallowed up in the linear trajectory of the outstretched arm—for otherwise, such contents would surely curve back into view sooner or later. The skull, that is, has apparently hardened along with the rest of the god's iconic form.

and renewed acceleration. We might think of cosmos in the Bhairava mode as teetering and tottering, wobbling on its axis as a direct result of having lost or emptied some measure of its capacity for ongoing self-creativity or self-correction. God as Beggar is asymmetrical, unsynchronized, terrifyingly awkward.

We must, it seems, come to terms with a notion of this deity as requiring, in terms of his own internal processes, some form of intervention that will heal his cracks and fissures and reconstitute him as a totality. Such a notion is, of course, an ancient one in India: Prajāpati, the creator, falls asunder each time he creates—as the sun fragments and dissipates at the closure of each day[67]—and needs to be ritually reassembled through human activity.[68] Such a process is, perhaps, the central, guiding vision or *raison d'être* of Vedic ritual. But what is distinctive about the south Indian sources that reformulate this problem in the light of the Dāruvana story is the insistence on movement, in the spinning dynamic of the *tāṇḍava* dance, as the primary mode of such healing. Moreover, this whirling motion embodies the existential geometry of middleness insofar as it moves the god through all potential axes and orbits. Indeed, were we to juxtapose all the southern versions of Śiva's journey through the Forest of Pines, we would see that each is another axis of movement through the middleness of cosmos. Each offers a possible life-course for this god; and each eventually removes him from a stretched-out linear segment of his existence and propels or twists him back into the continuous, rapid flow that we see in the Dancer—or in the interior of the *liṅga*. The self-emptying aspect of god as Bhairava, at the blurred edges of god's selfness, turns back on itself, curving into Naṭarāja. Here, then, is another possible definition of Śiva's 'self,' one very close to articulations we find in the Tamil Śaiva sources themselves, as that relation of god to his presence (*aruḷ*) created by god's going *into* and *through* himself, dancing in a middle space.

It is important to keep in mind that even this climactic stage in Śiva's mythic biography—the stage that takes him out of time, or takes time away from him—is itself far from indicating a state of balance or stable symmetry. There is a precarious quality to Naṭarāja's stance, as perhaps suits the whirling, twisting movement that has overtaken this god. He dances while poised, with one leg, on the back of Muyalakaṉ, that 'ancient blackness' congealed as a single mass that is identified with

[67] *Jaiminīya Brāhmaṇa* 1.7–8.

[68] See Malamoud 2002.

forgetting (*apasmāra*). So the axis of the dance rests on its opposite vector, the movement away from healing wholeness and toward fragmentation, loss of awareness, and jerky, discontinuous motion. Such is the foundation of Naṭarāja's spin; as the god dances, this dense, dark encrustation in cosmos melts and dissolves back into the fluid connectivities of Śiva's in-breath. Without Muyalakan̲, it seems, there can be no dance. A recent essay by Padma Kaimal plots the great bronze Chola Naṭarājas as radial compositions, the outstretched arms, spreading hair, and one leg dangling in the air (*bhujaṅga-trasita* pose) all articulating spoke-like radial lines unified within a wheel-shaped structure.[69] Such a wheel-like *yantra* grid can easily be read as expressive of either centripetal or centrifugal movement,[70] as also fits the breath-oriented model we have proposed. Yet we should not lose sight of the innate dynamism of this *yantra*, which even in its apparent arrangement around a centre (focused on Naṭarāja's navel) is turning and twisting so rapidly that the cosmos itself is in danger of being sucked inwards, as toward a vortex. Kaimal notes the destructive aspect of Śiva's *tāṇḍava* dance in earlier mythic and iconic forms and suggests a possible continuity with the refined Chola Naṭarāja.[71] The Forest of Pines, let us recall, could not sustain this violent dance for more than a few moments; and even if it miraculously goes on without interruption in Cidambaram, we can be certain that among the potential vectors it flings out there will be endless Bhairavas and Bhikṣâṭanas, hungry and flattened-out segments of divinity, as well as endless Muyalakan̲-like gaps and breakages under the god's feet. The best one can hope for, and one of the main purposes of the entire Cidambaram cult, is that these Bhairava and Bhikṣâṭana lines will curve or fold back into Naṭarāja, thereby resolving the entire tensile sequence and giving it intelligible meaning.[72] It is, however, not clear that Naṭarāja himself is entirely safe from the danger of being sucked into his own vortex and disappearing.

Māṟupāṭu: Sorcery and Resistance

Bhairava appears wherever there is blockage in the universe. Since there is blockage in every solid form and each externalized segment of space

[69] Kaimal 1999; see also Guy, in press.

[70] Kaimal 1999: 413.

[71] Kaimal 1999: 401–4. On Bhairava as a dancer, see Smith 1996; Kramrisch 1981: 113.

[72] Kaimal (1999: 408–10) notes a strong relation binding Naṭarāja, Bhikṣâṭana,

or time, Bhairava emerges, one might say, in every space and moment. This is fortunate, because only in this way can Śiva know himself. In such a system, awareness depends upon a factor of resistance strong enough to bring the parts of god back together. It is this process that we see in the all-too-human episode of the sages' rite of black magic, which runs parallel to Brahmā's hostile perspective on the infinite *liṅga* that stands before him. In both cases, Śiva intervenes to produce change in his opponents but is simultaneously transformed himself.

The sages commence a ritual defined as *abhicāra*, a blanket term for sorcery or black magic. The *Kanta-purāṇam* text also refers to it as *veḷvi*, a sacrifice (6.13. 99). This is a relation that needs to be clarified. In the *Koyiṟ-purāṇam*, the logic of the sages' action is set forth, in coherent terms, at the very outset:

> *Anger still unresolved in their hearts, they dug a fine pit before him—as if to obstruct him; as if inviting him to dance. They kindled a steady fire, they chanted mantras, they packed the enclosure with all kinds of poisonous things and, aiming directly at the unstained god whom even the heart cannot imagine, they fearlessly, or thoughtlessly, embarked on a rite of black magic.* (2.30)

They are angry; they want to block or obstruct this god (*takaivar pol*). We might expect just such an intention. They take up position 'before' or 'opposite' him (*ĕtir naṇṇi*), ready for confrontation. They are utterly unreflective, thoughtlessly (*avicārattu*) slipping into black magic (*avicāram*). They dig a pit, a hollowed-out space precisely corresponding to their own encrusted exterior that bounds and encloses inner vacancy.[73] The sages are empty shells, and the pit they produce is a dark hole that threatens to suck the cosmos, that is Śiva, into itself. The pit is empty of inner integration but packed with 'all kinds of poisonous things.' But it is at this very point that Śiva is impelled to begin his dance.

---

and Liṅgodbhava (the emergent *linga* of flame) on temples endowed by the famous Chola queen Sĕmbiyan Mahādevi (late tenth century)—perhaps not long after the full crystallization of the Cidambaram Naṭarāja cult and its initial expansion throughout the Cola area. The three *mūrti*s effectively recapitulate the Cidambaram triad of Bhairava (linked to Lingodbhava, as in the *Kantapurāṇam* text cited above), Bhikṣâṭana, and Naṭarāja. In the Sĕmbiyan Mahādevi temples, pilgrims following the standard sequence of circumambulation encounter Naṭarāja at the start and Bhikṣâṭana on the last wall (Kaimal 1999: 411)—a reversal of the pattern we have posited for the *purāṇic* texts. Perhaps this sequence returns the pilgrim to the known, experienced condition of cosmos (from breathing in to breathing out).

[73] Malamoud 1989: 74: '. . . quand, par magie noire, on veut attirer le malheur sur quelqu'un, on fait oblation dans un creux, un trou naturel de la terre.'

Indeed, the sages are, by virtue of their hostility, 'as if inviting him to dance.' Something here gives the god his final push into spinning movement. Opposite the pit, Śiva confronts the cosmos turned inside out, lacking any interior integrity, void of aliveness. The pit itself, in its empty solidity, is the aperture of a cosmos that has been breathed out. It thus needs to be 'taken away'—something only Śiva can do. His dance will restore the integrity of cosmos by reconnecting everything to everything else, for Naṭarāja is the god 'who joins and mingles.' The conclusion of the text says it simply: 'When God puts himself together, everything is fused and confused.'

What is it that makes the rite of sorcery into an invitation? Our texts speak repeatedly of a mode of opposition or resistance (*mār̲upāṭu*, *ĕtirttal*, *taṭuttal*, Sanskrit *virodha*) that serves the purpose of transformation. Bhairava 'transforms all that breathes' (*uyir mur̲r̲u' mār̲r̲i*, *Kanta-purāṇam* 6.13.194) as he transforms 'the egoism of the other gods' (*en̲aip pakavar tam akantai mār̲r̲a*, 6.13.164): the verb *mār̲r̲u*[74] is the transitive of *mār̲u*, 'to become changed, exchanged, altered, reversed;'[75] also 'to become false, to deny.' Closely connected to these meanings is the range of *mār̲upaṭu*, 'to be changed, to be opposed, to disagree, differ, to be discordant, to be in contrast; to be inimical.'[76] The latter root gives us *mār̲upāṭu*, 'resistance,' the sages' choice. Shifting emotional textures have various valencies, but *mār̲u* and its derivatives frequently tend, in relation to Śiva, to indicate friction, stubborn antagonism, and existential error.

Very often in the lyrical texts of devotion, the poet is both the victim and source of *mār̲upāṭu*: thus Māṇikkavācakar says to Śiva that

mār̲upaṭṭ' añc' en̲n̲ai vañcippa yān̲ un̲ maṇimalart tāḷ
ver̲upaṭṭ' en̲ai viṭuti kaṇṭāy

the five senses led me astray
so I became hostile and then
separate from your feet
soft as flowers—and now
you've let me go![77]

[74] Here as non-finite, *mār̲r̲i* or infinitive, *mār̲r̲a*.

[75] See Kampan̲, *Irāmāvatāram* 1. 561: *mār̲u* (nominal) as discordant or alternating contrast and shifting forms.

[76] *Madras Tamil Lexicon*, s.v. For Caṅkam-period usage, see, e.g., *Kur̲untŏkai* 101.

[77] *Tiruvācakam* 6.11.

Change in state, in particular the negative change oriented toward separation and distinction,[78] is the regular condition for subsequent forward movement. Dakṣa decides to carry out a sacrificial rite whose sole *raison d'être* is to oppose or subvert the offering of any portion to Śiva, the Beggar (*aiyam eṟṟ'iṭum vāṉavaṉ raṉakk' āvi māṟṟum pāṉmaiyāl).*[79] Such an intention by its very negativity serves to call up Śiva's presence and to generate breakthrough. An inner antagonism to the god congeals as resistance violent enough to produce his intervention or emergence; he is magnetically drawn to such points of blockage, and in overcoming them he reveals the hitherto invisible or unrealized truth of his nature. Such is also the sages' experience. It is crucial, however, for us to recognize that such resistance is also critical for Śiva himself in his own evolution. Sorcery, in other words, becomes in this context the essential condition or transition toward turning flat linear sequence back into a curve.[80]

How does it work? The sages launch weapon after weapon, in direct, linear motion, out of the fire-pit against Śiva. They are trying to kill the god; or, perhaps without knowing it, they seek to push him further along the empty vector of isolation on an ever more impoverished surface, one analogous to their own. Śiva changes these externalizing vectors into aspects or attributes of his own being, curving them back into himself. He skins the tiger and wraps its skin around his body. He curls the snakes around his waist. He hides the skull deep within his hair. The drum nestles in his concave hand. Through all these acts, Śiva is reshaping aspects of his self even as he is beginning to whirl and spin. The outer is curving into something inner and continuous.

But sorcery has its own logic and ontology. The Dāruvana story situates sorcery within the creative processes of phenomenal existence and

[78] Here *māṟupaṭṭu*, 'became hostile,' rhymes with *veṟupaṭṭu*, '[became] separate', at the start of the second line—the first state leading into the second, still more painful and consequential one.

[79] *Kanta-purāṇam* 6.1.14. Note that Dakṣa's sacrifice is precisely parallel to the Dāruvana sages' attempt to bewitch Śiva, with the added irony that Dakṣa seems intent on taking away Śiva's capacity *to take away* (this intention could serve as a working definition of south Indian sorcery). As with the sages, Dakṣa enhances resistance to the point where Śiva is compelled to break through it.

[80] Note that a very similar logic requires Śiva to disturb the detached and quiescent *kevala* 'selves' by immersing them in the world of form, with its endless friction and obstruction, in order to move them *through* this embodied (*sakala*) state

the formation of individual consciousness. In a sense, any self that has turned itself into an object, complete with contours, boundaries, and a systemic internal organization, is bewitched.[81] Being human implies consciousness; yet the free activity of consciousness depends upon possibility, upon the capacity to imagine infinitely (indeed, to imagine god). Conscious existence also depends, in this cosmology, on the interconnectedness and mutuality of all beings, all life. This connectedness is a function of the openness of beings to the imaginings of one within the other, one to the other, one about the other, one without the other. Awareness does not stop at the borders of individual beings; rather, beings flow through one another, changing one another, absorbing potentiality from each new interaction and interpenetration.[82] To slow down the flow of imagination, of possibility, of mutual impingement and interconnectivity—or to stop these processes altogether—is to kill consciousness. Such slowdowns or cessations can be called sorcery in south India.

Conversely, the removal of stasis is the beginning of aliveness. The sages use sorcery against Śiva in the Forest of Pines because the Forest is itself an ensorcelled place at the extreme limit of cosmic slowdown. Their own daily rites and disciplines are barren, frozen into blockage and stasis that exacerbate the obstructive forces of cosmic life. Their effect, as is always the case with sorcery, is to isolate the ensorcelled person, cutting him or her off from others—in this case, from the prime other, Śiva, who has himself become diminished through the sages' obsessions. Isolated, emptied into solidity, petrified into stasis, the victim of sorcery is closed off from the imagination of possibility; selfhood shatters into the death that is a monadic pseudo-autonomy, its horizon severely constricted, its awareness sadly impaired. We tend to think of the victim of sorcery as 'possessed' by some demonic agent—filled, that is, with a demonic presence—but a more general description of this state would focus on the hardening of the person into a solid emptiness

---

toward freedom. Only the *sakala* self merits the name 'human being' (*puruṣa*), with full soteriological potential. See *Śaivâgama-paribhāṣā-mañjari* of Veda-jñāna 5.84–7, citing *Pauṣkarâgama* 6.486–8; detailed discussion of the process in Schomerus 1912: 255–90.

[81] See Kapferer 1997: 14–21.

[82] Such themes have become prominent in the anthropological literature on south India: see Trawick 1990; Daniel 1984; Marriott 1989.

of feeling, being, or acting and the consequent freezing over of the transactional self. Such a self lives in a terrifying, entirely external, petrified hole, akin to the pit the sages dig for their violent rite.[83]

The bewitching of self is inevitable, a necessary consequence of living. Every movement toward otherness (indeed, the repeated imaginative creation of otherness) is a fluid shift from the interiority of being to its exteriority. Such movement is crucial to living in a net of dense, interdependent connectivities. Yet it also generates discontinuities that strain, attenuate, tear, and sever relationships. Every movement beyond the self exposes the self to such erosion, attenuation, and subsequent petrification. Whenever the self is totalized as an object through such emptying out into solidity, we can speak of sorcery. In the internal perspective of the Śaiva sources, such self-petrification exists at any given moment, in varying degrees, in every south Indian self. Even to use the pronoun 'I' is to indicate that this process has reached a certain point. In its extreme condition it is called possession and is subjected to exorcism—that is, the re-interiorization of a self made fluid again so that it can again reach out to others who inhabit the net of interconnectivity.[84]

We thus have a continuum stretching from extreme self-objectification to the rather milder states of what is usually called *ahaṅkāra* (Tamil *akantai*)—'I-ness,' the definition of self as a separate entity equipped with name, face, memory, and the recalcitrant illusion of an integrated, continuous, relatively autonomous existence.[85] All such states are bewitching extrusions, of varying intensity and solidity, from out of the inner whorl. This applies to Śiva no less than to us. Śiva as crystallized form (*mūrti*) is a diminution of the potential space of infinity. He comes to the surface as, let us say, the Beggar—another tear in the tissue of full potential, another deceleration in self-generative flux, another fragment or segment flattened out of the loop. As such, he is hungry, empty, and rather violent. Paradoxically, in such a system, the more surface becomes available, the more self can exist—but always a surface self, ensorcelled, self-possessed, knowing only itself, and thus more often

[83] For a counter-parallel from New Guinea, see Stephen 1996.

[84] See discussion in Shulman, in press (2).

[85] On *ahaṅkāra*, see the classic study by van Buitenen 1988: 53–73; also Padoux 1990: 101, 108 on the extension of the concept (*ahantā*, in relation to full objectivity, *idantā*) in Kashmiri Tantra. See *Kanta-purāṇam* 6.13.164, where Bhairava is asked to transform the gods' characteristic *akantai* (*ahantā*): above, pp. 52–6.

than not, innately mad, like the violent Bhairava who carries the skull of self-intoxicated Brahmā. Even decapitation is no cure for madness here.[86]

Or we could say that self-possession is itself the root condition of madness, an unavoidable consequence of the formation of surface. With the loss of fluid possibility, cosmos constricts into bewitched fragments, each intent upon perpetuating itself qua fragment within the confines of the gap or rent that it inhabits or comprises. In the Forest of Pines, these mad and hollow fragments assemble collectively to defend their separateness in an act of resistance so dramatic that it forces Śiva to become fully present to them and, no less important, to himself.

Śiva bewitches himself and his cosmos through self-evolution. He is susceptible to processes of self-diminution, encrustration, blockage, and fragmentation that produce the world as we know it. He also exorcises himself when he encounters resistance sufficiently powerful to put him into motion.[87] Yet the reverse movement of reabsorption, the re-internalization of the extruded cosmos, has its own dangers—for the fully fluid self, no longer susceptible to resistance, may flow away, lost, into sheer possibility. Śiva's existence, in this sense, is no less dizzying and precarious than ours.

Within this ontic frame, the sages' ritual of black magic has its natural place. Sorcery is linear and destructive, aimed at enlarging the obstructions and fissures in cosmos and god. Śiva accepts this linear order, including the sequence of the sages' weapons that he makes into his own; with his triumph over their greatest weapon—forgetting—he swirls into the vortex of his dance. Bhikṣâṭana has become Naṭarāja once again. Resistance has produced a change in god. This process repeats itself regularly. Straight lines are sometimes necessary, precisely because they are so destructive.

Now we can see more clearly the distinction between sorcery and sacrifice, despite the deliberate, perhaps ironic blurring of the two terms in the Tamil Dāruvana texts. Sacrifice is a causal ritual of transformation positioned at the deepest, or most interior, level. It creates by taking away, thereby opening up space. If you run a ritual of transformation in reverse, the inverted logic of causation should produce the opposite of the intended transformation.[88] In this case, reversed

[86] See below, pp. 163–80.
[87] See the more detailed development of this theme below, pp. 154–6.
[88] See Handelman 1998: 52–3, 156–8.

sacrifice would produce destruction through creation.[89] Exactly this sequence is evident in the sages' rite: from the pit of fire, which looks all too similar to the site of a Vedic sacrifice, a series of destructive forces are created with the express purpose of attacking and killing god. Sorcery creates in order to destroy. It is interesting to observe how this process exhausts the sages but fully revives Śiva, still in his Bhikṣâṭana mode; the latter fills himself with the destructive agents, recreates himself by using them as attributes and, through this bold reversal of direction that issues into the dance, liberates the sages from their state of petrification. Both parties to the interaction benefit. The sages have a glimpse of reality (albeit still partly veiled). Śiva, now whirling around his axis after removing the barriers they had set in place, has watched himself bend, turn, and curve.

The Bhairava moment, by way of contrast, is much closer to sacrifice than to sorcery. Here Śiva opens up space by taking away Brahmā's head. In so doing, Bhairava himself is partly emptied and made more skeletal in his composition (he extends the skull in his hand) as well as more linear in his movement (he walks restlessly through the earth, sometimes pursued by the driving, destructive force of Brahminicide, *brahmahatyā*).[90] In this case, we are witnessing a form of self-sacrifice that exacts a price from Śiva. Possibly whenever god destroys something vital in his cosmos, taking away in order to create, a potential hardening or flattening remains to haunt him. And even if Śiva, the fluid and subtle lord (*pati*) of creatures (*paśu*), is not affected by these processes in his innermost being, they can nevertheless cause him to veil himself more deeply, thereby rendering his contact with other living beings far more tenuous. South Indian Śaiva ritual addresses this possibility by conjuring up a greater aliveness and presence in the deity through various concrete actions, some largely contained within language. Such acts, repeated daily, are intended to work upon awareness on several levels, operating concurrently. From the perspective closest to our human exigencies, the practicing subject comes to know himself as Śiva, thereby emerging from the encrusted or hollow state that is the normal result of our entropic consciousness. From a perspective more deeply situated within the god-infused cosmos, Śiva comes through these ritual actions to know himself as Śiva, thus becoming Śiva. An external

[89] Malamoud 1989: 74 also speaks of 'le sacrifice inversé de la magie noire.'

[90] In the *purāṇic* sources from Benares, Bhairava walks toward Kāśī, where the skull will fall from his hand at the Kapāla-mocana shrine: *Kāśī-khaṇḍa* 31.

observer, were such a vantage point really possible,[91] would see the stone *liṅga* in front of the worshipper come alive as light.

The texts of the Dāruvana story offer us another, vivid cross-section of cosmos as Śiva as he undergoes these processes. We could, following the southern Śaiva poets, see these versions as a narrativization of the trajectory that brings the god fully into being. We encounter him first as Bhairava, his hand extended toward us, his worshippers; at its tip is the hard, dry skull that receives alms, and that is always empty (at least half-empty, or, more optimistically, half-full, as the narrator of the *Kanta-purāṇam* states). Sometimes he bears the skeleton of Viṣṇu's unfortunate doorkeeper, Viṣvaksena, impaled on his trident. Skull, skeleton, even the demonic Fury of Brahminicide that pursues him, are all empty or hollow forms, meant to be filled and left behind. Śiva's progress across this skeletal landscape is always linear, perhaps because its very hardness prevents attempts to penetrate it, demanding only that it be traversed. If, within the accordion-like frame we have described, we unfold the Bhairava-Beggar prototype into its proximate form as Bhikṣâṭana and magnify the coordinates, we see Śiva filling himself up in two ways—with the love and milky food offered by the sages' wives and with the hatred he elicits from the sages themselves. By inducing the sages to resist him to the point of practising sorcery—a reverse sacrifice—Bhikṣâṭana engenders Naṭarāja, who reintegrates cosmos from within itself, at least on the level of living beings. Naṭarāja, full of fluid self, is now more fully present, intricately engaged with everyone around him; all come to share the enveloping qualities of an awareness rich in mutuality, in subtlety and nuance, in unrestricted movement. As Viṣṇu says to Ananta when he describes this moment in the forest, '*I was alive as never before, my mind melting*' (*uyntu vaṇaṅkiṉaṉ maṉam urukum paṭi*, 2.42). The phrase nicely articulates Śiva's own restored or healed state.

Summary and Conclusion

In terms taken from our earlier discussion, perhaps a little too abstract, we might say that sacrifice re-establishes a capacity for middleness—in the sense of freedom, subtlety, and the ability to go in any direction.[92]

[91] Devasenapathi 1974: 86.

[92] This is what happens to Satī, who is initially stuck in her father Dakṣa's rigid world. By going into the fire at Dakṣa's sacrifice, she emerges as a different being.

This capacity is also a kind of knowing. The middle space that the Cidambaram temple opens up for pilgrims is, as both the *Cidambara-māhātmya* and the *Koyi̱r-purāṇam* tell us, a mode of awareness akin to that form of object-less consciousness that exists within the middle space of the heart in any empirical subject. '*Knowing is the space we inhabit. Awareness is not separate from us. What is real never leaves this world.*' But perhaps we can now say something more about such awareness. For one thing, like 'being,' it is never simply given, not even for god. It may have an *a priori* character, but still this 'knowledge' comes into play only when obstructions or 'stains'—*mala*, in the Śaiva Siddhânta terminology—are removed.[93] Something, that is, has to be taken away before consequential knowing can happen. We can posit a level of god-head that is not susceptible to such vicissitudes—a level where god simply knows, from within the middle[94]—but in practice, including the ritual practice of the Cidambaram temple, this level is not routinely available to Śiva in his perceptible or embodied forms. Indeed, he seems to assume such forms precisely in order to accomplish the complete process we have described, the process that unveils him to himself and to us.

In a cosmos whirling through ceaseless transforms, spinning erratically on its axis, god continually comes, or is driven, to the surface. His very breathing (the out-breath) requires this, indeed assumes form as emergent surface. Part of him—the feminine power of desire (*icchā-śakti*)—may even want it. The philosophers certainly think so. An active feminine piece of Śiva seeks to surface in the world *as world* and, in this very movement, to veil him from both world and self. Perhaps this movement should be restated, and surface defined, in a somewhat less dichotomous mode—for it is doubtful that any emergent surface can be

---

Note that Dakṣa typically resents, above all, the gift of a portion of the sacrifice to the Beggar (*aiyam eṟṟ' iṭum vāṉavaṉ*, *Kanta-purāṇam* 6.1.14)—so the whole purpose of his rite is to exclude this possibility. He clings to the encrusted surface and resists any attempt to revert to a fuller, more fluid state.

[93] Sivaraman 1973: 186 speaks of 'deobstructed knowledge.'

[94] Such a level is axiomatic in Śaiva Siddhânta: see Gengnagel 1996: 43, citing Aghoraśivâcārya. Yet to articulate such an axiom is in no way equivalent to addressing the *content* of Śiva's knowledge or to explaining the process of its activation. Modern discussions of Śaiva Siddhânta from Schomerus on frequently err in this respect, taking the attribution of knowledge to God, on principle, as a static property not in need of further, context-sensitive explication. See below, pp. 102–8.

truly or finally externalized in relation to this god. He extends beyond 'himself,' beyond the in-breath, into and through the exhaled cosmos in all its restlessness. No external vantage point is really available. Still, through this very movement of self-extension, parts of Śiva do undergo change; specifically, as we have seen, they tend to become attenuated and constricted. In a sense, there is a thinning out or flattening of Śiva's fullness. This may be what surface actually means—the thinning of space-time and its deceleration. God probably at most inhabits only the inner side or face of such a surface. Such a narrowing of cosmos from the inside, with accompanying elimination of potential expansiveness, is the work of the out-breath or, analogously, of that female component of Śiva that the Śaivas name 'desire.'

It is extremely difficult to define the nature of this desiring component of Śiva; in the Śaiva Siddhânta works, it has an irreducible quality, as if desire were simply desire, *tout court*. It is always possible to formulate its action in terms of a teleology of redemption—the enactment of cosmogonic process aimed at liberating trapped beings (*paśu*) from their trap (*pāśa*) through the ripening of *karma* and the operation of god's compassion—but even this rationale fails to resolve the problem inherent in the medial positioning of a god who is 'not two and not one,' 'neither the evident nor the never-evident.'[95] Indeed, the difficulty intensifies when we learn that this same desiring component of Śiva is defined as an aspect or evolute of knowledge per se (*cit-śakti*),[96] which is also *aruḷ*, Śiva's full and compassionate presence. We can hardly escape the conclusion that what Śiva desires is to know himself, whatever such knowing might mean in practice.

We will take up this theme in more detail in the next chapter, but certain elements can be formulated now on the basis of what we have learned in Cidambaram. Knowing, in Śivaraman's phrase, is 'only interior' to Being.[97] By now this is surely no surprise. Where else could knowledge of this critical sort reside? 'Knowledge that is known is Śiva himself' (*aṟiyum aṟive civamum ām*).[98] We are not dealing here with

[95] Śivaraman 1973: 198.

[96] Ibid., 99: 'The intelligent principle of *śakti* itself of the form of knowledge (*cid-rūpā*) is called *śakti* that desires (*icchā-śakti*) when in free collaboration with such factors as the requisite "ripening" of the *karma* of the selves it *resolves* "let me create" (*kariṣyāmi*).'

[97] Ibid., 201.

[98] *Civa-ñāṉa-potam* 6.2.39.

cognition in a more conventional sense, where splitting is always present. Ultimate knowledge is of a different order entirely from object-driven knowing. Yet what is 'knowledge that is known?' Conventional knowledge acts have two elements—the awareness of some specific content, and the awareness of this awareness.[99] If you do not know that you know something, you cannot know it. If you do not remember that you are remembering, you remember nothing.[100] But what is it to know oneself as self only insofar as that self emerges onto a surface that reduces, flattens, veils, maddens, or otherwise diminishes this same self?

Yet both the philosophical sources and the Śaiva narratives tell us that self-knowledge is indeed possible, and that the hunger for it drives this system through its twists and turns. There is a sense in which the curve can and must come to know itself as curve—by watching its lines bend and fold as the empty stretch fills up with space. The Beggar begins to dance. This moment belongs to the middle—more precisely, as we have seen, whatever is alive (*uyir*) is positioned between the dance (*naṭaṉam*) of *māyā* and impurity, on the one side, and the dance of Śiva and his *aruḷ*-presence, on the other.[101] (On another, perhaps deeper level, this living entity actually moves between Śiva and his presence.)[102] We can see the two simultaneous aspects of the dance that breathes out cosmos even as it breathes it in; in the pointed language of Umāpati's laconic *vĕṇpā* stanza, these are the 'dance of the body' (*ūṉa-naṭaṉam*, also the 'dance of deficiency') and the 'dance of knowledge' (*ñāṉa-naṭam*). Knowledge—god's knowledge of self in the sense just stated is the deeper, more primary state, an intra-divine potentiality that nevertheless, as the logical outcome of the initial, intuitive premises about god's nature, is activated and actualized under conditions of necessary blockage or resistance.[103]

In other words, in language closely bound up with the Cidambaram ritual system, it is not so much that Śiva is continuously present in his temple as Naṭarāja as that he is continuously *made* present there, by

[99] This standard Nyāya view has been elucidated by Matilal 1986: 141–79. See below, 3.1.

[100] See Narayana Rao and Shulman 2002: 187.

[101] Nirampav aḻakiya Tecikar on *Tiruvaruṭpayaṉ* 9.3.; see above, p. 42.

[102] This is Umāpati's final conclusion, as discussed above in 1.8.

[103] On God's self-knowledge in the perspective of Abhinavagupta and his Kashmiri Śaiva cosmology, see Handelman and Shulman 1997: 187. Śiva enters the game of dice at least partly in order to know himself.

ritual means, which include the factor of resistance. This process is the subject of the story the temple tells about its origins in relation to the original dance in the Forest of Pines. Similarly, it is not the case that Śiva always knows himself as the Dancer, or as the *liṅga* of space that contains the Dancer as its inner reality; rather, he is *made* to know himself as such, again through resistance as well as the love of his servants, Patañjali, Vyāghra-pāda, the sages' wives, and the constant stream of pilgrims. It is more than likely that even this latter quality of passionate devotion is not entirely free of resistance.

We do not know when the Cidambaram tradition assimilated the Dāruvana story to its vision of Śiva. It is likely that this integrated version of its origins was in place by ca. the late eleventh century, when Chola patronage added impetus to the fast-growing popularity of the Naṭarāja cult and to the place of Cidambaram as Naṭarāja's first home.[104] The Sanskrit *Cidambara-māhātmya* gives us a complete and polished narrative built around the relation of the Dāruvana dance to its more stable Cidambaram form; Umāpati, in the early fourteenth century, fixed this understanding of Naṭarāja's emergence in its classic Tamil expression. But we know that what became the *cit-sabhā*—the original *ci<u>r</u><u>r</u>'ampalam* or 'little space' at the heart of the shrine—was already in existence centuries earlier, at the time of the *Tevāram* poets, and already linked to Śiva's dance.[105] At the very least we can now understand something of the impetus that brought the Dancer of the Dāruvana into this open inner space. The Forest of Pines is that setting in which the impoverished Beggar is filled and set in motion in such a way that an unobstructed spacious fullness, curving and whirling rhythmically, becomes apparent to Śiva himself and to other selves who relate to him. Cidambaram makes this vision accessible in the unobstructed space within the temple, which is now framed in such a way that we—human observers—can stand it. This dance is the functional equivalent or, better, a precise, homologous re-embodiment of the *liṅga* of space that fills the same inner space. It is also an X-ray-like depiction of the inner workings of the *liṅga* of stone that we find in the *mūla-sthānam*, which Kulke believes to be the earlier cult focus at Cidambaram (to the north of the present-day *cit-sabhā*).[106] Whether there is a historical tension between

[104] See Sivaramamurti 1974; Kulke 1970; Kaimal 1999; Natarajan 1994: 31–95.
[105] See above, pp. 46–50.
[106] See Smith's objection to this sequence: 1996: 50.

the *mūla-sthānam* and Naṭarāja, or not, the relationship between the visible, stony *liṅga* and the invisible one expresses an enduring tensile vector within this god. This vector parallels the relation of the barely known to the deeply known, or of knowing to knowing that one knows. '*When god puts himself together, everything is fused and confused.*' When god puts himself together more fully, breathing in, drawing all into himself, fusing difference, he is less and less visible to us. The fact that this aspect is paradoxically enclosed in walls of fire-dipped gold, space enfolding space, light within light, shows us a certain self-imposed limit on the vortex comprising the dance. In this sense, too, the dancer is akin to the *liṅga* of stone.

We have to remember that Śiva apparently requires this progression from Beggar to Dancer in the interest of his self-knowledge, and that this sequence is probably repeated infinitely, with infinite variation. It is at least possible, and in our view more than probable, that the logic of the myth also recapitulates a historical sequence in the Cidambaram shrine. Bhairava, that is, may well have preceded both Bhikṣâṭana and Naṭarāja there. He is still there, in the gold-attracting *mūrti* in the *cit-sabhā*. A further stage in the evolution of this cult would take us to the Tantric mystery, *rahasya*, behind the curtain on the wall and to the crucial role of the goddess Śiva-kāma-sundarī. This is a part of Cidambaram's history that is still very much in need of investigation.[107]

Knowledge, especially self-knowledge, cannot do without resistance. Knowing is also intimately related to curvature, if only because the shaping of the curve turns it back toward itself, thereby relating movement to its own sense of becoming one with itself. Curvature also continues through itself, toward an otherness that inevitably becomes part of the curve. The body of the Dancer describes just such a trajectory. Naṭarāja, we can say, is drawn into his own movement, as is characteristic of the twisting, rotating process of his coming into being and retreating back into his inner depths while breathing out and breathing in. Śiva is 'drawn

[107] Kulke's study includes a reconstructed sequence relating to the worship of the goddess as it intrudes upon, and conflicts with, the male-oriented *linga* and Naṭarāja cults. There is, however, reason to posit a secondary and later reorganization of the mature Cidambaram grid, from the fourteenth century onwards, in terms of Āgama-based worship of the *śakti*. For related developments in this stage of Tamil Śaiva religion, see the sixteenth-century Tamil *Saundarya-laharī* of Vīrai Kavirāca paṇṭitar, with commentary by Ĕllappa nayiṉār; also Smith 1996: 135–60.

into the whirling movement of the dance,' accelerating to the point where dancer and dance are one. And this is 'only the beginning.' Śiva, the cosmos in movement, closing all gaps, becomes 'entirely present' not merely as a possible context for living but as the very ontology of all living movement, without which there is no existence. This is the condition of *aruḷ*, god in involution, looping in and out of himself, through himself, constantly re-creating a middle space. Insofar as everything else has been taken away from this space, it is 'pure.'[108] Notice that purity (*tūymai*), in this south Indian perspective, is thus not at all a matter of boundaries, as is so often stated, but rather of removing stains or obstructions—a state, in effect, of *no* boundary, no outer or inner edge. There is no outer ring around this Śaiva cosmos and no external vantage point from which to observe it. It does, however, have the capacity to regenerate itself as the middle in the sense of just this absence of external surface or boundary, indeed of exteriority of any kind. The middle opens itself up as an inner space moving still deeper inwards. In this space, presence can be intensified, as the Forest of Pines is turned inward by Bhikṣâṭana and as the eye becomes capable of seeing itself seeing,[109] the self of knowing itself as knowing. Surface issues into middleness that is experienced as presence; Bhairava issues into Bhikṣâṭana who is spun into Naṭarāja, the whorl of self that is understanding made of light. It happens moment by moment, with the help of the temple and its rituals, and there is no escaping the underlying, motivating premise: you first have to bring god to the surface if you want to reach the middle point where surface knows itself as depth.

[108] Thus Bhairava is naturally the Pure God (*tūyavaṉ*) in *Kanta-purāṇam* 6.13.197.
[109] See *Civa-ñāṉa-potam* 6.2.38. On this Wittgensteinian viewpoint, see Becker 1995: 162 ; below, 'On Not Knowing and Saying No'.

Exorcising Emptiness at Nelveli

Deny the mountain,
deny the earth,
deny the sky,
deny what you know,
and you will surely deny
yourself.[1]

On Not Knowing and Saying No

Of all kinds of knowledge, knowledge of self is the most unlikely and the most necessary. It may well be impossible to attain in terms of the south Indian Śaiva system, where even to think of oneself as one—a single, somehow coherent entity—is necessarily to split oneself into two. 'A living being would not think of itself as "one," and one who does think like this must be *other* than one' (*tāṉe taṉṉaiy ŏṉṟ' ĕṉa karutal veṇṭāmayiṉ aṅṅaṉaṅ karutum pŏruḷ veṟ' ŏṉṟu uṇṭ' ĕṉpatu*).[2] For similar reasons, a word such as 'I' is pregnant with epistemic disaster.[3] To know even a single, evanescent part of the self is to objectify that part and therefore kill it. What is knowable is, by definition, unreal[4] when compared to the unknowable but somehow familiar experience of being free. To be free, one has to take away. This experience is breath, *uyir*, moving inwards. Thus to know is to stop breathing in.

[1] *Tiruvaruṭpayaṉ* 4.7. *kĕṭu*, the principal verb here, can also be translated: 'waste;' 'neglect;' 'overlook.' Cf. *Naḷavĕṇpā* 73; Appar *Tevāram* 5.12.5.

[2] Civañāṉayokikaḷ, *Civa-ñāṉa-māpāṭiyam* ad *CÑP* 2, *vārttika* 1 (112–13): . . . *ekam ĕnil ekam ĕṉṟu cuṭṭuvat' uṇmaiyiṉ*.

[3] Cf. Sivaraman 1973: 191.

[4] *Civa-ñāṉa-potam* 6.1.

Philosophically, such a stance might conduce to scepticism. Indeed, doubt has its uses: by denying existence, by saying the very powerful word 'no,' the ultimate mantra, the doubter affirms, indeed effectively proves, his own existence.[5] On the other hand, somewhat surprisingly, there is knowledge free from doubt,[6] which is the only knowledge that counts. Knowledge not riddled with doubt is the primary criterion for truth (*pramāṇa*). What sort of knowledge can this be?

This question is particularly trenchant when we start to talk about Śiva and his apparently driving need to know himself. There is no reason whatsoever to imagine that Śiva can escape the paradoxes of knowing, though it is not clear in any of our texts just what it is that Śiva seeks to know. Omniscience can actually be a heavy burden or a hindrance, especially if it has, by definition, no real object. But seeking an object—something that can or could be known—is no solution. To enter into knowing of the object-oriented type is to fatally compromise omniscience. Stated differently, since 'knowing' and 'seeing' are mostly synonymous in this lexicon,[7] what the eye sees—even god's eye—is the objects that, by seeing, it has killed. Surely god's knowledge, which takes away and thus enlivens, liberates, and breathes, must have some other force or meaning.

We can, of course, restate the difficulty in the somewhat idiosyncratic terms that have emerged from our earlier discussion: thus we have the curve that comes to know itself as curve, or the surface that sees itself as depth.[8] These forms of knowing or seeing may take us away from the potentially lethal epistemologies of the everyday, toward a somewhat more promising goal. Perhaps such abstract formulations can even 'explain' why the god enters into the process we have been describing. At moments, reading and re-reading these texts, it seems that this logic might suffice. But even at such moments, we can hardly resist asking ourselves just what kind of knowledge this might be.

It is no use expecting the Tamil Śaiva Siddhânta texts to address these issues directly in purely logical terms. For historical reasons, we tend to demand an air-tight philosophical coherence from southern

[5] *Civa-ñāṉa-potam* 3.1. See *Brahmā-sūtra-bhāṣya* 1.1.1, end, and the *advaita* use of this theme; Grinshpon, in press.

[6] Sivaraman 1973: 306, citing *Pauṣkarâgama.*

[7] See *Śiva-jñāna-bodha* (Skt) 11.

[8] See the previous section.

Śaivism, more than from many other systems; but such a demand is often frustrated by the enigmatic or deliberately paradoxical statements of our texts, whether discursive–metaphysical or narrative in thrust.[9] Nonetheless, if we take the language seriously and listen to its nuances, certain key intuitions and expressive images do come clearly into view.

One of these is the eye that sees itself seeing. We will return to this image in a moment. Let us first prepare the ground by considering the carefully differentiated uses of negation, hinted at above. In the hands of the Śaiva metaphysicians, negation is situated at the very heart of knowing.[10] Why should 'no' be so critical and effective a word? For one thing, it sometimes takes away. 'No' is Śiva's word, or cry, from his first howl of protest upon being born to his angry retreat as the Pillar to Mount Muñjavat.[11] It is thus the creative word par excellence. It opens space. But in discursive contexts, there are many kinds of 'no,' neatly categorized by the Śaiva commentators. Tamil, like other south Indian languages, normally distinguishes between two major forms of negation, each with its own, somewhat artificial verbal 'root.'[12] One of these (*illai*) negates existence: thus *ulakam illai* would mean 'there is no world' (in relation, say, to a deeper reality). The other (*alla*) negates predication, attribution, or identity: *civa<u>n</u> alla<u>n</u>* '[X (masc.)] is not Śiva.'[13] What happens when we attempt to apply this distinction to Śaiva metaphysical contexts dealing with knowledge and oneness?

Civañā<u>n</u>ayokikaḷ, in the eighteenth century, offers a penetrating illustration. As we have seen, something that is entirely unitary will not think of itself as one, or rather *cannot* think of itself as one without splitting into two. But there are times when such a split is positively necessary if we are to define ourselves in lucid relation to the god.

[9] As recognized by Piatigorski 1962. For the contrasting view, positing air-tight coherence, see Schomerus 1912; Dhavamony 1971, inter alia.

[10] *Cūrṇi-kŏttu* [the old prose paraphrase appended to *Civa-ñā<u>n</u>a-potam*] 3.1: 'The knowing subject (*a<u>r</u>iv'uyir*) exists by virtue of saying no.'

[11] Above, pp. 33–5; Shulman 1986. Compare Rilke's famous pronouncement: 'Prejudiced as we are against death, we do not manage to release it from all its distorted images. . . . Life simultaneously says Yes and No. Death . . . is the true Yes-sayer. It says *only* Yes.' Mitchell 1984: 332.

[12] Chevillard 1996: 78 uses the term 'un verbe idéal.'

[13] See, e.g., Ce<u>n</u>āvaraiyar on *Tŏl. Cŏl.* 25. Chevillard 1996: 77 labels this 'la copule négative.' This type of negation parallels what Sanskrit grammarians define as *prasajya-pratiṣedha*.

So when the *vārttika* on *CÑP* 2 uses the term *attuvitam* < *advaita*, 'non-dualism,' to formulate the reality of god vis-à-vis the world and its living beings, the great commentator addresses the exact meaning of the privative particle *a*, 'non-'. Is this a denial of existence (*i<u>n</u>mai*)? That is, does the text want to insist on non-dualism as a total oneness characterizing god's relation to other living beings (*uyir*)? Does two-ness simply *not exist*? Is the 'self,' that is, entirely identified with Śiva without residue or excess? Certainly not. We know that Śiva and the living *paśu* or *uyir* are 'not two and not one.'[14] To insist on a complete unity of identity is thus actually to undermine the meaning of the word 'one,' whose use requires the cognitive split we have seen. Apparently, Śiva is himself susceptible to such a division, since he uses this word or at least allows its authoritative application to himself by Mĕykaṇṭār, the author of the *sūtra*s. This is an important conclusion, which Śivaraman aptly and cautiously paraphrases as follows: 'Meykandar's statement [about *advaita*] amounts to saying that God has not "told us" that He is in no sense self-conscious.'[15] Note the double negation, a characteristically intensified form of affirmation in this metaphysical milieu.

But if god is self-conscious, what exactly is he conscious *of*? In the Tamil Dāruvana texts, he seems to feel oppressed, at the start, by the very existence of the broken off and deluded pieces of himself—the falsely autonomous and loveless sages—and to want to reabsorb them into himself, recomposing himself as a whole. He would, that is, be conscious of points of blockage somewhere in his universe, that is, in his own being. He keeps smashing into such hard or crystallized pieces of self which, through their very opposition and recalcitrance, conduce to self-knowledge, as we have seen. But in that case, it seems we will have to opt for the second type of negation if we want to understand the word *advaita*, the denial of two-ness. It can only mean the absence of a predicated otherness (*ve<u>r</u>'a<u>n</u>mai uṇartti ni<u>r</u>kum*).[16] We are

[14] *Tiruvaruṭpaya<u>n</u>* 8.5, with Nirampav aḻakiya Tecikar's gloss on *attuvitam/advaita*: 'Those who say that god and the living self are one, and those who say that they are two, are both wrong. "Non-dualism" means that if you mix them together, there is no otherness.' See above p. 43.

[15] Sivaraman 1973: 495.

[16] *Māpāṭiyam*, *loc. cit*. We deliberately omit Civañā<u>n</u>ayokikaḷ's exploration of a third possibility, *ma<u>r</u>utalai*, i.e. the rejection of or opposition to the negated item: *advaita* would thus be a hostility or opposition (Skt. *virodha*) to any form of dualism, as *adharma* opposes *dharma*. Surprisingly, such a reading actually presupposes

thus precluded from calling god 'other' (*anya*)—at least insofar as he takes away.[17] He becomes other, or rather appears in this guise, only by creating (breathing out). In our terms, he is non-other when we share his unrealized potentiality but becomes other as soon as he objectifies any given strand of it, in language, thought, or deed.[18] In this sense, he is, indeed, 'non-dual'—not an undifferentiated unity, but also not subject to divisive attribution. Or, in terms of the habitual human perspective, he becomes other *when we know him* (as other). At no point, however, are we required to deny the *existence* of a dimension of displacement within god. Indeed, we know that such a dimension must exist. Language itself demands it by using a word such as 'one' with reference to god.

It might thus be best to avoid statements like 'god is one' altogether, were it not for the fact that the Upaniṣads and much subsequent literature are rather full of them. But once again, there is an advantage to such usages, since they inevitably give rise to the need to say something more specific about what it is that god knows, or that we can know. See how naturally Civañāṉayokikaḷ slips from semantic analysis to this epistemic or existential level: 'If we stick with the meaning of non-predication [for the word *advaita*], so that the phrase now means "he [Śiva] is not two," we must understand that he is *not other* in relation to two-ness but rather remains constantly *with* [us].'[19] So god is characterized, despite his tendency toward displacement, by his constancy in 'being with' (*uṭanāy niṟṟal*). 'Withness' (*uṭan, uṭanpāṭu*)—another deeply rooted element of the late-medieval Tamil conceptual universe—is not a technical, primarily spatial or temporal matter.[20] It is, rather, a derivative of presence (*aruḷ*). As such it is not a given in the normal sense but more an experience or form of knowledge that can be activated, actualized, recognized, or enhanced. If we think, again, in ritual terms, the living being who wants to be free, perhaps in the course of *becoming*

---

a kind of dualism. The passage has been discussed, not entirely satisfactorily, by Sivaraman 1973: 142–3.

[17] See discussion of this same *sūtra*, in its Sanskrit form, above, pp. 59–60.

[18] We wish to thank Yohanan Grinshpon for remarks on this point.

[19] *aṉmaippŏruḷ paṟṟi iraṇṭ' allav' ĕnap pŏruḷ kŏḻḻiṉ iru-pŏruḷkaḷum veṟ' aṉṟi uṭanāy niṟkum ĕṉap poruḷpaṭum*, 113.

[20] As Sivaraman correctly notes, 1973: 493, n. 22. Cf. *Civañāṉacittiyār, cupakkam* 2.1 (90).

free, applies himself to making god present in order to know him as *being with*, which really means *being within*, perhaps by *breathing in*.

It is at just this point that the Śaiva Siddhânta makes its boldest statement. Like the Buddhist Mādhyamika, Śaiva Siddhânta is, perhaps at base, a radical, self-subverting epistemology. It stands and falls on its theory of knowledge, and *knowing* is the experiential dimension of its teleology. 'Being with,' the actual experience of Śiva's presence, is a special kind of knowing. Here the eye sees itself seeing, like the 'inner heart that is shown to the eye that sees' (*kāṇuṅ kaṇṇukuk kāṭṭum uḷam pol*) and, being seen, moves toward loving.[21] Specifically, the 'self'—that which breathes, *uyir*—knows itself as Śiva's knowing. It is *never* the self that knows—we are speaking of knowledge worth having, that is, self-knowledge—but Śiva who knows and is known to know. In the language of the canonical Śaiva texts, this form of second-order knowledge is called 'not forgetting' (*maṟavāmai*).[22] As in other South Asian epistemological systems, as we have seen, knowledge always has at least these two aspects—knowing something, and knowing that one knows.[23] But here the something that is known is not an object but an experience, and to know that you know is to know Śiva as knowing for you.[24] Since all such knowledge is a matter of identity in its fullest sense, I know that I am I only because I know that the one who knows is not I, yet non-other than I. Such is freedom. This statement could also serve as a definition of consciousness itself.

But there is one further aspect involved. For here we can, at last, give a tentative answer to the question about what Śiva knows when he knows himself. In a moment of freedom such as we are describing, probably ritually achieved, something profound happens in the god who

[21] *Civa-ñāṉa-potam* 11. The corresponding Sanskrit *sūtra* reads *dṛśor darśayitevâtmā tasya darśayitā śivaḥ*, 'it is the self that gives sight to the eyes, and Śiva gives sight to the self.' Śivâgrayogin naturally equates seeing with knowing, or showing with teaching (*darśayitā jñāpayitā*) and, following the *sūtra*, connects this moment of giving sight or knowledge with the inner sacrifice, *antar-yāga*. A similar transformative reciprocity of seeing and being seen *while seeing* appears at the culmination of the Dāruvana version of *Kūrma-purāṇa* 2.37; see Appendix.

[22] e.g. *Tiruvuntiyār* 18.

[23] See Matilal 1986: 141–79; above, pp. 97–8.

[24] Thus *Cūrṇi-kŏttu* 5.2: 'All living beings know through Śiva' (*araṉāle uyirkaḷ ĕllām aṟiyum*). Cf. *Śaivâgama-paribhāṣā-mañjari* 5.102: it is not the eye, but Śiva, that sees for human beings.

knows himself as knowing for us. Doubt-free knowledge emerges at this point and only at this point. Veiling has done its job and can rest. The god dances on Apasmāra-puruṣa—demonic, or epileptic, forgetting, the failure to know that one knows or to remember who it is that knows. A movement of far-reaching mutual interpenetration, utterly remote from any stasis—as it is remote from deadly discursive understanding—spins the god into the self that knows him as knower. What is required is an entering in (*uḷam pukutal*).[25] Separation is ruled out (*piripp' in̲ri*), displacement displaced. World, self, Śiva are 'not one and not two.'[26] They flow together in the middle. The god is self-aware insofar as the self is aware that Śiva knows.[27] Śiva knows himself by our knowing that we know ourselves as his knowing us. Splitting collapses or melts,[28] cracks and contours coalesce and are drawn back into the whorl. Weaving god into self as god's awareness of our self as knowing him, we enable him to *be with* us, and thus with himself, turning on an axis that is generated out of this radically interdependent form of knowing. Being with us, his devotees, he comes to the surface; but the surface has become a spinning whorl indistinguishable from whatever could be called or known as depth. Such movement always indicates a profound existential shift within god, achieved in part through our acting upon ourselves. Still, within this whorl we can perhaps notice another, inner spin, revolving at its own rhythm—the spin of knowing how and what the self, circling or twisting through Śiva, can know of itself. It is this knowing that we call exorcism, the Śaiva answer to sorcery, hence a trenchant statement about freedom.

Tirunelveli: Seeing All There is to See

The most explicit statement in Tamil about exorcism in connection with the Dāruvana, and at the same time the most extensive, complete version

[25] *Civa-ñān̲a-potam* 2.1.9. Cf. *Māpāṭiyam* 438.

[26] Above, p. 44; cf. *Cūrṇi-kŏttu* 2.1.

[27] *Māpāṭiyam ad CÑP* 9 (433–6); *Cūrṇi-kŏttu* 5.2; see Śivaraman 1973: 413–14. And cf. Daniel 1984: 234 on 'synthetic knowledge' in Tamil, which seeks 'to discover the self in the other or to know the self by getting to know in the other that which is also in the self.' See discussion by Nabokov 2000: 26–7; also Trawick 1990: 116, on Śiva seeing through the eye of Kaṇṇappan̲: 'In order for you to understand my heart, you must see through my eyes. In order for me to understand your heart, I must see through yours.'

[28] *urukki uṭaṅk' iyaintu*: *Civa-ñān̲a-potam* 2.1.9.

of the Dāruvana story that we have from south India, comes from Tirunelveli, in the far south of the Tamil area. Like all other large shrines in the south, Nelveli has grown through a long process of accretion, assimilation, and integration to its present luxuriant state, where the pilgrim comes face to face with many forms of divinity. Again like other major temples, Nelveli offers a relatively coherent fabric of historical and thematic relations among these diverse faces of the god, so that we can, in effect, read the mature temple map as text. This is not the place to attempt a developmental synthesis, but we can at least sketch in something of the cultic background to the identification of Nelveli as the original Forest of Pines.

The earliest literary evidence we have from Nelveli is a single *Tevāram* decade ascribed to Tiruñāṉacampantar (perhaps seventh century), celebrating the 'rich god who lives in Tirunelveli' (*tirunĕlveliy uṟai cĕlvar*).[29] It is very striking that already here there is prominent reference to the forest: Śiva at Nelveli has the habit of seeking alms from loose women (*cĕṭicciyar*):

It would be more than difficult
to think his nature (*iyalpu*)
is always the same,

but it is in his nature
all the same
to mount the bull and go begging
from loose women,
house by house.[30]

It is of some interest that *iyalpu*, 'nature,' 'property,' 'propriety,' 'conduct,' is derived from the root *iyal*, which expresses notions of harmonious composition, possibility or potentiality, and also movement—'to go on foot, to move forward;' 'to walk about gaily;' 'to dance.'[31] Like most phenomena, the god is composed, we might say, of movement. Indeed, so unstable and changeable is he that it is 'more than

[29] Tiruñāṉacampantar *Tevāram* 3.92.

[30] *ĕṉṟum or iyalpinar ĕṉa niṉaiv' ariyavar eṟ' at' eṟi / cĕṉṟu tāñ cĕṭicciyar maṉaitŏṟum palikŏḷum iyalp' ituve*, 3.92.2.

[31] *Madras Tamil Lexicon*, s.v. These latter meanings are well attested from very ancient times. See, e.g., *Aiṅkuṟunūṟu* 175. Cf. *Tŏl. Ĕḻuttu* 47 (the *iyal* of phonemes denoting themselves).

difficult' to think of him in any fixed or unitary form. It is in his nature to change, to flow, to twist, and this propensity finds immediate confirmation in his identification as the Beggar in the Forest of Pines. The rich god (*cĕlvar*) is filling himself up with their gifts—needs these gifts, no doubt, if he is to be rich. His wealth lies in begging. The women there are somehow spoiled (*cĕṭicciyar*, a strong epithet < Tamil *cĕṭi*, 'that which is decayed;' 'vice'), no doubt because they respond to the god's seduction. He is playing with them, tantalizing and misleading them:

> Smeared with ash,
> spinning a snake hissing fire,
> the sliver of a moon, and the Ganges
> into his tangled hair, he comes on foot
> to tease women, their voices sweet
> as a parrot's, as if to steal
> their hearts.[32]

Notice the spin and the tangle. *Kiṟipaṭa*, 'to tease,' is sometimes clearly erotic;[33] it can also suggest something deceitful or deluding, thus the refractory drift of a heart ignorant of the god.[34] But here Śiva himself, spinning and turning, at once masked and transparent, adopts this mode; the phrase is precisely parallel to another, *mātarai maiyal cĕyvār*, in verse 6 of this same decade: 'he confuses (or intoxicates, drives mad, deludes) women'—this god with a woman in half his body (*maṅkaiy or paṅkiṉar*, in the preceding line of the verse). That he is androgynous to begin with only intensifies the paradoxical and maddening quality of his begging: he has, one might think, all that he needs, both male and female components of self, but he is still driven to fill himself up from the outside, as it were, by re-internalizing a feminine part lost in the forest and confused by this apparition of a needy bisexual completeness.[35] This deity, as we have said, is usually unable to regenerate himself from within.

The female component of Śiva at Nelveli is the goddess Kāntimatī,

[32] *pŏṟi kiḷar aravamum poḻ iḷa matiyamun kaṅkaiy ĕṉṉum*
nĕṟipaṭu kuḻaliyaic caṭai micaic culavi vĕṇṇīru pūcik/
kiṟipaṭa naṭantu naṟ kiḷimŏḻiyavar maṉaṅ kavarvar polum. . . . 3.92.3
[33] Thus *Tiruvācakām* 41.10.
[34] Ibid., 5.32.
[35] See Cuntaramūrttināyaṉār *Tevāram* 36.5 (on Tiruppaiññīḻi).

the 'radiantly beautiful;' it is customary to visit her first upon entering the temple, *before* seeing the male god, Nĕllaiyappar.[36] The goddess appears in full wedding attire, for this couple agreed to give Agastya a vision of themselves as bride and bridegroom at Nelveli, as this sage made his way south to Mount Pŏtiyil.[37] Directly in front of the goddess is the Swing Chamber (*uñcal maṇṭapam*), where Kāntimatī swings for three days after her annual wedding ceremony, in the month of Aippaci; this large hall also contains a huge standing mirror.[38] We note in passing that the Tirunelveli temple complex is graced with an unusual spaciousness, repeatedly experienced as one moves from one part to another. Thus connecting the Kāntimatī shrine to the male set of divine embodiments is the Corridor of the Chain (*caṅkili maṇṭapam*),[39] with its great pillars and sub-shrines to Subrahmaṇya-Murukaṉ and Kāśī Viśvanātha, Śiva as Lord of the Cosmos.

Once inside the domain of Śiva as Nĕllaiyappar, we find many familiar faces. A stone Bhairava (the 'Child Bhairava')[40] stands in the north-east corner, very close to the innermost sanctum; Naṭarāja and Śivakāmi appear nearby as large bronzes, and Naṭarāja dances here in another of his localized dance-halls, the *Tāmra-sabhā* or Copper Space.[41] A fine bronze of *Kaṅkāla-mūrti*, the Skeleton or Skeleton-Bearer, is situated to the west of the sanctum in the first *prākāra*.[42] The Skeleton, as we know, is a multiform of Bhikṣâṭana, another derivative of

36 Pāskarat Tŏṇṭaimāṉ 1967: 184.

37 Agastya was sent south by Śiva to balance the earth, which had tilted downwards in the north-east (the Himalayas) when all the gods and other beings came to see Śiva and Pārvatī's wedding. Because Agastya missed this happy event in the north, he was promised a personal vision of the newly-weds on his route south.

38 Puṉṉaivaṉanāṭa Mutaliyār 1966: 6. Our thanks to Sascha Ebeling for making this booklet available to us. See also Umāmakecuvari 1990: 91–2. The Swing Chamber is dated 1635.

39 Constructed in 1647 by Vaṭamalaiyappap Piḷḷaiyāṉ: ibid., 8.

40 Pāla Vayiravar: ibid., 12.

41 Analogous to the *cit-sabhā* + *kanaka-sabhā* at Cidambaram. See Dorai Rangaswamy 1958: 1: 440–1. There is a set of five such *sabhā*s, the other three being at Tiruvalankatu (*ratna-sabhā*), Madurai (*rajata-sabhā*), and Tirukkurralam (*citra-sabhā*).

42 See Balasubrahmanyam 1975: 185–7. The Nelveli shrine, a Pāṇḍya foundation, was substantially renovated during the reign of Rājarāja at the end of the tenth century, partly to allow the addition of the massive sub-shrine to Viṣṇu as Paḷḷikŏṇṭāṉ (ibid.).

Bhairava;[43] we will return to this image, which plays a central part in the Nelveli Dāruvana story.

Like at Cidambaram, Nelveli sets up a strong tension between two *liṅgas*: the Root Liṅga (*mūla-liṅkar*), in a sunken level of the first enclosure, perhaps the most ancient cultic focus here; and the *liṅga* that is today the major embodiment of Śiva at Nelveli, known as Venu-vana-nātha, 'Lord of the Bamboo Grove,' and also Veṇṭa vaḷarnta nāyakar, 'the master who grew upon request.' He is also Nĕllaiyappar, 'god of Nĕllai = Nelveli.' All these names have important resonances. Nelveli, to begin with, is literally 'bounded by paddy.' If at Cidambaram the god is enclosed in a chamber made of gold, at Nelveli he is hemmed in by growing rice. But the *purāṇic* story, in fact, makes Śiva himself the 'fence' or 'hedge' (*veli*): A temple priest named Veda-śarma left paddy to dry in his courtyard when he went down to the Tamraparni River for his bath; while he was gone, a strong rainstorm suddenly came up, threatening to wash the paddy away. The priest came running home, but he found his courtyard still dry—for Śiva himself stood there as a boundary beyond which not even a single raindrop could fall.[44] Here is the god as containing, not contained—or, as we shall see, as reaching outward toward a certain edge or limit.

This same god of the Limit has another important property or aspect. He has a tendency to shoot up, like a plant, and to continue growing. Once, before the stone temple was built, he was hidden as a *liṅga* in the midst of a bamboo grove; the bamboo trees were the Vedas, who took this form in order to offer shade to Śiva.[45] A cowherd known as King Rāma (Rāmakkon̲) used to go everyday to milk his cows in the cowpen located nearby; on his way home with a pot full of fresh milk, he would pass the hidden *liṅga*. Each time his feet would get entangled in the undergrowth and, stumbling, completely unaware, he would pour the milk over the god. Eventually he took an axe and started to cut away the undergrowth; in this way he revealed the god—by actually cutting off his head. Today this lopped-off head graces the sanctum and is known as 'the master who grew upon request,' since the cowherd

[43] See above, pp. 52–8.

[44] Pāskarat Tŏṇṭaimān̲ 1971: 187; Cuppiramaṇiya Mutaliyār ad *Pĕriya Purāṇam* 2784.

[45] As Umāmakecuvari 1990: 233 says, the bamboo grove is thus apparently the Forest of Pines. Perhaps in Tiruneveli, bamboo is as close as one gets to a Himalayan pine.

begged the god to grow to an immense size, seated upon a throne (*pīṭam*) that includes within it twenty-one smaller thrones.[46] Moreover, the happy cowherd had now seen whatever *can* be seen in this universe—so the full name of the deity is Mul̲utu kaṇṭa rāmakkon̲ukku muttiy aḷitta ven̲uvan̲anātar, 'the Lord of the Bamboo Grove who gave freedom to Rāmakkon̲, who had seen everything there was to see.'[47] In Rāmakkon̲ we can recognize the necessary figure of a 'first king'—very often a cowherd[48]—and in the 'throne' holding the ever-growing *liṅga* in place we may see a *yoni* in perpetual movement, generating and repeatedly extruding this *liṅga* that grows through or beyond its wound.

So Nĕllaiyappar Śiva, hero of the Forest of Pines, inhabits an unusually expansive and spacious domain, which he bounds, on the one hand, and shoots through in an organic, upward moving form, on the other. In the latter guise, he is the head cut off from the root, this act of self-sacrifice being, it seems, the very condition of his continued growth. The root remains present in the sunken *liṅga*, the originary generation of godhead here, adjacent to the main shrine. You cannot have one of these forms without the other, just as the *mūlasthānam* at Cidambaram must eventually link up with the *liṅga* of space. But the set is not complete. A short arc connects the Child Bhairava in the corner with the Root Liṅga, the Lord of the Bamboo Grove, the splendid Skeleton-Kaṅkāla slightly behind the latter, and the Dancer in the Copper Hall behind the Skeleton. These five male forms of Śiva are aligned in linear proximity along a slightly curved axis—or is it a vector indicating the direction of inner evolution in this deity, from the full potentiality of the Root Liṅga to the visible but wounded Bamboo Lord and thence to the Skeleton and the Dancer?[49] We now have to add one further male identity, critical to the god's adventures in the Forest of Pines. For immediately beyond the Lord of the Bamboo Grove and effectively intersecting the latter's enclosed space is Viṣṇu at Nelveli, Nĕllaikkovintar or Paḷḷikkŏṇṭān̲. Although, as stated, this sub-shrine took its present contours during Rājarāja Chola's rule, we can assume that Nelveli, like Mamallapuram, Tiruvarur, and many other Tamil sites,[50] contained

[46] Pāskarat Tŏṇṭaimān̲, *loc. cit.*; Pun̲n̲aivan̲anāta Mutaliyār 1966: 12.
[47] Ibid.
[48] As at Cenci and Tirupati: see Hiltebeitel 1988: 57–64
[49] Just as Bhikṣāṭana at Cidambaram moves the god toward the dance: above, pp. 46–8.
[50] Shulman 1978.

a much earlier symbiotic doubling of Śiva and Viṣṇu at its core. The male deity here, in other words, is actually split into two primary, complementary identities, the left-hand (northern) Viṣṇu suggestive of a certain centripetal, outwardly emergent 'male femininity,' like the female segment on the left of Śiva as the androgyne, Ardha-nārīśvara. In this guise, Viṣṇu will appear as Mohinī in the Forest of Pines. The right-hand (southern) segment, a centrifugal Śiva persona, fissures and reproduces itself in the entire, rather unbalanced series we have outlined—Bhairava, Root Liṅga, Bamboo Lord, Skeleton, and Dancer. Outside the male compound we find a more uniform 'female femininity' in its own space, but deeply bound to the self-segmenting male. This set of relations has a systemic aspect evident in each of the major iconic condensations and driving the latter through their transformations relative to one another. One question that emerges naturally from even so rapid an overview, and that achieves expression in the Dāruvana variant from Nelveli, is the following: Is the male hidden by a female exterior, the male *within* the female, a more fundamental form of the godhead than the female appearing as active female—that is, than the female aspect of god that devolves into 'presence' or 'awareness' (*cit-śakti*) and thence into the phenomenal world?

Tirunĕlvelittalapurāṇam, Tārukāvaṉaccarukkam

We owe a monumental compendium of Tirunelveli tradition to a Veḷāḷa poet named Nĕllaiyappap Piḷḷai or Nĕllaiyappak Kavirāyar, who completed his Tamil *kāvya*, the *Tirunĕlvelittalapurāṇam* in 120 chapters and 6912 verses, in 1829.[51] He claims to have based himself on a Sanskrit text (*vaṭa nūl*) from the *Sanatkumāra-saṃhitā* of the *Skānda-purāṇa* (*kāntam*), which he turned into Tamil *viruttam* verses.[52] A preface composed by Putūr Vaḷḷināyakam Piḷḷai mentions a Sanskrit *māhātmya* on Tirunelveli that was given to the poet, following a dream revelation, by one Nīlakaṇṭa Cāttiri, who also explicated this Sanskrit text to Nĕllaiyappaṉ.[53] The god of Nelveli himself corrected some of the poet's mistakes and helped him out from time to time when he became stuck in

[51] Zvelebil 1995: 492. An earlier *purāṇa* on this site, the *Veṉu-vaṉa-purāṇam* (attributed to Nirampav aḻakiya Tecikar), was unfortunately not available to us.

[52] *Tirunelvĕlittalapurāṇam, avaiyaṭakkamum pāyiramum*, 8.

[53] *ciṟappuppāyiram* prefaced to our edition, verse 25.

a verse.[54] The first public performance of the *purāṇa* must have aroused some opposition—by no means a rare occurrence at such occasions—for a certain Nākappan̲, who attacked the book, died of a stomach disorder soon thereafter; on the other hand, a Tiruvaṭiyappan̲, who read the work and praised it, was healed of leprosy.[55] Tamil poetry of any real intensity and status is regularly accompanied by such effects.[56] We might bear this facet of the poem in mind as we read the long chapter that, while narrating the events in the Forest of Pines, focuses on human hopes for exorcism, healing, and understanding:

> Gateways, towers, temples of burnished gold, pools paved with jewels, banners waving in the sky, incomparable homes, pavilions, fragrant gardens—you can see them all on Mount Kailāsa, where god lives. The very streets are inlaid with precious stones, with temples on either side. Snakes and ghouls everywhere: also ashrams for performing *tapas* in delightful surroundings, and halls where Vedic Brahmins and astrologers can sit. There are crowds of strange creatures—Rudras, Kinnaras, Kimpurusas, Yogis, the gods who oversee the directions of space. The lucky ones have achieved the same form as god himself. Pillars inlaid with the nine gems stand in golden palaces interspersed with banana groves, betel and sugarcane. And every day the most enchanting women dance and sing and play the vina. Those are the goddesses: ordinary women, by the millions, light the lamps for worship. You can hear, at all hours, the chanting of Veda and other texts, amidst the cries of the parrots and the mynah birds beside the pools and the divine drumming that throbs in the streets. Peacocks spread their tails in the gardens, white parasols close off the sky. Devotees who have reached the deep ecstasy of freedom sing to god, who lives there—unbroken in self, with the Woman as half of him and snakes on his arms.
>
> To be precise, he sits, with Pārvatī, on a throne more luminous than a million suns, in the very middle of that mountain peak. His sons, Gaṇeśa and Kumāra, flank him on either side, and there are innumerable ghosts and spirits and devotees at his feet. He is the king, dense with compassion.

[54] Pūn̲naivan̲anāta Mutaliyār 1966: 17.
[55] Ibid.
[56] Shulman 2001: 1–18.

Once Viṣṇu came to worship, right after killing the two demons Madhu and Kaiṭabha. Ushered in by Nandikeśvara, he bowed to Śiva and sang his praises. Śiva said to him: 'We're very happy that you have come, especially after you tricked those two demons to their death. If there is anything you would like, just tell us.' Viṣṇu replied: 'Generous lord of Nellai,[57] is there anything your devotees cannot achieve? The demons died through your flowing goodness. Master: I would like to know your form as Kaṅkāla-Mūrti, Lord of the Skeleton—the form you took, out of love, when you lifted the corpse of an earlier, dead Viṣṇu onto your shoulder.'

And Śiva at once agreed, promising to give him that knowledge, in love. With the delicious Pārvatī inside him, Śiva looked steadily at Viṣṇu and said: 'In the far south, to the east of the Malaya Mountain,[58] there is a place called Nelveli, where the goddess performed *tapas*, and the Vedas performed *tapas*, and other wonderful things happened. The very first *liṅga* is there. Kāntimatī, the goddess who grants life in that world and in this, lives there. The Porunai river opens the way to all who bathe there. We showed Agastya our wedding in that place, and from there we—the great goddess Umā, or Parā, or Ambikā, and myself—guard the world. It is also known as the Ancient Site of Wholeness (*brahma-vṛddha-pura*). Many gods and sages have gone there to perform *tapas*; even at the time of the universal flood, it survives as home to the Virgin Goddess—also known to the Vedas and Āgamas as the Forest of Pines. There are many places in the world that are dear to me, but that site is Kailāsa—heaven itself. Anyone who lives there, or is born there, or dies there, or even just thinks of it in his or her heart, wins freedom. There, in Tirunelveli, we will show you the ancient Skeleton Form that you want. There, too, you will find Lakṣmī, who has been worshipping us fiercely and happily for a long time.'

That was the promise, and Viṣṇu welcomed it and worshipped Śiva and the goddess in her form as the Ultimate. At that, the famous sage Nārada arrived in Kailāsa, eager to report to Śiva about the many novel things he had experienced in various shrines. With vina in hand, he passed through the many gateways leading to the palace until he reached the gatekeeper Nandin; and, at Śiva's command,

[57] = Tirunelveli.

[58] i.e., east of Kerala.

Nandin ushered Nārada into the god's presence. Nārada prostrated himself at Śiva's feet, praised him with joy and steady desire: 'My great happiness,' he said, 'flows from you, Father.'

'I know you,' said Śiva; 'you have come here to tell me about some form of action (*karumam*). Speak.'

'O androgynous God,' said Nārada, 'there is no act (*karumam*) that you do not know. Still, I must tell you: In the southern land there is a place called the Forest of Pines, a place of proper conduct (*nīti*). The sages there have no sense of the real way (*nĕṟi*). They think that performing ritual acts without error is what really matters (*kotil karumame pŏruḷ ām*). They do *tapas* but without thinking of you. They insist that Vedic ritual is all about achieving an elevated state and doing away with the bad parts of existence. They never speak of all the Śivas. They utter various mantras, but never the five syllables.[59] In fact, they never even say the name "Hara."[60] Though they understand many arts and sciences (*kalai*), they believe that the rituals that each one performs individually will lead to heaven, and that there is nothing to be gained through Śiva. I tried to tell them that they had no appreciation of the real state of affairs—that no matter how many rituals they performed, they would achieve nothing without *you*. But they refused to listen; they even mocked me. "We've never heard that Śiva gives results without our performing fine rituals," they said. "There is no wisdom in this. Anyone can get results—by the painstaking, and painful, work of sacrifice and other forms of *tapas*. That is what works. Why should we bother to think about Śiva?"

'I tried to argue with them. "There are two kinds of action,"[61] I said, "that emerge and have consequences, and it is Śiva who brings them both into being. That is what the Vedas say, and what all the Āgamas and Śāstras reaffirm as truth." But they would hear nothing of this, fixed as they were in their non-way. Still, I kept telling them that the Veda enjoins the worship of Śiva as right action (*karumam*). And yet no matter how many times I said this, they just kept on with their fixed, steady series of rituals, their hearts empty of you. They may be great experts in *tapas*, but they are utterly confused.

[59] *namaḥ śivāya,* 'homage to Śiva.'

[60] = Śiva.

[61] *iru viṉai*—good and bad karmic acts.

Fine human beings may still lack all understanding—may fail to worship you properly, or to meditate on you according to the way, or to know you. Then, lacking your love, they fall to hell. Is that a good thing? They know how Dakṣa, who once abused you verbally, ended up, but they go on, still today, scorning you with words. One can lecture them with endless examples, but they just won't learn. I know—I tried. First Lord, Three-Eyed God: you live without likes or dislikes, and yet I ask you, in your flowing goodness, to send Viṣṇu, here, to them; I beg you to make this egoism of theirs, that turns all their *tapas* into suffering, disappear.'

And Śiva laughed. Meanwhile, Viṣṇu also urged him to do as Nārada advised; this was the boon Viṣṇu sought. Gently and sweetly, Śiva spoke: 'O Dark god, O wise sage, we will destroy the egoism of the simple-minded sages in the ancient Forest of Pines, which offers release without end, in Nelveli, nestled in the midst of rich paddy fields. It will be as you have asked, and for the good of all the world.' He ordered Nandikeśvara to bring him his bull, and, when the bull, beautifully adorned, was before him, our god, red as sunset, mounted it and said, 'Just as one day, long ago, we danced with Kālī in the Forest of Pines[62] and overcame her self-absorption,[63] we will now do away with the self-absorption of those sages.' Umā, mother of the universe, joined him on the bull; ghouls unlimited surrounded him, and Nārada walked beside; obstinate Kuṇḍodara, 'Pit-Belly,' raised the begging bowl high as they set off in the direction of the Forest of Pines. Vedic Brahmins were scattering flowers, and there was singing and the music of the vina; women sang, courtesans danced in turn; gods and sages surrounded them, offering praise. Parasols, fans, flags were waving; yak-tail fans cooled the god; the ghouls and spirits were making rather a lot of noise—in short, it was as if they had taken everything they had on Kailāsa with them. Devotees, in great flocks, were performing every possible service, waving their insignia. Śiva, his long hair sleek, as if streaked with lightning, examined all the Śiva temples on the way.

After passing through many shrines, they reached Mount

[62] The dance with Kālī is here set in the Dārukāvana—perhaps a reference to Kerala and the story of Kālī and the demon Dāruka?

[63] *akantai* = *ahaṅkāra, ahantā*, literally 'I-ness.' Similarly in the previous verses of Nārada's request and Śiva's response.

Govardhana. Here Śiva left Pārvatī behind, with Nandin for her companion. Riding now in a flying ship formed of the syllable Om, together with Viṣṇu, Śiva continued southwards to Cidambaram and many other shrines, as well as many pure rivers. He arrived at Madurai, with its towering *gopurams*; then at Tirukkurralam, and the Porunai river; everything he saw gave him joy.

At last they reached the Forest of Pines, its tall buildings rising up out of the trees. He entered his own shrine and looked at the foundation-*liṅga* there—the long *liṅga* formed in the very beginning. And he gazed at the goddess Kāntimatī, and at the golden open space.[64] Putting off their celestial forms, Śiva and Viṣṇu assumed other forms and went sightseeing in the streets—first those thronged with devotees, and then those where the accomplished sages lived, lacking, as they were, the true understanding of love. Then Śiva looked at Viṣṇu and said: 'I have assumed the Skeleton Form, *Kaṅkāla-veṣa*, the one the sages' wives adore. You, too, wished to see it: look at me now, with desire.' Śiva concentrated his mind on that Skeleton Guise, and at once he stood there, as if millions of love-gods had come together as one. This was a guise to make women sick with pangs of separation. Not even the Vedas could express such powerful beauty. Would you like to hear about it more precisely?

Let's begin with the long hair—gleaming with gold, like a thousand million flashes of lightning. The crescent moon hung over his forehead, which was covered with luminous white ash, with a mark of vermilion in the middle. His mouth was coral, flowing with sweet elixir of life, his teeth bright as pearl. On his face there was a play of moonlight—from a thousand million moons. Earrings hung low over his cheeks, and his eyes were like three brilliant lights, his forehead—a shimmering bow. His neck was dark with poison, radiant as black diamond. He had four long, golden arms, and his hands formed the signs of fearlessness and generosity.[65] On his chest you could discern the deep impressions left by Pārvatī's taut and golden breasts. He wore a garland of cassia flowers, and *rudrâkṣa* beads, and burnt ash; another garland, of bleached skulls, quivered and

[64] Perhaps the *Tāmra-sabhā*, the 'copper hall' where Śiva dances at Nelveli. Kāntimatī is the goddess of the Nelveli shrine.

[65] *varadamoṭ' apāyam.*

shimmered upon him. In his hands were a trident, a skull, a vina, and a small drum. A belt was gleaming, like the moon, over his navel, and he had a tiger's skin tied around his waist. His thighs were long and tapering like an elephant's trunk. You could see him as Bhairava, who had plucked off Brahmā's head. Gold sandals adorned his feet. Everywhere around him—filling all space—there was a deep and heady fragrance. His chiming anklets seemed to be calling out to all women. Thousands of suns upon suns: that was the Skeleton Guise—pure, ravishing, radiant. Even disciplined women who came to see him, and who could discern from the graceful playfulness on his face the signs of his inner thoughts, were overwhelmed.

Viṣṇu, the Tall One, standing there, was steeped in thought within his heart, for at last he had seen the Skeleton—seen the feet he had sought, in vain, on the day he married Śrī.[66] He bowed to those feet. His whole body was tingling with desire. He was out of control, crying out to Śiva: 'Unstained lord, husband to the perfect goddess, sweet and ancient god, handsome bearer of the axe—today I have seen your Skeleton Guise with the whole of my being. Only eyes that you have given count as eyes. What greater happiness could there be? It is through this vision, that brings understanding,[67] that I have become Puruṣottama—the Ultimate Male.'

Standing there, overcome by the god's beauty, surging with desire, Viṣṇu got his Tamil name—Māl, the Bewildered. Śiva, standing beside him, was happy. 'Now that your heart is full of love,' he said, 'you must remain here, in Nellai, at all times. And because we are pleased with your praises, you may choose—wisely—whatever you want.' So Māl, the Bewildered, asked that Śiva stay in this crafted form in that shrine, giving freedom to devotees, poets, gods, sages—whoever worshipped him with love in his mind; and also that whoever worshipped the Skeleton Guise in Nellai would be released from suffering and shown the good way.

Śiva readily granted these requests. Then he looked lovingly at Viṣṇu's face and told him clearly what was to be done. 'I want you to take the seductive form of Mohinī, with her beautiful long hair,

[66] A reference to the story of Viṣṇu's failed attempt to reach the root or bottom of the *liṅga* that appeared before him. Our text connects this story to Viṣṇu's marriage to Srī/Lakṣmī.

[67] *potam = bodha.*

and destroy the *tapas* that fills up, from within, all the sages of this place, who fail to think of us continuously in their hearts.'

Māyan̲, who sleeps on the snake,[68] was happy inside. Respectfully, he took his leave, determined to do this thing. I, who tell the story, know exactly how it happened, and how he looked. Let me describe it. First, he concentrated in his heart on that Mohinī Guise, perfect for unsettling sages who think ritual acts are the real thing.[69] At once, she was there: a long braid black as the monsoon clouds, filled with murmuring bees and redolent of jasmine and campak; a face lit up like ten million moons; darting eyes, dark as nelumbo flowers; speech flowing like wine; a forehead curved like the crescent moon, marked with musk and vermilion; two rainbow-shaped eyebrows; flashing earrings, a ravishing smile, formed from glistening pearls; gems and jewels covering a body that could stupefy sages, could turn them into slaves; in the midst of all this luminescence, like gold crowning sugarcane, or like two mountain peaks made of soft gold, or like silk-cotton buds, two full, round, dancing breasts. Her shoulders and arms were slender, soft as *kāntaḷ* blossoms; her fingers, shoots of coral; and in the middle of her body, descending from the exquisite tummy, there was a line of hair, flowing like honey. A golden belt dangled, heavy with jewels, from her waist; her thighs were luscious as the plantain, her shanks like a quiver of arrows, her feet soft as the radiant red lotus. Anklets, bells, and toe-rings tinkled and moaned as she moved, filling the earth with fragrance, toward the sages intent on their *tapas*. Her huge breasts quivering as she walked, she was all woman—and full of love for Venu-vana-nātha, the Lord of the Bamboo Grove, that is, Śiva in Nelveli, whose hand she had touched. Smiling shyly, she approached the sages. Her eyes were shooting glances, like spears, from under her eyebrows, curved like bows; and there were smiles rich as moonlight, the flash of jasmine-white teeth, as Mohinī walked through the streets of Nellai town.

She went right into the place they were doing their rituals, secure in their belief that regular sacrifices, *tapas*, and other fine practices would bring release. She was proud, and also bashful—enough to

[68] Māyan̲ = Māl, Viṣṇu, who sleeps the sleep of yoga on the great snake Ādiśeṣa. See above, p. 68.

[69] *karumame pŏruḷ ĕn̲ru.*

drive anyone crazy. She kept silent and chastely covered her breasts as she went forward; but her dark eyes were penetrating everyone, like arrows aimed by the god of love. And they saw her—the sages saw her and knew real desire. The rituals were disturbed; they fled the place of offering; their minds were split wide open, as they gave up on all the cumulated *tapas* in which they had so delighted. Inside, they were melting down, their bodies steaming. They wanted only to embrace her; they were jumping and dancing and moaning, like the bird that feeds on moonbeams at the moment of moonrise. They sobbed, they wailed, they ripened, giving up all that rich *tapas*, all their chants, the root-mantras in their special sequence. They had no thought for Śiva, with poison in his throat; now they were clustering around Mohinī, staring, in stunned amazement, at her beauty.

'Is she from the world of Indra? Or from that of the Yakṣa spirits? Or from the moon? Could she even be from Earth? Tell us, is this possibly the astounding Mohinī form taken once, long ago, by Māyaṉ?' They were actually wailing as they fixed their eyes on her beauty. Hit by desire, they were sick to the point of dying. They ran around, shedding their clothes and all possessions; in body and mind, they grew weak. They glued their eyes on her, they spoke of her as the very essence of womanhood; some sang, some cried, 'Look!' and other plaintive words. Some prostrated at her feet. Some begged, 'Make love to me!' Some covered her long hair with fragrant garlands, others smeared sandal paste on her, or kissed her breasts, or applied vermilion to her forehead, as they cried, 'Come to me.' Still others lay down on her feet to study their beauty, while others marvelled at her tapering waist. They were sighing as they approached her, fighting each other off with clubs and sticks. They grabbed at her, they thronged around her, they touched her; they treated one another as enemies. Like the gods fighting for the drink of immortal life, they mobbed her, as they gave voice to their sorrow, their longing, their wonder:

'My body is yours; just take it, free of cost.'

'She's a goddess.'

'We should worship her feet with flowers.'

They were all over her, scrambling, hugging, their hairs standing on end all over their bodies.

'Her hair is dark as night, and her speech like elixir.'

'Is she some Nīli demoness from Nellai? Is her heart a rock?' They argued with one another.

'We can only go on breathing if she shows us a smile.'

'She'll make love only to one of us. So the rest of you, clear out at once!'

The ones who saw her golden garments couldn't take their eyes away; they failed to see her splendid breasts. The ones who were staring at her waist failed to see her eyes. Those looking at her ornaments didn't see her face. 'The one certain thing is that she is playing,' they said, in surprise.[70]

'Her feet are perfect lotus flowers.'

'Her eyes are spears—and so desirable.'

'Her face is the full white moon.'

'She is as patient as the Earth itself.'

Some went further, cursing shamelessly, obscenely. 'Damn those staring eyes!' They were sweating and steaming, shouting, dancing, all around her. 'Only idiots,' they were yelling, 'give themselves to worship, to devotion, to visualizing the deities, to the *liṅga*, to those carefully uttered mantras or to all kinds of *tapas*. Only you, dear Mohinī, can bestow freedom.'

'She's holding her saree to her breast with one hand, and waving the other hand, but won't her tender feet stumble on these pebbles?'

Perhaps they used to be clever, but now these sages were going wild in the streets. Some lay on the ground, panting. Some closed their eyes in alarm. Some pushed themselves forward, singing, their body quivering, 'At last our *tapas* in this flowering forest has borne fruit!'[71]

They worshipped her: 'Her eyes are the arrows that burned the demons' Triple City.'

'Do away with our weakness, born out of desire.'

'Immortality itself has taken this feminine form.'

Some coaxed her softly. 'Come, this is my house.'

'Come in, later you can leave.'

'We have loaded you down with garlands and painted the dot on your forehead. Can your fragile waist bear these burdens?'

'In female charm, in character, in richness of experience, in sheer

[70] *ma<u>n</u>niyat' ivaḷ ŏru māyai kŏl ĕ<u>n</u>par*. 105.

[71] We omit v. 111.

brilliance, she outstrips even Rati, the wife of Desire. If she would only come into our space,[72] we could make love to her there.'

Some painted kohl around her eyes, saying, 'You are life itself to us.' They pleaded, they melted, they toyed with her hair, they spread flowers on the ground to protect her tender feet. 'Could anyone—even those who have given themselves to long *tapas* in the wilderness, even the gods themselves—forget their longing for her, once her eyes have pierced them?'

And so on—weeping, boiling inside, they followed after Mohinī, who had by now destroyed all their *tapas*. They lost all dignity. Now I've told you—you who are sages yourselves, flawless in wisdom—all about this moment, about how those great sages who scorned Śiva became full of lust, about Mohinī's dazzling beauty and her actions. I think it's time to speak of Śiva's greatness.

After sending off Māyan̲, Śiva, wearing the Skeleton Guise, intent on redeeming the world, set off by foot for the houses of the sages' wives. He was carrying a fine begging bowl and twirling his trident. He was singing the Veda, to a sweet tune. Dancing, his eyes alight. He came to stand at the entrance of house after house, in the long street, with a brilliant smile on his lips—very hungry for alms. His melodious voice drew them to him, and they understood. There was no one else in the street. Flocking there, they saw him directly—the god unseen by the lucid Veda. People say women are rather simple, or even simple-minded, and it must be true, for their bodies simply gave in. Garlands quivered over their breasts. They had no wisdom in sight: their hearts were shaken. There is an ocean called 'god's beauty,' and they were drowning in it.

Do you think there is anyone who can tell you truly about all the wild things they did in their confusion? Still, I will do my best, following my teacher, the learned Vyāsa. I'll tell you the little that I know.

'His body is glowing like sunset. At least we've had a glimpse. But it is the music of his vina that has bewitched us. Won't he even consider merging into us? He's come here to play, that is certain. He's guised for a game.'

A few of the women went up to Kuṇḍodara, the dwarf attendant, and lovingly and joyfully ladled out rice with golden spoons into

[72] *cālai*—the sacrificial arena?

the begging bowl he carried. And they also spoke of their bewildered state. 'There is no one like him. He's no *tapas*-driven Yogi. And somehow it doesn't feel like he's really come to beg. More likely, he just wants to drive women to distraction, to "undo" them.'[73]

'What city are you from?' they asked. 'In any case, the mere fact that you have come here, to where we live, shows that our *tapas* has paid off.'

They came there, they served him, they were happy, they fought each other with their eyes. They praised him, they spoke of their intoxication. And you know what was most amazing? Although they were disciplined women, experienced in *tapas*, educated, properly married, and so on, still not one of them sounded like any of the others.

'He came here, and our clothes have slipped off by themselves. Only this belt is irksome,' said one.

'Melt down my breasts,' said another; 'make me happy, fuck me now.'

Flashing smiles, dense as moonlight, were met by answering smiles. 'I'll stop sulking if you'll make love to me,' said one.

'What a beauty!'

'What a pleasant game!'

'Are handsome men always so cruel?'

'He could do away with all this suffering, this sharp pain of longing and confusion—but will he?'

'Not even the God of Love himself could paint his image.'

They threw all their jewels and golden bracelets and fine ornaments into the streets, knowing they were useless. Every time they caught sight of him, their eyes clouded in passion. They were utterly helpless. They stood there, flirting shamelessly. 'If he acts like this, he must have no ability to think,' said some. The ones who saw how beautiful he was in front pressed toward the front, while those admiring his back stayed back.

They were lost. 'He knows how much we love him, want him, how desperately we need him right now, and still he won't save our lives.'

'We know we are remarkably attractive women, wonderfully feminine, but it's all shattered now, destroyed.'

73 *vikāram mayal kūra*, 126.

'Our strong breasts are yours for the taking.'

'Can those golden feet of yours stand walking on the earth?'

'Let us perfume you, cool your body with sandal paste. Come into us in love, naked as you are,' they cried. Pure as he was, I should remind you, he was covered in white ash.

Some simply couldn't stand it. From their houses they brought out rice cooked with milk and served him, their bracelets of shell jingling. Their golden houses, golden garments, other golden things—none of this mattered to them any more. Although their husbands had maligned him earlier, they—the wives—were looking only for him.

'You dance, you play the vina, you sing, but you don't have the graciousness to look us in the face. You're looking for something: if it is goodness you seek, then enter into us.'

'The sweet south wind enfolds us, desire is pricking us, and inside we are shaken—and you don't even notice. Black-Neck: send away the god you once burned with the eye in your forehead.'[74]

Lovingly they offered him flowers, sandal paste, sweet white rice—which melted down in the heat of their desire until it looked like white ashes; they covered their bodies with it. They followed him, their bracelets ringing, their sarees slipping from their bodies. They were entirely infatuated, their minds spinning. '*Karma*,' they thought, 'is god.' He was beautiful beyond imagining, with the crescent moon on his crest; seeing him, they could see nothing else.

'If we ask you to embrace us, you just smile and say nothing. Is this fair? Could you tell us what was written on our forehead, at the beginning of our lives?'

They no longer thought about *dharma*, or prudent conduct, or what was right or wrong, or about ritual acts.[75] Overwhelmed by passion for the god with Umā inside him, they were melting down in confusion, pleading with him to make love.[76] They had lost any wisdom that could hold things together; they had gone beyond oceans, gone beyond mountains. They were murmuring, babbling: 'The sages won't be coming home now. This is the time to make love to us.'

They danced, they sang, they quivered like streaks of lightning; they turned away, they addressed him: 'You have come to beg

[74] Kāma/Manmatha, Desire.

[75] *karumam* = *karma*.

[76] Omitting 144.

alms—by locking onto our golden breasts.' They complained: 'His long hair, flowing like a river; the vibrant music he plays on the vina, his full shoulders—we are mired in all this beauty. His body is covered with white ash, and he wears the sacred thread—and here he is, looking for alms in the groves and fields around Nelveli, the home of Venu-Nātha.[77] He is utterly without shame, and that isn't right. He is brighter than light itself, purer than light. And if he doesn't make love to us on a soft bed sharp with fragrance, sharp with joy, he'll simply kill us.'

'He dances, he amuses himself with subtle sounds. Crooked as he is, he won't look at us with anything like friendship. He thinks he can escape us, but how can we let go?'

'With his long penis, white ash on his forehead, those gentle legs dancing the *tāṇḍava* dance—this whole amazing apparition—he might as well be Śiva, the god who lives on Kailāsa.'[78]

'This feast is for all for you. Come into our houses, eat this most delicious, inner food, and go, in love.'

'You have a body that anyone—chaste women, and innumerable men—would desire. You have the great gift of imparting joy, so why come begging here?'

'We are only women, and inside us a fire of longing is burning, while you just stand there. Or are you like that god who burnt the Triple City of his enemies—with his smile?'

They went on and on, preaching at him, sulking, coaxing: 'Either give us back our clothes, or make love to us.' Others were busy dishing out white rice, with a golden ladle, into his begging bowl. Just seeing his luminous red body was enough to drive them mad with yearning.

Meanwhile, Śiva himself was walking back and forth, singing the Veda, pounding on the little drum in his hand, dancing as if overflowing with energy. He would come close, take up the vina, make up a song in praise of Śiva, as if he were a devotee. Deeply distressed, they pressed against him, declaring their bewildering passion. 'It just isn't fair. You make a complete ruin of our self-control and our strength, and then you coldly refuse to embrace us. You don't know how to live. Let's go away now.'

Some said to one another, 'Listen, ladies: he might be the god

[77] 'Lord of the Bamboo,' Śiva at Tirunelveli.

[78] Omitting 152.

who has a woman inside his body. You can see the traces of a breast (or is it a *liṅga* turned into a breast?).[79] And if he does happen to be the god who embraces Śaṅkarī-Pārvatī, what chance is there that he will make love to us?'

'He could be Śiva, who burned the Triple City and has now come to burn our city—not to cover our breasts in flowers.'

'Now that you mention it, his body *is* of coral, smeared with ash. Look at his feet, soft as the lotus. Look at the trident. He's a dancer, too. He must be the god who swallowed poison from the sea.'

'But where is the eye on the forehead that burned the god of desire?'

'He's just hiding it from us. There's no doubt that he has three eyes.'

'Maybe so, but then where is the garland of skulls?'

'The whole point is to confuse us: that's why he came here, so beautiful he could kill.'

'But we see no trace of the white conch earring, or his female half, or the neck black as night.'

'That's because god, who is always everywhere, has now come here to break us.'

'In that case—if he really is Śiva, rider of the bull, conqueror of passion, who has come here in love—then we should worship his feet, lest he go away.'

So said some, but for the most part those women, wives to the idiot sages, showed no devotion, and failed to praise him, though god himself was standing right before their eyes. They were trapped in the net of wanting. 'It's springtime,' they said, 'season of love; the cuckoo is cooing, the south wind fragrant with new buds, the *an̲ril* birds in riot. Passion is hard.' They were moaning and lamenting,[80] hanging on to him, following him as he passed through their street, that was littered with their clothes, their jewellery, and ornaments. They were in love with god, and love[81] possessed them: everything else had fallen away, everything like control or nobility of spirit or *karma* or *dharma* or feminine beauty; it was all cluttering that long street together with the flowers and bracelets and conch-bangles and splendid garlands that they threw at his feet, and with

[79] *kŏṅkai mevu kuṟiyum uṇṭo*, 161.
[80] Omitting 171.
[81] *aṟpu* = *an̲pu*.

the arrows of flowers that the love-god was shooting without pause. I might just remind you of something I said before, that Viṣṇu himself went crazy with love, from the depths of his heart, when he saw Śiva's form as the Beggar; that's why we call him Māl, the Bewildered. So you can imagine what happened to the women. No one could possibly describe it.

And what about him—god himself, standing in front of those crazed women who were in touch with the whole goodness of the divine? He looked at their faces, and his face flowered into a smile, full of gentle love. They loved him back, yearning for him; desire stretched out endlessly inside them. Now, deep within them, their wombs held babies. Painlessly, they gave birth to 48,000 marvellous children.

It all happened in the blink of an eye. Those children bowed at Śiva's feet and worshipped him. He said to them, 'Perform *tapas* in wisdom, while keeping us in your mind.' They were already wise, so they took their leave at once and happily went off to the forest, mindful of god, wanting him, as they gave themselves to *tapas*. No sooner had they left than the women once again surrounded Śiva, who stood among them in the street like a golden mountain rising up from the sea.

He had the sweet-spoken goddess within him. Suddenly sages versed in the great texts and rites, committed to performing good works out of love, arrived—men such as Bhoga, Khaḍga,[82] Atri, Kṛtu, Pulastya, Pulaka, Kāśypa, Bhāradvaja, Kaṇva, Bhṛgu, Jambu, Śuka, Sumantu, Gautama, Vaiśampāyana, flawless Paila, unfettered Kumbha(yoni?),[83] Aṅgiras, and Durvāsas. These were men with love for Śiva, and they were honest, great in *tapas* and Yoga; they had devotion for Śiva, and never forgot him or left him. Now they surrounded him, singing his praises with deep understanding. Their wives came, too, and lovingly offered food to the god. There was no end to the compassion that Śiva showed them, looking at them; then they all went back to their homes.

When they were gone, the others—those women mad with passion—were still there, still moaning, stripped of their bangles and their clothes. 'Our desire is ripe; we are lost; please just fuck us,' they said, huddling around the pure god.

[82] *kaṟkar*?

[83] Agastya.

Viṣṇu saw it all, in his female form, the one the sages had pursued like madmen. He came there, bowed at the golden feet of the god of Nelveli, praised him. Śiva didn't want those sages to see his Skeleton Guise, so he took it off and assumed another form: he stood stark naked, singing songs, hiding his real beauty from the eyes of those hysterical women. Mohinī-Viṣṇu stood beside him. And the idiot sages arrived, too, the ones who had scorned god. There were those who had only water, and those who lived on the wind; very dharmic and pure, some had taken a vow to stand in the middle of five blazing fires. Some ground grain between stone for their food, while others consumed only wind, water, dried leaves, and boiled rice. There were 60,000 of them: Their long hair was coiled into braids, and they knew little of desire, although these were the ones who had madly followed Viṣṇu as Mohinī. When they saw their wives, they said, 'These women, just like us, were confused by passion. They saw this man and at once let go of their clothes and their modesty.'

As soon as they had formulated this for themselves, their confusion passed. They saw to what a pitiful state the women had been reduced, and this distressed them deeply, so that they began to wail in shame: 'Who is this fellow? Just look what he has done. Some man took the form of a Play-Woman, came here, and drove us mad. Meanwhile, some other male, by some strange game or trick, overpowered our wives.' They thought it over, and clarity came. 'It must be Śiva, with the moon in his hair, who demolished the self-control, the sense of shame, and the physical strength of our lovely women. And the one who came winking at us coyly from under those curved eyebrows, the delicious woman with lush red lips who demolished all of our *tapas*, must be Viṣṇu, husband to Śrī. But Viṣṇu, by himself, would have no interest in ruining our discipline; he was certainly only following orders that came from Śiva. Anyway, despite the loss of what we had before, we can put our bodies back to work and stock up on more *tapas*, as much as we need. But what Śiva did—coming here with great beauty, his body glowing like sunset, and then, by magic, stripping our women of their clothes and all shyness—that story will last on earth as long as the sun and the moon. He took a certain beguiling form, and he made Viṣṇu take another. Only Śiva, with the eye in his forehead, who burnt the demons' three cities—only he could do this.' They stood there, hurt and angry, aflame.

Boiling with rage, they spoke to the women. 'Whom do you think you are following? You have lost all self-control, which alone shows the way. Why are you standing around here? Get back home at once.'

Hearing this, the women said to themselves, 'Anyone who sees god becomes free. This is goodness. Moreover, no loss can ever come to such a person. These foolish sages sound completely crazy.' Śiva heard and looked at them, a glance flowing with love; and, taking this gracious god into their hearts, they happily went home, totally free of knots.

The women were gone, but Viṣṇu still stood, in his female guise, close to Śiva. Brahmā and the other gods came to see what the sages, heedless of Śiva, were thinking of doing, now that their *tapas* had been lost. As the gods worshipped, Venu-Nāyaka, the Bamboo Lord—Śiva at Nelveli—waited quietly, with compassion. The sages were shooting fiery glances at him; they wanted to kill him. They hurled harsh and angry curses at him, but these curses failed to reach him. When they saw this, they wondered what to do next.

Among them were some wiser men who, after contemplating matters, said: 'Notice that your curses have gone astray. Why waste words? This person standing opposite us is Śiva himself. Who could kill him?'

'No,' the others responded, 'he is some wicked fellow who first disturbed and humiliated our women and then stood shamelessly before us. Would you say this is proper, or customary? Is there any worse disgrace?'

The real Yogis replied, 'There is no-one on earth like you—who still believe that *tapas* is for real, and who just go on, without any thought for the god who burned the Triple City. Actually, he must have come here, and must have made all these new, strange things take place, in order to remove this very flaw. No action, good or evil, bears fruit for anyone unless Śiva gives it energy. Any *tapas* that is done without thinking of him is utterly in vain. He makes entire worlds, and turns them to dust in a split second.'

'Very nice,' sneered the sages. 'If he really *is* Śiva, how can you explain what he did—the ruin of our women and the destruction of our rituals, sacrifices, and all our pure, good, wonderful *tapas*? No, no. This man is someone else. If he's just crazy, why impute any form of greatness to him? Or you might say that he's some kind of drunk—but in that case, what power does he have? There may be something wrong somewhere, but this business of coming here like a beggar and then blasting the women just can't be right.'

'No,' answered the Yogis. 'He is god, and he came here because there was a flaw in you, a flaw he wished to heal, if necessary with a little coercion, but basically out of compassion. The women saw it, worshipped his feet, and experienced immense, dense happiness. You should try worshipping him too.'

'If he is Śiva, so where is his trident? Or the poison that should be in his throat? Or the tiger-skin around his waist? This fellow has no notion of how to behave. He teased passion out of the women, brought confusion, and started begging. You think we should worship *him*?'

Then they looked straight at him, at god, and said: 'Just who are you? Where do you live? What is your name? Our wives were perfect, and you reduced them to less than that. Did you have a reason? What's the story? Don't be lazy, speak!'

God smiled. 'Very well. I have no father and no mother. No relatives either. This world, which is really one, everywhere, is my world. The great throngs of living beings are my family. Happiness and sorrow have nothing to do with me. And there is one other thing I have to tell you. This ravishing woman, Mohinī, is my wife. She cares nothing for anyone else. She is chaste and restrained. Many have died seeking her, with her long black hair, pearl-like smile, mouth red as coral, her languorous walk. I make universes upon universes, out of kindness, and then, with a single spark, a single sign,[84] I turn them to dust. I don't want anything, even goodness, and I do *not* want anything either. Not wanting is also a flaw. Even Yogis of sharp perception can't perceive me. That is why I am here, full of love, in this world—eager to give joy to all who have wisdom. Moreover, this particular shrine is the Siddhi-Sthānam, the Site of Perfection: so I thought it was only right to come here, to bring perfection to people like these.'

He is the master of inner life, but the great sages scorned his words. 'If you really are the god of all three worlds,' they said, 'how

[84] *pŏri*—sign, spark—the *liṅga*?

could you have sunk so low as to seduce our wives? Are we enemies, we and you? Who really did this deed? And who, exactly, are you?'

And among themselves they said, 'This man used mantras and other magical devices to drive our wives mad. He has that power. Moreover, he can no doubt use other effective means, such as *yantra* diagrams, to ward off all our curses. That's why we have to kill him. Let us think carefully and set in motion a ritual of black magic.'[85]

Flames surged within them as they went to a site to the west of the pure Bamboo Grove and, wicked at heart, dug a pit for the raging sacrificial fire. With logs soaked in ghee, they lit the fire. Among them were some who had achieved greatness in *tapas*, real kings with long matted hair; but the rite they were performing had only one aim—to kill the god with the moon in his hair. As the flames crackled and hissed, there arose from within the fire a great tiger, with blazing eyes, cruel to behold—violent, fierce, angry, with a gaping mouth, a twisted tail, a terrifying roar. The sages worshipped this tiger as soon as they saw it and ordered it to put an end to the three-eyed god. Yet as it sprung at him, the god caught hold of it and flayed its skin with a flick of his hand; as the sages stared at him, he draped himself in this fine new garment.

Now an axe emerged from the flames, and again the sages directed it at the god. Fire, sky, and earth merged as the axe flew toward him, but Śiva took it in his gentle hand and made it into his own weapon.

The sages were furious. They produced a huge elephant, mad with rut, from the fire and ordered it to kill the Madman. So off it went, raging, a terror to the whole world; and Śiva flayed it, too, like the tiger, and covered himself in its skin.

The sages were rather amazed. At once, a deer emerged from the flames with a roar that shattered the cosmos. Śiva lifted it in his hand and said to it, 'Roar into my ear, until your rage is exhausted.'

No sooner was this danger averted than bright snakes came, hissing, at him. Śiva, the ultimate god, added them to the snakes that had long ago sought refuge on his body from their enemy, the Garuḍa eagle. The gods, seeing this, sang hurrahs.

So now the snakes, gleaming, slithering, full of movement, were

[85] *apicārav-omam*, sacrifice of sorcery.

Śiva's servants. Like a thunderbolt, a torrent of noisy ghouls came pouring from the fire. 'Kill Śiva' cried the wily sages, and the demons rushed to attack the god with Umā inside him. Then something truly amazing happened. As they came at him with the gods watching, Śiva turned a sweetly compassionate gaze upon them. 'Strong as you are,' he said to the ghouls, 'you are just right to become my guard of honour. Surround me at all times.' They fell in devotion at his feet.

Now Śiva had an army. From the sacrificial fire, a bleached skull arose, grinning, as if it had swallowed the entire cosmos. It raced, howling, toward Śiva, who took it in his hand, placed it on his head, to remain there forever, and said, 'Please keep on making what must happen happen.'[86]

The sages saw the skull happily, even lovingly, ensconced on Śiva's head. 'We can't fight him,' they said, their hearts shaken, shuddering. They thought of all the mantras they could remember and hurled them at the flawless god, to kill him; and these mantras coalesced into a radiant drum, beating out a rhythm that overpowered all the worlds. The gods understood the nature of this drum and shivered in fear. They saw it approach god, the Trident-Bearer. To their shock and delight, a strange thing happened: Śiva lifted it up gently in his delicate hand, soft as a flower, and whispered to it, 'Beat your music each day right into my ear.'

The sages saw it all happen, but they still could not figure it out. It did not occur to them that no matter what they tried, it would not work. They were burning inside, determined to destroy the god who is never destroyed. So they poured more butter in the fire, and the flames leapt higher, and a really powerful being, named Muyalakaṉ, exploded outward—like the end of the world. They praised him, entreated him: 'Take the fire of this unending sacrifice and put an end, please, once and for all, to Black-Neck, the one who ruined our wives.'

Śiva, ablaze himself, with flames in his hand, saw him coming. Raising his foot, gracefully bent and poised, like a red lotus, Śiva kicked Muyalakaṉ over onto his stomach and then stood, with one foot, on his back. All the universe was singing except for the sages

[86] *uṉṉāl āṉatu cĕyvăy nīy iṉi*, 228.

with evil in their hearts; they were boiling over with rage and grief and despair. 'We performed this ritual according to the secret rules of the Veda, and still he transformed everything that came out of the fire. He's still standing there, victorious, unscathed.' So they said but, since they still hoped to kill him somehow and couldn't see any other option, they tried the curses again. Could curses touch the pure god? He was smiling the same smile that once shattered the demons' three cities.[87] Seeing him stand there, alive, unbounded, they finally saw that there was no way to destroy him. They gave up anger, but now they were bewildered, shaken, afraid. 'This must be the fruit of our *karma* from a former life,' they thought. They could say nothing more. They were sobbing, deeply perturbed.

The gods, on the other hand, were full of hallelujahs. 'So much for the ripe wisdom, the intelligence, of the sages! They exhausted themselves with this ritual aimed at the endless, endlessly auspicious, evil-less god. They have lost everything—the glory of *tapas*, and the rite itself.'

As for the sages, they looked at god and said, 'We now know your power and your greatness. Have the graciousness to inform us what kind of *tapas* we should do to rid ourselves of the shame of our wives' faithlessness.'

They still had no real knowledge. Śiva laughed. 'I know your customs, and your true *tapas*. That, in fact, is why I targeted the integrity of your blameless wives. You have to know that whatever you do without thinking of me—whether it is carefully considered *tapas*, or dharmic action, be it ever so full of feeling; whether you bathe in sacred waters, or meditate on various themes—none of it is any use, and all of it will perish. The Vedas tell us this. Moreover, if I attempt something or other, not even Viṣṇu or Brahmā can easily block it. Nothing alive can move, in any direction, without me. The ones who find the true way are those who worship me with their own hands. That is what you should do, every day, though you know nothing about such loving service to the father, though you are confused and in pain, caught and choking in the noose of deeds. Those who desire and worship the Root Liṅga in ancient Nellai, according to rite—who praise it and serve it and walk around it—end

[87] The Tripura, burnt by Śiva's smile. See Narayana Rao and Shulman 2002b: 174–82.

up in Kailāsa, in the group of my servant ghouls. So my advice to you is to direct your love to that *liṅga*, to think about me as you do *pūjā*, and in this way to accumulate perfect *tapas*.' With this, Śiva, with Umā inside him and Mohinī beside him, disappeared.

Actually, he went into the middle space, the inner depths alive with life, of the Root Liṅga, together with Umā. The sages could no longer see him. The gods also went away, now that Śiva was gone. Most of those who live on earth, and sages, too, praised god, but the sages of the Forest of Pines could not hold him in their heart: they were really lost, and dishonoured, too.

At this moment there were earthquakes and many other bad omens. The sages trembled, afraid, uneasy in their mind, wondering what kind of game—what illusion[88]—they were seeing. So they gathered together in the Great Hall[89] to discuss Śiva's acts and his disappearance with the unique Yogis who were there. 'First there was the matter of our wives' disgrace; then Māl ruined all the wonderful *tapas* we had garnered; then all those things came out of the sacrifice, until Śiva destroyed it. Śiva is the only truth; there is nothing real in the world except him. He came here for our sake and stood before us, hardly knowing himself, as we, in our weakness, failed to know him or ourselves.[90] Maybe Agastya can help us at this juncture.'

Everyone was happy with this suggestion. They were by now bubbling over with the hope of winning Śiva's mercy; they were weeping with desire to see him again. Crying out 'Śiva! Śiva! Hara! Hara!' they all rushed to the feet of the dwarf sage Agastya,[91] a true devotee of the Nelveli god as well as an incomparable master of Tamil poetry. They told him the whole story. 'Until recently, we used to think that *karma* and *dharma* were the keys, and that Śiva was without reality and did not count. But that was only until Śiva himself came to the Forest of Pines and, by doing many strange, new things, showed us the real state of things. He put up with all our mistakes, and still we failed to serve his feet. Then, just like that, he disappeared. We want to see him again, and that is why we are here, seeking your help.'

[88] *māyamov itu*, 247.

[89] *per avai*—at Nelveli?

[90] *ta<u>n</u>mait tā<u>n</u> a<u>r</u>iyāmal*, an ambiguous phrase probably referring to the sages, but possibly to the god himself.

[91] Agastya, born from a pot, is the size of a thumb.

Agastya considered the matter, in grace and courtesy. 'Clearly, he came to rid you of your so-called knowledge, which was really a slippage—opposed to the Vedic way. But if you want to see him again, we must go to consult Brahmā.'

They accepted this advice and set off, with Agastya, for Manopati, Brahmā's world. They found him seated on his lotus; they bowed, they offered worship, and Agastya told him all that had happened—the sages' ruin at the hands of Mohinī, the loss of their wives' dignity, the destruction of the sacrifice. Brahmā listened carefully and said, 'You forgot the deathless god. You should have been meditating on his feet, and instead you lost all your *tapas* and your householders' dharma. By coming here with Agastya, you seem to have given up evil and to have achieved love for Śiva, in all his purity. Let me tell you about him. You have been living right there in the Forest of Pines, but you never thought about the Lord of the Copper Hall,[92] with his fiery eyes. You paid no worship to Mother Kāntimatī. You never went to see the Root Liṅga. Śiva knew this, and still, out of love, he came to you as a beggar. You should have taken delight in his presence, but did you? No, not you. You scorned him. You got mixed up. You lost your *tapas*. I don't care how much *tapas* a person does—if he isn't thinking of Śiva, the god of Nelveli, it's all wasted. Worse than that, he becomes ridden with anxieties, he grows weak inside, and ends up wandering like a beggar from place to place, until he dies and falls into a burning hell. Take Dakṣa, for example: just like you, he paid no heed to Śiva. He tried to carry through a great rite, and Śiva destroyed it along with Dakṣa and all his family and wives and the gods who joined him. Ever since then, it is well known that whoever does not think about Śiva is a traitor to the god. Guess how we would classify you!

Once Viṣṇu and I were talking in a confused and egoistic way. Śiva stood before us and said, "See if you can see my top and my bottom." Viṣṇu became a boar, I became a goose, and we went through whole universes, millions of them, but could not reach *his* limits. That's the same god who stood right in front of you, whom you failed to recognize in the dizziness that passes for your awareness. If a beggar comes to your door, he should be honoured, seated, and regally fed: definitely not cursed! I'd like to tell you Pine Forest

[92] The *tāmra-sabhā* at Nelveli.

people a story about someone who actually gave his own wife to a beggar. He was a Vedic Brahmin named Sudarśana, and there was nothing he did not know. His wife, with lovely darting eyes, a voice like honey, long tapering neck, and splendid full breasts, was chaste as Arundhatī. As for her waist—maybe it was there, maybe not. Just like the classic images of the Goddess of Beauty. Her husband used to say to her, "Our God, with Umā inside him, sometimes comes disguised as a beggar. So you should treat any guest who comes your way like a god, and give him whatever he asks, unstintingly."

One day Death came, as a Brahmin, to test her love and loyalty. Her husband, of course, was out. She welcomed the guest, bowed to him, seated him, fed him rice and ghee. He ate happily, and then he said to her: "You are unbelievably beautiful. I am stricken with love for you. Please make love to me." She was taken aback, but then she remembered that it was her duty to give a guest anything he asked for, and to do so happily. Besides, her husband had ordered her: this was the real meaning of chastity. So she was prepared to agree. Meanwhile, her learned husband returned home. Death looked at him and said, "Great sage, please allow me to immerse myself in your lovely wife." So the Brahmin joyfully gave him his wife.

There was a small bedroom to one side of the house, and that is where Death took her, putting her to bed without touching her fine body. He was only pretending to make love. Really, he had explored this woman's self-discipline and the sage's mind. When he got off the bed, he put aside the Brahmin guise and appeared in his own form, as Death, to the husband. "It was just a test," he told him. "I know how wise you are. Even if I were to offer the kingdom of the gods, or all the gold and wealth that can be won by *tapas* in this world, who but you would be capable of giving me the wife he lives with? I don't want this woman: you live the householder's life with her, with all her graces. Anyone who even utters your name will be freed from repeated dying." And Death went to his home.

That, my friends, is the way a guest should be treated.'

The sages heard Brahmā's story and understood. They were unnerved: 'We now have the grief that comes of having insulted god. We even cursed him. Why go on living? You, who know the truth, are our only hope. Help us see him again and serve him, the god adorned with snakes.'

Brahmā said, 'By now you know that sacrifices and *tapas* work, in this world, only for those who concentrate on the god with the woman inside him. Everyone else gets caught in the snares of Death and ends up in Hell. You mocked Śiva when he came to release you from your chains. What exactly did he say to you?'

'He told us,' they said, 'never to forget the great Root Liṅga that is light and ultimate truth—the *liṅga* in the Forest of Pines. He told us to see it and praise it with love each day, keeping him in the centre of our hearts as we did *tapas*. That is what he said, but when he saw our continuing self-absorption, he disappeared. That is why we sought you out. We want you to make us feel love, so we can see him again.'

Brahmā meditated on the god covered in cassia flowers, who had come in search of such fools. Then he said, 'Do just as he told you. Worship the *liṅga* in Nelveli. Make *liṅga*s of copper and gold. Stay here with Agastya, immersed in what is right. Bathe in the Water of Flowers, Cintupunturai. Do *tapas* and praise the beautiful *liṅga* once worshipped by the god of Dharma himself. After this period is over, the god without end will come again, like before—in the month of Māci.'[93]

So Agastya and the sages took their leave of Brahmā and returned to the Forest of Pines, where Śiva lived, at peace. As Brahmā had commanded them, they bathed in the Porunai river and entered the god's shrine; they worshipped the *liṅga* there day by day. Each of them, all 60,000, set up a *liṅga* that bore his name. They were constantly immersed in love.

A year passed. It was the month of Māci and, like before, Śiva came to them in the Skeleton Guise, carrying a golden skull. The sages fell at his feet. They praised him, they circled him, they sang to him. 'Supreme Lord of Nelveli, with the goddess inside you: you are more stunning than ten million gods of desire. No wonder you drove our women mad when you walked through the streets of Nelveli, making music, in the form of the Skeleton that is sweet to the eyes. When Māl and Brahmā sought your limit, you were an endless pillar of fire. When we hurled mantras at you along with the drum, the tiger, the deer, and the axe from the sacrifice, you began to dance on the back of the great hero, Muyalakaṉ. Today

[93] February–March.

we praise you as you dance in the Copper Hall, crowned by ten million suns.'[94] They were weeping, begging for his goodness. Compassionate, he gave them wisdom and real knowledge, and he revealed to them his astonishing form, more brilliant than suns upon suns. They took in this wisdom; they dived into an ocean of deep happiness as they saw with their own eyes his all-encompassing oneness. 'This is too much for us,' they said to him; 'we are afraid of too much light. Please appear to us as you are on Mount Kailāsa, with the goddess inside you.'

He did: twelve arms, the goddess merged in him, black poison in his neck, riding the bull. They celebrated him in this form. They danced, they sang: 'You have shown us this true bodily form so we can worship you as you stand before us. Those who hold you constantly in their minds are the only ones who become free.[95] Śaṅkara! Sthāṇu of Nelveli! No one—not even Brahmā or Viṣṇu—knows your great truth. And we, too, who spin helplessly in the net of painful delusion, have no easy way to speak of this truth, though we feel it now, and thus may be said to know it. We are very small, and we were terribly foolish. Please forgive the mistakes we made. We want to stay here forever at your feet.'

With the woman within him, god looked at them as they bowed, fell, rose before him. He asked them to choose whatever gift they wished. They said, 'We want you to stay in this Forest of Pines in your Skeleton Form, together with Vaṭivuṭaiyāḷ—the Most Beautiful Goddess. Anyone who gets a glimpse of the Skeleton in Nelveli should have the joys of Kailāsa, god's heaven, a radiant state: free from being and becoming, they will come to understand, and to maintain in their hearts, the only reality that is truly real, and that works—that is Śiva.'

He agreed. Moving to the west of the unique Root Liṅga, he took his place as the Skeleton and said in a mode of compassion filled with delight: 'Anything feminine in the cosmos belongs to Umā, and anything male belongs to me. Therefore, no one should be in pain, and no one, of whatever caste, should be scorned. Those who cover themselves in burnt ash and carry the *rudrākṣa* beads will assume my own form and become free. Anyone who mocks my devotees,

[94] Verses 306–14 have been condensed.

[95] We omit verses 321–4, a formulaic *stotra*.

even in his mind, will endure the tortures of hell as long as the sun and moon survive.[96] And as for this Forest of Pines—not even Brahmā, not even the Vedas, can tell you about its importance. This is the Siddhi-sthala, the Site of Perfection: the *liṅga* here is pure empty space, and the goddess, Vaṭivuṭaiyāḷ, is pure light. At first she came to do *tapas* in a cave by the Kampai river,[97] then she married the god; it is she who is present here. Other defined forms of ours can also make you free; we came to show them to you. But there is no other *liṅga* in the world like this one.' He pointed at it with desire, like the dawn of a million suns.[98]

At this point Viṣṇu put aside his Mohinī form and resumed his own. He was smiling at Śiva, who said to him, 'You successfully bewildered all the sages in the Forest of Pines and ruined their *tapas*. I am pleased. Choose a boon.'

'There are two things I want,' said Viṣṇu. 'I was in love with you when I was Mohinī, and I want you to make love to me. In addition, I want to see again the Skeleton Form—the one you used to beg for alms in this place, and the Terrible Skeleton you became to rid me of pride when I came down as a Dwarf.'[99]

Śiva addressed him. 'When the ocean is churned to produce the drink of immortality, you will become Mohinī again, to give this drink to the gods. At that time we will make love joyfully and passionately, and a son of ours—Hari-Hara-Putra, the son of Viṣṇu and Śiva—will be born. As for the Terrible Skeleton of Nelveli, which is the Southern Kailāsa,—come stand close to me and look.'

Then he showed him the Skeleton: skulls of many Viṣṇus and many Brahmās hanging around his neck, and that gentle smile, soft as moonlight, playing on his lips. Black poison stained his throat; he held a deer and an axe in his hands; an eye was staring out of the middle of his forehead. He was all black fire, with many

[96] Verse 335 omitted.

[97] In Kancipuram.

[98] Verses 341–5 omitted.

[99] The Vāmanâvatāra: Viṣṇu came as a dwarf to ask the demon king Bali for the gift of land—what could be covered by three steps. Given this gift, swelling into immensity, he reached the end of the world with his first step, and the limit of heaven with his second; the third step crushed Bali into the Nether World. A local version of the story seems to add a role for Śiva who, as Aghora-Kaṅkāla, overcame the Dwarf-God's pride. The two skeletons are identified here.

thousands of universes dangling from the tip of each hair on his head; the skeletons of endless Viṣṇus and Brahmās were tied to his waist. He was covered in the flayed skin of an elephant, and he was dancing, very gracefully, on top of Muyalakaṉ, born from the sages' sacrifice. He was Bhairava, the Terrible Skeleton: Viṣṇu's bones were impaled on the trident he held in one hand. Viṣṇu, seeing this, wept: 'At last,' he said, 'I have seen your limit, that I failed to find so long ago.'[100]

The gods and sages sang Śiva's praises. 'Lord,' they said, 'every time we look at this Skeleton, at once beautiful and terrifying, we are afraid. Could you kindly merge it with the powerful light that fills the *mūlasthāna*—the original centre of this shrine, the Root Liṅga? We ask you to stay here in Nelveli, where everyone—Brahmins, gods, sages, snakes, and ordinary people—can serve you.'

Śiva smiled. 'I accept these requests,' he said. Then he revealed his form inside the great *liṅga* and thus became Bhairava, with trident and skull, his body smeared in ashes white as milk. He stood in the eastern corner of the shrine. He has a tank of water there, too—the Skeletal Bhairava Well. Demons and spirits flee in horror from anyone who bathes in that well. In fact, hordes of Bhairavas are always attacking the demons who possess people; gnashing their teeth and snarling, Bhairavas pin the arms of such demons behind their backs, turn them upside down, and pummel them with clubs until these demons scream in pain. The trick is to get the possessing spirit to tell you his name: as soon as this happens, the demon or ghoul runs away from the body he has entered, with Bhairava chasing him from behind or spinning him in the air. The same applies, by the way, to other forms of sorcery[101] and to the haunting spirit of a crime like the murder of a Brahmin. With Bhairava's help, anyone possessed by such a demon can become healthy and free and live a normal life at home, devoted to this god.

Right behind the shrine of this Skeleton Bhairava there is a Vaṉṉi tree, the tree of fire, that has the very form of Śiva. He stays there in the shade of that tree, creating worlds and caring for them. This

[100] When, as a boar, Viṣṇu dug through the earth seeking the root of the *liṅga* of flames.

[101] The demons involved are *pey*, *pūtam* = *bhūta*, *pilli*; the *vacanam* adds *picācu* and [*pilli*]*cūṉiyam* [the latter analogous to Sūniyam in Sri Lanka; see Kapferer 1997].

tree is to be watered and worshipped, with lamps, each day, because if its leaves and fruits ever dry up, the entire cosmos will feel the pain. If, on the other hand, this tree lives forever, the earth will also survive. Śiva brought all the sages of the Forest of Pines, now free of lethal action, into the shade of this tree, and he gave them lessons there.

At a certain moment, the gods asked him to dance before them, again, in the Copper Hall, with the goddess as witness. Śiva readily agreed: as the Skeleton, poised on top of Muyalakan̲, he began his dance. And as every bone of Muyalakan̲'s was crushed, in turn, worlds upon worlds were shaken from their place. Everyone saw this, and the god saw it, too—so he ceased dancing and went, still a Skeleton, with the goddess, into the *liṅga* shrine. He is still ensconced there on a royal throne, to the west of the *liṅga*. Outside, Nelveli is well protected by his rowdy ghouls, and also by fierce Kālī, by Bhairava and Durgā, by Viṣṇu, dark as the ocean, and by the hero known as Karumpan̲ai Vīrar. Śiva, wearing the freshly flayed skin of an elephant, sits happily within.[102]

So now I have told you, as best I could, the whole story of how Śiva came to the Forest of Pines and excited love in the women there. You, too, are sages; and now you know all about the Skeleton Guise, that gods and human beings serve. My advice to you, as the Storyteller, is to go and see it for yourselves. Hurry, now, to Nelveli. Enter that forest.

Edges of Self

'Nothing alive can move, in any direction, without me.' Anything that lives, that has an inner composition that is natural to it and that resonates harmoniously with other living beings—*iyalpu* —is in movement in relation to Śiva, who has put it into movement. But Śiva, as we saw in the *Tevāram* poem on this shrine, has his own *iyalpu*, which moves him toward the forest. This god is in continuous movement in relation to himself. He is, that is, playing or toying with himself, in ways that are usually tantalizing or deluding when seen from some theoretically external perspective, such as that of the sages in the forest at Nelveli. What they see is described in sufficient detail to allow us to extrapolate a set of possible rules for this game.

102 Omitting 366–74, 380, 392, 394–6, 398–9.

The Nelveli text clearly attempts a wide-ranging integration of Dāruvana materials. All the themes that we isolated in the first two chapters appear here, sometimes in very detailed form: the double encounter of Mohinī with the sages and of Śiva with their wives, with the by now familiar scenes of wild infatuation and subsequent disappointment; the progression from seduction and conflict—the sacrifice of black magic—to enlightenment through the dance; the richly elaborated notion of exorcism that follows from this progression; the relation between Bhikṣâṭana and the *liṅga*, in particular the Root Liṅga that is identified with the middle space whose inner depths are 'alive with light;' the fixing of this tableau in the Tamil shrine or, more precisely, the assertion that it repeats itself regularly at this site. The metaphysics of the curve and the twisting surface, seen as projecting shorter linear sequences, are still very much in evidence. Questions of recognition and of knowing, on various levels, arise in much the same manner as at Cidambaram, where the self is made of understanding that is light. The god transforms himself along the lines we have seen, in interactive reciprocity with what the sages and their wives are undergoing.

In addition to these elements, very much in the line of Kacciyappar's *Kanta-purāṇam* version, the Nelveli narrative has absorbed significant features from the north Indian Dāruvana variants. The most conspicuous of these is the sages' curse against Śiva, the ostensible cause of the *liṅga*'s fall to earth. We have explored the antecedents to this motif in the epic's myth of Śiva as Sthāṇu, the Pillar.[103] It is striking that this curse, which has given way to the sacrificial rite of sorcery in the main Tamil versions of the story, reappears, in this most comprehensive of existing tellings, as if the poet were reluctant to exclude any known element relating to the forest. He has also taken his detailed description of the sages, in their many poses and diets, from well-known Sanskrit versions.[104] In particular, Nĕllaiyappap Piḷḷai, or his source, seem to have a close dependence upon the well-known Sanskrit text of *Kūrma-purāṇa* 2.37,[105] where both the repetition theme and the presence of enlightened Yogis are important. Add to this the short but evocative inset about Sudarśana, who offers Death his wife—an episode taken from *Mahābhārata* 13.2.36-85 or its further extensions in the classical

[103] Above, 1.7.
[104] *Brahmâṇḍa-purāṇa* 1.2.27; *Kūrma-purāṇa* 2.37. 93–7.
[105] See Appendix.

purāṇas.[106] Perhaps for the first time in the southern tradition of the Dāruvana we are exploring, Śiva's journey to the forest comes to include an overt intention to put the sages to a test. The Beggar is akin to Death insofar as the latter makes outrageous requests. To penetrate this guise—or, for that matter, to act selflessly toward the unsettling guest even without recognizing him—is here the initial step toward freedom.

We could easily continue separating out the textual strands that have gone into the making of the Nelveli master-narrative,[107] but there is another, perhaps more fruitful method of interpretation. For Nĕllaiyappar takes us still deeper into the forest than either of his predecessors, studied above. The integrated sequence he presents reveals, upon reflection, a further level in the south Indian vision of this god's internal process. Above all, it shows us the direction this process necessarily follows and another aspect of the logic guiding its unfolding, in particular with respect to the issue of Śiva's self-exorcism and the probable human contribution to this ideal goal. Let us attempt to formulate the pattern empirically, closely following Nĕllaiyappar's own words.

We begin with directionality. In the Nelveli text, Śiva's movement follows a meaningful trajectory amenable to analytic formulation. Here, as the text ends, he is not dancing—not yet, at any rate. He is not, that is, accelerated to the point of sucking entire universes back into himself. Nelveli, unlike Cidambaram, is not a steady-state whorl made visible. The dance in the forest is part of a somewhat wider project. Moreover, Nelveli *is* the original Forest of Pines, again unlike Cidambaram. So in going to Nelveli, Śiva is going *somewhere*. The poet implicitly draws a line from Kailāsa to southern Tamil Nadu. A certain minimal linearity must be taken as given. Moreover, Śiva is no first-time tourist. He is *returning* to the forest, and he returns a second time in the course of this telling. An aspect of repetition defines the trajectory.

The journey has other distinctive features. Along with the strong sense of directionality and repetition, the god's process entails his

106 Thus *Liṅga-purāṇa* 1.29.44-63; *Śiva-purāṇa* 2.3.35.10. The Sudarśana episode has been discussed in some detail by (Doniger) O'Flaherty 1973: 197–8, unerringly linking it to the Forest of Pines.

107 Note the integration into the story of Agastya, the Vedic sage seen as the foundational figure for medieval Tamil culture, but here a teacher capable of correctly recognizing Śiva; Agastya is situated on Potiyil Mountain, not far to the south of Nelveli.

emergence as Kaṅkāla-mūrti, the Skeleton Guise. This grimly seductive image marks a limit. It is the most beautiful of all the god's forms, 'pure, ravishing, radiant.' Only eyes that have seen it count as eyes. It alone brings understanding, *potam/bodha*. The Skeleton is Śiva's 'real beauty,' which he hides from the sages by becoming naked. In the forest as elsewhere, nakedness is a highly effective mask. It is the Skeleton who is real and, as such, only rarely visible. Yet here, too, we find the god repeating himself, reappearing as the Skeleton to the sages during his second visit, in the winter month of Māci, and yet another time to Viṣṇu, who correctly states: 'At last I have seen your limit, which I failed to find so long ago.' A 'final' revelation takes place when the Skeleton subsumes the dancing Naṭarāja. He is thus both Beggar and Dancer in their true guise. Kaṅkāla-mūrti, 'at once beautiful and terrifying,' also merges, at the request of the gods and sages, into the light that fills the Root Liṅga. He is, we are told, what is actually inside this *liṅga*—so we are privileged with another penetrating X-ray or cross-section of the interior. The Skeleton is also Bhairava and, as such, the secret weapon of exorcists. He could be seen as the form or means with which Śiva exorcises himself.

But why should the god have to exorcise himself—and of what or whom? By now the answer should not be far to seek, but the text helps us by lucidly setting up the problem in the initial verses. Something has happened in Śiva's space. He sits in Kailāsa, supposedly his 'home,' but he is absorbed in the memory of another, original Kailāsa, the 'heaven itself' that is Nelveli, the Forest of Pines. These two paradisiac worlds should, one might think, be perfectly correlated, capable of coalescing with one another. In fact, however, they are separated by considerable metaphysical as well as geographic distance. Kailāsa is Nelveli and yet not quite Nelveli. Śiva lives in Kailāsa, but the Root Liṅga is in Nelveli, where all good things happened: Śiva and Pārvatī married there; Kāntimatī lives there; Śiva and Umā guard the world from there; Nelveli survives even the universal flood. Nelveli is Kailāsa and yet not quite Kailāsa, for Kailāsa is 'here' and Nelveli is 'there.' In effect, the Himalayan Kailāsa has to move south to visit the Tamil one, so that by the close of this version of the story they can come together again. The south Indian Kailāsa has apparently moved away from its point of origin as *brahma-vṛddha-pura*, the 'ancient site of wholeness.' Something has been lost or attenuated, and the god wants to reattach or restore it. To do so, he has to move outward toward what we might think of, somewhat ambiguously, as the very edge of his self. The Skeleton, we are told repeatedly, is as far as he can go.

Surprisingly, the limit of self seems to be located in the middle (not the centre) or to point toward the middle. We will argue that the Skeleton is a compacted form of middleness-—always emergent in front of Śiva as his horizon; always coming into being, somewhere between form and non-form, between not-two and not-one. In this sense it contrasts with the *liṅga* that, while generative of infinite realities, never itself 'becomes.' The Skeleton is uniquely male, mostly untouched by the feminine force of *māyā-śakti* and its material effects. All bones and the space between them,[108] he is a potent amalgam of hard surface and the empty fullness characteristic of god in the deeper reaches of himself. More precisely, he is god brandishing aloft, on his trident, this emblem of his evolving nature, *iyalpu*. The god of Nelveli is the field of force between the Skeleton and the Root Liṅga, and between both these realities and the presence of the goddess Kāntimatī. He is also the wounded *liṅga* that 'grows upon request.' If we study him in this somewhat eerie light, as he seems to need to study himself upon his arrival in Nelveli, we may be able to say something tangible about the content of his awareness.

All this suggests that by coming to Nelveli Śiva is moving toward the middle, and that in doing so he is both exorcising himself and unfreezing the sages and their forest. It is in the nature of the Skeleton Guise to draw out the innerness of being, to bring what is inside to the surface, to erase the distinction between interior and exterior. The wives of the sages experience this process directly: the Skeleton sucks their selves to the surface of their being, where they relate to the god as self to self, without otherness, in the space between not-two and not-one. The sages resist this shift: they are on the outer surface of the god and eager to stay there. They, too, mark a limit and a danger. They show us the cosmos devolving rapidly toward a congealed two-ness, heavy with temporal gaps. We could describe the entire Dāruvana programme, *in nuce*, as an intervention by Śiva to keep two-ness from coming fully into being in a universe that is contracting outwards into flat, linear sequence; his goal, which applies to his own internal process

[108] Like Bhṛṅgin, the skeletal witness to the dice-game and to Naṭarāja's dance: see Handelman and Shulman 1997: 113–16.

no less than to any externalized object, is to curve cosmos back into itself, to reopen the depths of middleness.

The outside, we should remember, begins somewhere inside; it becomes outside only as this inside begins to harden. In this sense, the outside is still a continuation of the inside, though it is shifting from infinity to finitude, acquiring names, selfhood, knowledge, and a surface with two distinct sides. One of the problems endemic to the forest is the need for both Śiva and the sages to peel away an inner mask, a mask that has hardened somewhere inside and still faces inward, thus making it nearly impossible for Śiva to know himself except by means of this false guise. On one level, this inward freezing into a face is the god's most persistent, indeed maddeningly recalcitrant, riddle or challenge. Once, at the wholly fictive origin of the cosmos, god held space and time within himself, and human beings related to god through the middleness of not-two and not-one; Śiva and living beings looped through one another without becoming one another. Now they have shifted disastrously toward two-ness, separation, and difference. The ancient site of wholeness is moving away from god. Śiva has to remember it before he can revisit it. He is caught, at the point where our text begins, in the looping movement of time. Pieces of his world, and of himself, are no longer connected. Parts of him have slowed down unbearably. Split-off fragments, astonishingly solid, have come to think of themselves as entirely autonomous, thus damming up the god's self-transforming flux. There is far too much knowledge, all of it a slowing toward stasis; there are many, too many, straight lines. Even Śiva has a name.

The forest has left Śiva, its trajectory angling away from god rather than curving through him. The further the forest travels in this direction, the less its inhabitants recognize themselves as parts of god's self. Śiva, too, is not quite what he was in the forest that was. Even his knowledge seems outdated; he has to be briefed by Nārada. He sits, reminiscing, on Kailāsa, while the sages pursue their dessicated rites without him. The curvature of the cosmos has twisted into a line, along which god and human beings are moving away from each other, with little awareness of one another. The Root Linga is still in the forest, but the sages have no knowledge of it. Under these conditions, Śiva's vocation is to act against his own nature as the cosmos emptying itself out. He will, in short, have to take something away if he is to return to the middle. Think, then, of a god who contracts, slows down, hardens, freezes, grows dry, becomes empty, forgets, remembers, begins to speak in the first person, acquires contours, corners, wrinkles, lines—all this as he moves toward his edges, where the Skeleton may reappear.

Sorcery Redefined

Strange things may happen in the middle. For example, Death may turn up as a guest seeking love. A person might correctly recognize god, standing before him, without actually seeing him or understanding the purport of his presence. Unexpected kinds of knowledge emerge spontaneously—often to mislead. Sorcery can rebound upon the sorcerer. God, like human beings, will appear to be less *as himself* than he is in his imagination of himself.

The middle is the space of meeting, where otherness becomes selfness. As Nirampav a̲lakiya Tecikar tells us, 'If you mix together, there is no otherness.'[109] Yet even to utter a word like 'self' is to make the self other, just as counting 'one' immediately implies 'not one'—thus at the very least, two. Hence the very striking confusion consequent upon recognition in this version of the story. Both the wives and the sages actually recognize Śiva as Śiva, yet this knowledge, which rapidly becomes definite and certain, seems almost irrelevant to what happens to each of these groups. First the women's hypothesis: 'With his long penis, white ash on his forehead, those gentle legs dancing the *tāṇḍava* dance—this whole amazing apparition—he might as well be Śiva, the god who lives on Kailāsa.' Notice the subjunctive. A discussion ensues among these women, mad with desire:

'He must be the god who swallowed poison from the sea.'
'But where is the eye on the forehead that burned the god of desire?'
'He's just hiding it from us. There's no doubt that he has three eyes.'
'Maybe so, but then where is the garland of skulls?'
'The whole point is to confuse us: that's why he came here, so beautiful he could kill.'

They are, of course, right: this is a god intent on 'fusing and confusing,' as we have seen. The women are already well advanced in the stages of this process and thus, in a sense, free from the exigencies of knowing:

[109] Above, n. 14.

> *For the most part those women, wives to the idiot sages, showed no devotion, and failed to praise him, though God himself was standing right before their eyes. They were trapped in the net of wanting.*

If this sounds less than ideal, remember that they 'had lost any wisdom that could hold things together; they had gone beyond oceans, gone beyond mountains.' They can therefore see the god directly in the most beautiful of his guises, the Skeleton. But this very intensity puts the women somewhere on the other side of the god: they want oneness while he, embodying the middle, wants to move them toward this middle space. He is drawing their interiors toward himself, toward the surface, at the same time opening himself, as only god can, to the self they offer him. He reaches out to them, begs from them, fills himself with their awareness of him, with their longing and madness. He wants them to see themselves as he sees them, from his situation in the middle. Such a perception is not only a matter of melting and flowing, as we might conclude from the two earlier versions of the story that we have cited. At Nelveli the women retain something of their individuality: 'Although they were disciplined women, experienced in *tapas*, educated, properly married, and so on, still not one of them sounded like any of the others.' Here the principle of not-two and not-one becomes concrete and generative: something new is born in the middle space, a third-ness that takes the form of 48,000 children, born mindful of the god. Śiva has filled the women's empty wombs by moving into and through them, even as he himself has been filled by the force of their desire. The women are now free, like 'anyone who sees god,' and can go home—without losing the entire range of their self-experience. One kind of blockage has been removed with only minimal relation to the domain of knowing.

As to the sages, the path to the middle goes through very violent resistance. Recognition first engenders hate. These pedantic, obsessive men—some of them committed to a diet of wind or water, others to a slightly more elaborate cuisine of dried leaves and boiled rice[110]—achieve insight at a relatively early point in the story. Overcome by the seductive Mohinī, they have lost all control; they are restored to their usual arid state when they see what has happened to their wives. So intense is their humiliation that their minds suddenly clear completely, and they can make the necessary analytical deduction:

[110] See above, n. 104.

'Who is this fellow? Just look what he has done. Some man took the form of a Play-Woman, came here, and drove us mad. Meanwhile, some other male, by some strange game or trick, overpowered our wives.' They thought it over, and clarity came. 'It is must be Śiva, with the moon in his hair, who demolished the self-control, the sense of shame, and the physical strength of our lovely women. And the one who came winking at us coyly from under those curved eyebrows, the delicious woman with lush red lips who demolished all of our tapas, *must be Viṣṇu, husband to Śrī. But Viṣṇu, by himself, would have no interest in ruining our discipline; he was certainly only following orders that came from Śiva. Anyway, despite the loss of what we had before, we can put our bodies back to work and stock up on more* tapas, *as much as we need. But what Śiva did—coming here with great beauty, his body glowing like sunset, and then, by magic, stripping our women of their clothes and all shyness—that story will last on earth as long as the sun and the moon. He took a certain beguiling form, and he made Viṣṇu take another. Only Śiva, with the eye in his forehead, who burnt the demons' three cities—only he could do this.'*

The deduction is correct, the conclusions catastrophic. They first hurl curses at the god—very much like the sages of the northern versions of the Dāruvana, as we have noted[111]—and then, when this fails to have any perceptible effect, they move toward the sacrifice of sorcery, *apicārav-omam*, which is meant to kill him. In between these two episodes, there is an argument with the 'real Yogis' who suddenly appear, replete with knowledge about Śiva. Faced with this degree of certainty, our sages have their doubts: would god act in this way? Can the Beggar really be Śiva? Where are his attributes—the trident, the tiger-skin, the poison in his throat? When the Yogis insist on the identification, the sages mock the Beggar with pointed but insulting questions: 'If you really are the god of all three worlds, how could you have sunk so low as to seduce our wives? Are we enemies, we and you? Who really did this deed? And who, exactly, are you?'

In other words, how could god be less than complete? The sages' disappointment goes to the heart of the matter. They have effectively recognized Śiva—recognized even his self-diminution into the Beggar's volatile state—but this act of sterile, surface knowledge fails to conform to their axioms and assumptions about god. Hence the terrible hatred, fuelled by conflicting strands of awareness: this man who beguiled and humiliated them is god, but also apparently much less than god. A lethal

[111] See surveys by Jahn 1915 and 1916 and Kulke 1970: 57–67; for one example, see the Appendix (*Kūrma-purāṇa* 2.37).

doubt flickers in their minds. There is no way out of the predicament except to kill the bewildering amalgam standing before them, a hybrid of wholeness and fragmentation that they are determined to see as located outside themselves. Bewitched themselves, rigid, straining, and far too full of lucid intellection, they resort to sorcery as the weapon of choice.

In what sense are these sages bewitched? We have addressed their state several times before, mostly in terms of petrification and stasis, on the one hand, and of the necessary dimension of resistance and opposition, *māṟupāṭu*, on the other.[112] The Nelveli text, by its sheer richness of detailed description, but also by its culminating statements linking the Dāruvana directly with the praxis of exorcism, allows us to formulate a somewhat more comprehensive statement. This formulation should address the level of intimate collusion between Śiva and the self-deluded sages, since both parties undergo forms of exorcism in the forest and thereby become free.

The sages are intent upon *tapas* that, as Śiva himself tells Viṣṇu at the briefing on Kailāsa before their mission, is a kind of solid: it 'fills them up from within.' It is Mohinī's task to melt down this solid state. The radical misperception of the nature of *tapas* with which the sages begin speaks eloquently of their actual emptiness. They are trying, rather pathetically, to fill themselves up in this way. The more solid, the more empty: the principle holds true for the world as a whole. There is no room for self in a space encysted and frozen solid. The rituals these men perform are, in their own view, 'the real thing' (*pŏruḷ*), the emphasis being on the false substantiality, the 'thingness,' to which they are committed. A certain anxiety naturally accompanies ritual reified and rule-bound to this extent; this anxiety comes into play, in a massive way, when Mohinī disturbs the sages' practice.

Mohinī hardly 'does' anything: simply by being present, she washes away the sages' discipline, their ability to differentiate, discriminate, categorize, compartmentalize—all critical components of Vedic ritual process. They melt, boil, jump, moan, dance, and wail, a set of discordant, spasmodic movements akin to the epileptic discontinuities of the demon Muyalakaṉ. Mohinī has become the sages' religion: 'Only idiots give themselves,' they say, 'to worship, to devotion, to visualizing the

[112] See above, pp. 14–16, 87–95.

deities, to the *liṅga*, to those carefully uttered mantras or to all kinds of *tapas*. Only you, dear Mohinī, can bestow freedom.' Wrong again. There is no communication between the seductive Viṣṇu in disguise and these raging men. Mohinī remains entirely other—remote, cool, distinct. The meeting has nothing of mutuality or of mingling. Twoness still reigns intact. Mohinī stands in the same relationship to the sages as did the deities of their former ritual practice; in both instances, there is no contact between god and man. God becomes that which man imagines him to be.

If Mohinī has taken something from them—they are, after all, 'melted down'—she has not replaced this with anything. She has not opened the space of middleness for them. Indeed, the gulf between the sages and god may even have widened. Propelled out of their self-contained, self-sealing ritualism, the sages become acutely aware of someone who is beyond their encapsulated world; but still they cannot reach her. Mohinī can do what she does to them because they have driven their capacity for love into a hidden corner of their selves and walled this off. They are locked into isolation, utterly unable to connect with a reality beyond their impoverished vision of themselves. Such is sorcery, *tout court*.

Notice that Mohinī, for her part, is also a relatively impoverished surface self concealing a theoretically male self underneath.[113] The female, that is, is held within the male or moves outward from within him as the active *śakti* linked to wanting, knowing, and acting (*icchā*, *jñāna*, *kriyā*). In the present case, this active and seductive aspect of the godhead is identified with Viṣṇu, a female male gifted with unusual generative potential: Viṣṇu as Mohinī gives birth to Śiva's son Harihara-putra in an act of strangely involuted sexual conception (Śiva in effect impregnates himself as male to produce a male child).[114] This same Mohinī-Viṣṇu hungers for the Skeleton, the autotelic male who is all bones—but who seems to have space between these bones where self can relate to self and gender can alternate and transform. Once again, we are looking at a productive or transformative middle. On another level, we could say that what we are calling the middle allows the *liṅga-yoni* continuities—the two potential modes of male and female continuously flowing through one another, thrusting out, sucking in,

[113] She thus contrasts starkly with Gaṅgamma at Tirupati: see Handelman 1995.
[114] See *Viṣṇu-māyā-vilāsamu* of Rosanūri Veṅkaṭapati-kavi.

exploding, weaving, and imploding—to emerge on to a surface through the mediation of the Skeleton. In this case, when the Skeleton enters the Root Liṅga, as happens in the final crescendo of the Nelveli text, exorcism becomes complete. But we anticipate.

Something has crystallized in the forest: Mohinī leaves the sages even more occluded, frozen, and lost than they were at the outset. She has intensified their blocked, resistant state to the point where it has to burst into an active, hate-driven attack, powerful enough to stimulate Śiva to exorcise himself. By now we know why this process is ineluctable. Sorcery, we have said, is precisely this walling off of the self—a loss of connectivity, an encrustation, fragmentation, isolation, a pseudo-autonomy that is always accompanied by opaque perception and a slowing down of inner process. Relations are severed, borders made solid. But in a deeper sense, sorcery, including its common embodiment in possession, is an attack by the self on the self.[115] We see this most clearly in the complementary process undergone by Śiva and the sages. The latter create a 'sacrifice of sorcery' out of which the god's lost attributes emerge to attack him. How did he lose them? We cannot know. Perhaps Bhairava had something to do with it. Śiva as Bhairava violently takes away pieces of his own cosmos (Brahmā's head, for example, though this head then clings to the god's outstretched hand). Sacrifice is always this 'taking away,' which opens a creative, in our terms 'middle,' space. Tamil regularly chooses this idiom. But Bhairava's sacrifice is necessarily self-sacrifice, since what he takes away belongs to his own cosmos—to himself, that is. By taking away aspects of his cosmos, Bhairava may lose certain inherent parts of himself—parts that are, no doubt, externalizations or objectifications of god's being. As Bhikṣâṭana, he first begs them back, then reclaims them from the sages' rite. Without knowing what they are doing, the sages are emptying themselves in order to reunite god with himself.

There is a certain lack of synchrony in this process. Bhairava, as we have seen, is Śiva moving toward oneness by 'taking away.' (Were he able to pursue this direction to the end, Śiva would perhaps lose himself in the hidden recesses of self.) The sages, however, are initially trapped in two-ness, the antagonistic world of separation and illusory autonomy. In this mode, they unintentionally move toward recomposing

[115] See Shulman, in press (2).

the god by restoring the very parts that, as Bhairava, he has taken away. Śiva's drive toward unitary wholeness or fullness anticipates and conditions the course the sages will follow in their resistance, *mārupāṭu*, and its eventual healing. But the two complementary sequences are somehow at odds in temporal terms, another indication of the sages' failure to attune themselves to Śiva's evolving presence. On the other hand, we have to remember that the two sequences eventually overlap not in the achievement of oneness but in the middle dimension where both parties are not-two and not-one. Bhikṣâṭana, emerging out of Bhairava, actively begging from those who have cut themselves off from him, is the trigger and key to this achievement.

Bhikṣâṭana-Śiva is thus attacked by aspects of himself, which he tames and reabsorbs, curving them back into his body. On the surface, this confrontation is the product of a violent otherness. The sages are sacrificing in the mode of *abhicāra*, black magic—a destructive anti-sacrifice that seeks not to 'take away' in the classical sense of opening up the middle range of potential movement but rather to 'take away' middleness itself, thus killing god. Were the rite to succeed, time, if it still existed at all, would be entirely linear; twists and curves would vanish; space would be as empty as the sages themselves. Or we could say that the sages' path is to attack the self with itself, to enclose selfness within aspects of self that are clearly known, hence dead, defined, locked into stasis. The effect is to block all avenues of the self's movement, so that self is imprisoned within self and effectively alien to itself. Sorcery blocks the self's capacity to become aware, self to self, of an otherness never fully separated from the self, an otherness that folds back into selfness, ceaselessly re-creating the latter. Sorcery is twoness concretized. Even more important, sorcery is two-ness felt or experienced as oneness, the isolation and self-enclosure of an autistic inner world. In this sense sorcery is the dark shadow of sacrifice—an intentional walling off of the originary power of sacrifice. It creates gaps where fluid connection should be. It segments an innerness that is turned against itself, thereby losing coherence along with the capacity to see itself as simultaneously autonomous and interdependent, open to autonomous otherness that is experienced and known from within.

Sorcery produces the solidity of emptiness. At its extreme limit, in possession, the self ceases to imagine itself as anything *but* other—a separate being that takes up all inner space, utterly denying movement.

Such deadly, constricting otherness is the true opposite of the interwoven selfness that the women achieve. In cases of full-fledged possession, as the Nelveli text states, 'the trick is to get the possessing spirit to tell you his name: as soon as this happens, the demon or ghoul runs away from the body he has entered, with Bhairava chasing him from behind or spinning him in the air.' Naming creates an entity distinct from the possessed, an entity that can then be driven out, as it were, with the help of Bhairava, the Skeleton. Demonic possession implies forgetting—forgetting who one is or was, who one imagines oneself to be, who it is who knows the self as self. But possession of this sort, which can be healed by sacrifice, is perhaps only an extreme, intensified form of the existential condition always implied by merely having a name.

This turning of the self against the self, the deceleration and definition of immovable pieces of self that thereby become alien, are integral to life as a conscious being. In one sense, this movement is also the condition for self-knowledge. Śiva thus goes to the forest because parts of his being are cut off, encrusted, and empty—as happens to any living being emerging on to a surface. These processes are essentially self-generated, and it is the special merit of the Nelveli *purāṇa* that it makes this point very clear, thus offering an implicit rationale for the entire sequence of the forest. The other side of a false autonomy is a false heteronomy—the mistaken belief that we have been invaded from without, made subject to an alien will. Possession often looks like this and is, indeed, often classed as such, as we have just seen in the language of the Nelveli text itself;[116] but in the end it is doubtful if heteronomous acts as such can ever transpire in this meta-psychological world.[117] What does transpire is the continuous interweaving of self-possession and self-exorcism, the latter usually requiring conflict, severe resistance, and some form of sacrifice. The forest offers one forceful paradigm. The sages exhaust themselves in black magic; by the time they have restored Śiva's attributes to the god in this antagonistic mode, they have emptied out their own emptiness, thereby filling him. A deep reciprocity marks this exchange despite contrasting intentionality. The sages are exorcised as they exorcise Śiva; or he exorcises himself as he frees them from their obsession. Note that at base this business is

[116] See discussion in Nabokov 2000; also pp. 164–73.
[117] As argued in Shulman, in press (2).

not, contrary to common views and the usual lexicon, a matter of taking someone or something out of the possessed person. Quite the opposite is true: it takes something or someone *into* her or him. In principle sorcery empties out being just as it dries up fluidity, disconnects the continuous, and decelerates movement and time. Exorcism, on the other hand, *fills* being with the fluid, the organic, the self-transformative, and the interactive. It undoes forgetting in the specific sense mentioned at the start of this chapter.[118] By the end, Śiva thus dances on the back of Apasmāra-Muyalakan̲, forgetting personified. Once again, dancing is fullness, a magnetic emptying of everything outside by sucking it inwards, so that the dancer swells and fills. Sorcery is transformed into exorcism, and the empty sorcerers—the sages—are themselves prepared to be filled.

Within this scenario, which we have now studied in three closely related sources, the role of desire suddenly makes new sense. In the case of the sages' wives, matters are somewhat more straightforward: desire for Śiva transforms and ultimately removes the residual blockages they may still be experiencing. They stream into the god, and he fills them with fertile seed. Mohinī somewhat similarly awakens the sages to desire, which in this case seems opposed to a brittle ritualism. Without feeling, without desire, there will be no sorcery; and without sorcery, there will be no escape from the occlusion that cuts these sages off from Śiva and from all other selves. An initial intensification of their resistance, driven by desire, will eventually issue into renewed connectivity and the recognition that goes with it. In the first instance, feeling per se (love, hate) connects. In the second instance, hate separates, love relates. But underlying the catalytic role of desire in general is, it would seem, a wish and need to unblock. In the forest as in other south Indian social worlds, desire, outwardly directed and hence not wholly self-contained, is the natural antidote to that isolation that leaves the self stranded, impoverished, bewitched.

Return

At Nelveli, the Skeleton Kaṅkāla stands slightly to the west of the Root Liṅga. Both are permanent presences that set up a certain tensile, highly energized relation. Or we might think of it as fragile equipoise, very

[118] Above, p. 107.

similar to Naṭarāja's, always on the point of driving the deity through another sequence such as we have seen, from self-possession to self-exorcism, from emergence outward as the Skeleton to reabsorption within the light-filled *liṅga*, from breathing out to breathing in. Kaṅkāla and the Root Liṅga show us very subtle moments or potential modes within these processes. But they do not inhabit quite the same level of reality. At the very end of the narrative, the Skeleton enters into the Liṅga, defined as 'pure empty space,' that is, as fullness uncongealed, not split, entirely free. Both formed and formless aspects of infinity merge in a healing domain, the very antithesis of possession—the 'middle space, the inner depths alive with light,' into which the Skeleton has disappeared once before.

Demons do not do well in the presence of this spacious god. An infinity of Bhairavas attack them from inside the *liṅga*. Most vulnerable, it seems, are the predatory village demons, the *pey*, *bhūtas*, and *piśācas*, as well as the very prevalent and dangerous *cūṉiyam*, whose very name means 'emptiness.'[119] Note that *cūṉiyam*, for the Tamil Śaiva philosophers, is equal to anything knowable by empirical 'pointing knowledge,' *cuṭṭ'aṟivu*, that vanishes in the presence of true knowledge, *uṇarvu*.[120] The metaphysical coincides completely with its objective local embodiments. There is also a Skeletal Bhairava Well at Nelveli, equally abhorred by such demons—since this water is fluid and interconnected, the opposite of petrified pseudo-existence. Similarly, outside the shrine we find the Vaṉṉi tree, that is to be watered and worshipped daily: 'If its leaves and fruits ever dry up, the entire cosmos will feel the pain.' Is cosmic evil finally just this, the pain the cosmos experiences when a living piece of it goes dry? Perhaps not surprisingly, Bhairava dwells in the shade of this fluid, ever-growing tree, akin to the *liṅga* of Venu-vana-nātha that continues growing on request; here the god gives lessons—in metaphysics?—to the reformed sages of the forest. One hopes they ask many pointed questions that have no logical answers.

It is very striking that in this version, unlike the others we have studied, Śiva agrees to remain forever in the forest. He stays on as the Skeleton, the most ravishing of all his forms and the most susceptible to further movement toward and from the middle. Entering the *liṅga*,

[119] On Sūniyam in Sri Lanka, see Kapferer 1997.

[120] See Dhavamony 1971: 209.

he heals the possessed in the paradigmatic act of exorcism. He does this again and again, since he must repeatedly exorcise himself. He fits all too well the description Brahmā gives the befuddled sages when they come to him for advice after the failure of their sacrifice of sorcery:

> *I don't care how much* tapas *a person does—if he isn't thinking of Śiva, the god of Nelveli, it's all wasted. Worse than that, he becomes ridden with anxieties, he grows weak inside, and ends up wandering like a beggar from place to place. . . .*

Like Bhikṣâṭana, Śiva grows empty, or hungry, and begs to be filled, as if from the outside; he is unable to fill himself until he has erased some inner dimension of self-alienation. In this skeletal form, he has the 'body full of holes, needing to be fed'[121] that Tamil poets so often identify as peculiarly human. Śiva, that is, is not always thinking of Śiva. His awareness of himself, as we have seen, is a goal, an always temporary result achieved through interactive process, never simply given. Moreover, such self-knowledge has the special character we defined earlier in the wake of the Siddhântin philosophers. It is not a *knowledge of* but, at best, a *knowledge as*. It only happens through a strong mutual interpenetration of potential knowers. Like any form of wisdom or perfection, it exists between not-one and not-two.

The incompletion of such a process, or its self-regenerative and repetitive aspect, is suggested by the Skeleton's decision to return to Nelveli (in the month of Māci, a year after the confrontation with the sages) and by his need to remain there. Nowhere else can we see so clearly the accordion-like effect of this cosmology: the forest is Nelveli, which is Kailāsa, which is the cosmos, which is Nelveli (dislocated from its original situation as the Site of Perfection). These locations are, in theory, capable of being superimposed without disjunction; in fact, they keep sliding slightly away from one another as gaps open up, distance congeals, and a tenuous set of selves and named beings crystallize into presence. The mere act of breathing out enlarges these gaps. As god breathes out, he ensorcels himself, and galaxies fall out of focus.

Hence the need to return. In fact, there was never a first time. Each appearance of Bhikṣâṭana in the forest is a repetition (also a premonition, a sign of impending re-emergence). Each time it ends with the

[121] *pucippat' or pŏḷḷal ākkai*: Appar *Tevāram* 4.45.2.

dance that approximates the in-breath. But the dance is never allowed to reach the point of infinity in which the cosmos would disappear, sucked into the whorl. Śiva breathes out—as part of this dance. The tension between the two directions of breathing may well keep the god in movement. We, the onlookers, integral both to his self-exorcism and to his emergence into a powerful presence in which self-knowledge will also be present, help him in this respect.

It is normally not so difficult to acknowledge the pain of two-ness. Two is the number of splitting and otherness; the recalcitrant otherness of other beings lies at the core of loving, as the Śaiva poets constantly remind us—they want to be reborn many times so as to endure, over and over, the sweet torture of longing for an often absent god.[122] Notice that these poets thus nicely articulate the often much less evident catastrophe of oneness. Final fusion is an option utterly inimical to the god's inner movement, which demands self-extension into some form of otherness, a temporary encrustation of molten infinity.[123] The existence of Śiva as Śiva, as a living presence emerging within a matrix of relations, depends on a moulded, hardened cosmos that is momentarily separated from his sentient yet hardly differentiated inner being. Southern Śaiva ritual is strongly oriented toward this same process of drawing the god toward us from out of the *liṅga*,[124] at once exorcising him and the worshiper's own self, perpetuating the precarious movement of the dance on this side of the infinite without letting the dancer accelerate past the limit. Indeed, Śiva at Nelveli is, as we have seen, just such a limit, which he proclaims in his very name. If we want to speak about knowing, our point of departure is here.

[122] As Cekkiḻār says, 'loving hurts.' *Pĕriya Purāṇam* 18. 16 (1056).

[123] Even in the state of ultimate release we find a triad of relations: the god who offers the taste of freedom, the living self that experiences this taste, and a residue of encrusting or staining *mala*, without which no tasting is possible. See *Uṇmai viḷakkam* of Maṉavācakam Kaṭantār, 51 (*mutti taṉil*). Here the *mala*-crust replicates in miniature, in a more harmonious context, the necessary function of resistance (*māṟupāṭu*), as when the sages attack Śiva: see Devasenapathi 1974: 306.

[124] See the lucid description by Brunner 1986, including the notion of *sakalīkaraṇa*, constructing the body of Śiva in place of the *māyā*-body of the practitioner that has been emptied of metaphysical reality. To produce a present and visible (*sakala*) body for the god through mantric praxis and visualization is, on one level, to repeat the cosmogonic impulse; yet it is the special feature of the Tamil *purāṇic* texts of the Dāruvana that they implicitly restate this Āgamic ritual in terms close to exorcism, on both the divine and human levels.

To draw the god out of his *liṅga* and toward us is to affect his inner composition and his awareness, at once re-creating him within our world and lifting the constriction that has kept him bound. Where is he at the start of this process? He cannot be entirely one, for in that case we would not exist. He may be caught in a subtle two-ness that is balanced in our direction yet also absent from us, thus relatively unaware of himself. The ritualist, who *is* aware, draws him into a mirror-like dimension in which he can see himself in or through our eyes, that is, he can see himself seeing. This is the moment his bewitched state gives way to something richer and deeper, though we, for our part, may remain ensorcelled when he suddenly appears among us. Usually, we fail to recognize him. In another sense, we are ourselves the mirror held up to this deity. Hence, perhaps, the heightened ritual moment of attaching eyes to a divine image. One often reads that such moments are dangerous—that the god's gaze is potentially destructive. Yet these are the moments when god sees himself seeing insofar as he sees us looking at him—the charged and delicate moments when he can be said to begin to know.

Knowing, that is, is effectively a form of exorcism. To know is to unblock the hardened parts of self, the parts that cut self off from others or that render selves utterly other, discontinuous, self-contained. Śiva tells Nārada and Viṣṇu, near the beginning of the Nelveli text: 'Just as one day, long ago, we danced with Kālī in the Forest of Pines and overcame her self-absorption, we will now do away with the self-absorption of those sages.' Self-absorption is, apparently, all too close to sorcery, a kind of demonic possession that blocks all potential movement among selves. The full self depends on the interaction of selves that know themselves through the other's knowledge. Moreover, such knowledge, to be real, is never an object. Śiva knows himself only through whatever it is he is in the process of becoming, and we know him when he is becoming whatever he has made us, just as he knows himself through us in this manner. In other words, not even god is likely to know himself as X in advance of moving into or through X. In this sense human beings share 'selfness' with god, an overlapping, organic process of simultaneous emergence that is, however, visible to the eye, human or divine, only in some specific sequence, one self at a time.

Thus when Śiva returns to Nelveli, he first studies himself, from the outside, as the Root Liṅga. When he becomes the Skeleton once again, he positions himself in relation to this same *liṅga*. When he re-enters the *liṅga*, the forest that *was* becomes the forest that *is*. Kailāsa closes the gap between the Himalaya and Nelveli. Time collapses without disappearing—for inside the *liṅga*, the Skeleton can still be clearly perceived. We would use a word like 'reflexive' to indicate that these processes did not carry so strong a connotation of dissociation and splitting. One that knows itself as one is no longer one—but Śiva who sees himself as Śiva through the eyes of those others who see themselves as Śiva is *no longer dissociated at all*. He is rather woven into a middle space that allows movement in any direction. Knowledge of this kind is knowledge that matters, in the sense of working change upon cosmos and god.

Nĕllaiyappap Pillai has drawn in the main contours of a process enabling such integrated and object-free knowing. Some are familiar from the earlier Tamil versions we have studied; others achieve stark articulation here for the first time in the context of the Dāruvana story. The paradigm of melting down dissociation by 'reflexive' doubling or repetition of this special type is present in many small details, right from the start—for example, in Viṣṇu's request to see the Skeleton, 'the form you took, out of love, when you lifted the corpse of an earlier, dead Viṣṇu onto your shoulder.' He of course achieves this vision at the very end of the chapter, when the Skeleton reveals himself with 'many thousands of universes dangling from the tip of each hair on his head' and 'the skeletons of endless Viṣṇus and Brahmās tied to his waist.' In this stance, as Viṣṇu sees himself replicated without end, closure of sorts becomes possible for the recurring spirals of experience. A similar result may flow out of the moment that Śiva studies himself as the Root Liṅga or sings songs about Śiva while begging from the women in the forest. The Nelveli of the past momentarily fuses with the Nelveli of the present. The act of seeing in such a moment blends the content of perception inextricably with its frame.[125]

It is never the case that a single observer sees his singular self at a singular moment; the skeletons of endless Viṣṇus are certainly the norm. Viṣṇu is central to this process and as such beautifully complementary to Śiva's role, just as he is intimately tied to the *liṅga*-shrine within the male half of the Nelveli temple complex. At Nelveli, Viṣṇu

[125] On braided frames, see Handelman in Shulman and Thiagarajan, in press.

is reconstituted as male via a long but necessary detour through a female surface persona. Śiva frees himself through Viṣṇu's guise and unmasking and through the effects of this process upon the lost parts of his own self. Such is the manner and rationale of his self-exorcism. This god is in the process of remaking himself. Not everyone can see it. The sages are blind, as, all too often, are we. Still, while repetition never repeats exactly, god can, it seems, become free by precisely such a progression, looping vision into vision, turning the eye back upon itself. There are moments when one knows that god is not two and not one and, not being either, is 'unbroken in self'[126]—*our* self, knowing itself as him. Such a moment may be close to what the Śaiva Siddhântins mean when they speak of 'seeing god, the unthinkable, as thinkable' after all.[127]

[126] Above, p. 115, end of first paragraph in the translation of Nĕllaiyappap Piḷḷai's text.

[127] *acintitaṉāy niṉṟa patiyaic cintitaṉākak kaṇṭu vaḻipaṭum āṟu*: *Civa-ñāṉa-potam* 12.1.

Feeding and Madness

Those who see that in and out
are one
have nothing left to scorn.[1]

Is God Sane?

In all the Tamil texts we have examined, the god who comes to the Forest of Pines is a god who needs to grow, to move, to come alive, and who cannot do any of this alone. At the heart of both the philosophical and the ritual systems put in place around this god is the effort to enable these processes to take place within him, or to enhance their effect, thereby reversing the opposite processes of slowing down, stopping, or dying. Stated negatively, and very starkly, on the verge of sacrilege, at the heart of these systems we find a strong anxiety about a god who tends, at times, under everyday conditions, to go dead. In this respect, Śiva is very much like any human self. It is always possible to find oneself surrounded by dead objects or to create a world made up of such objects. Such a world, which does repeatedly come into being, in experience, because of the entropic and self-diminishing processes within the godhead, is a constant danger for anything alive. If Śiva comes to a stop, the cosmos itself disintegrates into a state of suffocating blockage and pervasive isolation; beings can no longer connect to one another or to him. Of course, even a blocked and object-laden universe is still made up of god, but such a face to god is of no use and little interest to the south Indian poets and metaphysicians. They want a god who is in movement and, rather like the wives of the sages, they are prepared to facilitate this change by filling Śiva

[1] *Tiruvaruṭpayaṉ* 10.6: *uḷḷum puṟampum ŏrutaṉmaik kāṭciyarukk'/ ĕḷḷun tiṟam etum il.*

up in various ways, including the apparently effective device of telling him his story.

It works: Nelveli is home to the god 'who kicked Death to death' (*kūṟṟ' utaittār*).[2] Śiva comes alive in this shrine and brings life to other living beings in the circumstances we studied in the last chapter. At Nelveli, this god grows (after being decapitated) and dances (after being fed). He moves toward a limit or edge that he produces in or through himself. He meets enough opposition and resistance to force a change in the direction he is evolving. His left-hand, male–female self moves through a trajectory of masking, seduction, and unveiling.[3] All this is necessary if Śiva is to be free and to open up space for *our* freedom. None of it is simply given. Ritual and cognitive or meditative effort on our part is essential if god is to be made present to himself or to us. It is time we left behind the still prevalent, rather timid readings of Tamil Śaiva Siddhânta, with their fixation on the notion of god's 'pure being' or 'pure knowing' as a steady state always available to his worshippers. Whatever is pure in this conceptual system is made so by taking something away, something that has ossified or frozen within the moving god. As to Siva's 'knowing,' we have seen something of what this may mean.

There are, however, many other possibilities for Śiva as he moves into the Forest of Pines. The Tamil texts present us with a relatively coherent set of perceptions, and we have attempted to draw out their implicit logic. The narrative itself is largely constrained by a set of classically articulated coordinates. But if we move only a short distance to the north, into the Tamil–Telugu boundary area of South and North Arcot, Chittor, Nellore, and Anantapur districts (the latter three in present-day Andhra Pradesh), we find another strikingly consistent set of variants, very close in some ways to the Tamil series we have examined but with a fascinating change in focus. Here, too, there is a strong interest in the problem of feeding the god and putting him into spin. Another important temple—the shrine to the highly energized and attractive Vīrabhadra at Lepaksi—formulates this theme in its own way. Village myths from the Senji area take the problem further, once again drawing

[2] *Pěriya Purāṇam* of Cekkiḻār, 2784 referring to Tirunelveli.

[3] A principle is involved: the surface guise (*porvai*) that Śiva adopts cannot be seen by human beings for what it really is, *i.e.*, a decoy (*pārvai*) set up to trap and entice. *Tiruvaruṭpayaṉ* 5.5. Cf. *Tiruvātavūraṭikaḷ purāṇam* 1. 2. 63.

a link with sorcery, possession, and exorcism but also explicitly speaking about madness in relation to the god. We examine a classical statement very close to these materials in the fifteenth-century poetic version of the Dāruvana myth by the Telugu poet, Śrīnātha.

It is one thing to be hungry; to need to be filled from the outside, but quite another to be so empty or, in contrast, so full that you become literally mad or wild or out of control. Occasionally, our texts speak in such terms about Śiva or about others who are close to him or implicated in the process he is undergoing. The sages embark upon their rite of sorcery with the express aim of killing 'the Madman.'[4] Viṣṇu, seeing the Skeleton, goes crazy himself—and hence is known as Māl, the Bewildered.[5] The sages' wives, frenzied with desire, wonder if the naked beggar is not both maddening and, perhaps, mad himself.[6] A dimension of madness, expressed in several distinct ways, is deeply present in the Dāruvana story. In this chapter we observe more closely this god who has gone beyond the bounds of the culturally delimited norm and is clearly identified as insane. Such a notion is an ancient one in south Indian Śaivism.[7] We will connect it to the problem of Siva's coming face to face with himself, or, indeed, of having something like a self. For if self-awareness is always tinged with sorcery, as we have argued at some length, then it is perhaps understandable that even god's ensorcelled consciousness can, when experienced as such, drive god into states outside ordinary, that is 'sane,' existence.

To illustrate, we cite first an extremely widespread pattern of northern Tamil village myths about Śiva, in which the god is cursed to wander as a lunatic beggar with Brahmā's skull attached to his hand. This Bhairava-like guise is now the result of an unsettling moment of mirroring: five-headed Śiva confronts five-headed Brahmā and tries desperately to distinguish himself by cutting off one of the latter's heads. This violent act only makes matters worse. The god is burdened with Brahmā's skull, a voracious, driven entity that is inseparable from Siva's body. He is expressly said to be crazy, homeless, without rest.[8] He needs

[4] *Tirunĕlvelittalapurāṇam, tārukāvanaccarukkam* 223.

[5] Ibid., 73, 174.

[6] *Koyiṟpurāṇam* 2.21; *Takṣa-kāṇṭam* 6.13.59.

[7] See Yocum 1983. Cf. Sontheimer 1989: 50–8, 61–6 and 1989a for Deccani parallels to the Vedic materials.

[8] Among many recorded variants of this pattern, see Brenda Beck's instance from the Konku region in north-west Tamil Nadu: O'Flaherty 1973: 127 (with

the direct intervention of the local goddess to find relief from this state. To put the matter simply: God, insofar as he is male and alone, without the goddess, and insofar as he approaches the village that tells his story, is experienced at least initially as insane.

Perhaps we should not be surprised. Tamil Śaiva narratives sometimes speak of madness as a form of play. Thus when Śiva, guised as an old man, interrupts Cuntaramūrttināyaṉār's wedding by claiming the bridegroom as his slave, Cuntarar insults him and calls him crazy (*pittā*). But the claim is authenticated by a palm-leaf document signed by the bridegroom's grandfather. Cuntarar is forced to follow the old man until the latter disappears, suddenly, into the temple of Śiva. Now Cuntarar knows: he is, indeed, the slave of the 'madman' who came to the wedding. He wants to sing a Tamil poem in praise of this god, but how should he begin? Śiva himself whispers the answer: 'Sing to me as you called me then.' So Cuntarar's first poem begins with this address: 'Madman, crowned by the crescent moon! (*pittā piṟai cūṭī*).'[9] Madness of this sort is relatively benign; also quite familiar. The god is playing with his human intimates, revealing himself to them, or *in* them, in a game that stretches them as it stretches him. Norms and conventions are undermined or, to use our earlier language, curved or bent or twisted, and as a result god becomes present in the labile modes that are natural to him in his more autonomous, 'fuller' self. We will have more to say about this pattern, but its distinctiveness in relation to the far more threatening and unhappy beggar of village mythology should already be evident.

If we wish to understand the latter case, we have to listen carefully to the way the story is told. Here is one fairly straightforward account as recorded and translated by Isabelle Nabokov from Mel Malaiyanur, near Senji:

> Paramacivaṉ (the god Śiva) had five heads. The angels, the sun, and the moon used to regularly ask the god to grant them favours. Even the god Brahmā came and asked for one. He wanted a fifth head too. Śiva granted his request.
>
> No sooner was Brahmā endowed with his fifth head than he began to fulfil wishes as well. Śiva felt bad about this. At the same time

---

discussion of *purāṇic* parallels, 123–6). Here Pārvatī also takes the head in her hand and becomes mad.

[9] *Pĕriya Purāṇam* 1.1.28–74 (174–220).

> Īshwari (Śiva's wife) complained that she could no longer distinguish him from Brahmā. Śiva replied: 'What could I do, he came and asked for five heads and I granted him the favour.'
>
> As Brahmā was becoming arrogant, and in the eyes of Īshwari too much like her husband, Śiva cut off one of Brahmā's heads. But another grew in its place. When he cut off that one, another replaced it, and again and so on.
>
> The god Viṣṇu appeared, announcing that he had given a special boon to Brahmā that enabled his head, if chopped off, to grow back. To cancel the boon Śiva would have to keep the head in his hand. Śiva followed Viṣṇu's advice and once more cut off Brahmā's head, but this time he held it in his hand. Brahmā fell down but when he got up he cursed Śiva for having broken his promise. 'You will become a naked beggar and hang around like a madman. You will never be at rest again.'
>
> Unable to get rid of Brahmā's head, which stuck to his hand, Śiva suffered the curse. He wandered like a homeless, crazy beggar. When he reached the cremation ground of Malaiyanur, the goddess Īshwari followed the advice of her brother, Viṣṇu, and took the form of a scary-looking being (*akora rūpam*). She became Aṅkāḷaparamecuvari and threw two lumps of blood rice at Brahmā, and one to the head that was stuck to Śiva's hand. Then Brahmā's head fell off and rolled on the ground where Aṅkāḷaparamecuvari stepped on it. Delivered of the head, Śiva came back to his senses. He and Īshwari resumed their happy life as husband and wife.[10]

Each stage of this rather complex internal evolution deserves scrutiny. Śiva begins in a state of apparent completion: five is a number of wholeness, suited to the spilling outward of godly fullness in gifts and boons. Brahmā properly benefits from this initial state but then comes to resemble Śiva, the source, far too closely. Brahmā can also give boons, and the goddess can no longer distinguish one five-headed male from another. Brahmā appears to be too much like Śiva in another sense as well—he is arrogant or, in our terms, self-possessed. Śiva attacks him. But like the *liṅga* at Nelveli that grows upon being decapitated, the heads that Śiva takes away simply grow back. There is an answer to this problem of infinite regeneration: Śiva has to hold fast to the

[10] Nabokov 2000: 89–90.

head that he removes. God becomes distinct from his mirror image only in his grasping, already incipiently hungry mode.

A curse follows: Śiva will be restless, like a madman, a beggar. He wanders to Mel Malaiyanur. He is glued to the skull, constricted in direction, obviously in need of help. Now the goddess can intervene, filling the fissure that has opened up. Brahmā is fed, as is Brahmā's erstwhile head, which drops from Śiva's hand, rolls on the ground, and is stamped upon by Aṅkāḷammaṉ. Her movement, apparently reflecting her recognition of her husband as well as her filling up with her terrible *aghora-rūpa*, reminds us of the dance. The goddess has, that is, swollen into a self that is in movement. Freed from the extra head and its demands, Śiva's head or heads become clear. He rejoins his female persona, probably mingling himself into her. Something like a balance—or is it a state of reciprocal interweaving and mutual knowing?—is, at least temporarily, restored.

One head too many is madness. As Nabokov remarks, Śiva is 'effectively "possessed" *by* an additional identity.'[11] But how many heads are a reasonable compromise with the overflowing fullness? When does the series become too much to bear? And why should this god have to suffer the curse of restless lunacy?

Let us look at another, more elaborate version from the same area, collected by Eveline Macilamani-Meyer:

> 'It happened once, when Pārvatī was returning to Kailāsa, that both Śiva and Brahmā were sitting there. Since both of them had five heads, she was not able to tell them apart, and thus she prostrated herself in front of Brahmā, thinking him to be her husband, and she received his blessings. Brahmā thereupon started to laugh, which made the Ammaṉ very angry. She said to him: "So you are laughing because I have now lost my faithfulness as wife to Śiva! I am cursing you that your head shall be cut off." Īśvara, who also was angry, plucked off one head, he plucked off 99 heads of Brahmā. After he had cut off one thousand heads, Brahmā said: "You have plucked off my head, therefore you shall go to the cremation ground and wander around there without food, without sleep, like a beggar you shall go around." Thus Brahmā cursed him. Because of that curse, Śiva had to go around begging. With a begging bowl he asked for

[11] Ibid., 90.

alms. When he received the offerings, the *kapālam* (that is, the skull of Brahmā, the begging bowl) which had gotten stuck to his hand, ate everything. Thus without food, without eating, he was rolling around in the ashes of the cremation ground. As he was rolling around in the ashes like this, he finally came to lie down in the cremation ground here in Malaiyaṉūr [South Arcot district, a central site for Aṅkāḷammaṉ].

At this time the Ammaṉ, who was doing *tavam* (= *tapas*), saw Civaperumāṉ (Śiva). She thought: "Whom should I appoint as guard? He (Śiva) is mad, and he might get up and go somewhere else. What should I do, if he left? It is in this place that I have to get his left side." What did she do? She started to think: "How long should I reflect? Whom should I place as guard? Right, let it be Vināyaka (= Gaṇapati). He is the right person; because he has a big belly, he can sit there." "You, Vināyaka, sit there! People will bring you *kolukkaṭṭai* [cakes of rice flour with coconut scrapings and sugar] on Śivarātri. You eat these and stay there and watch," she said to Vināyaka and continued her *tavam*. At dawn she had to go to the cremation ground. She needed some *kolukkaṭṭai* for Vināyaka. When at dawn the lame Cempaṭavar (inland fisherman) came, she told him: "Appa, you have to bring me *kolukkaṭṭai*." As soon as he had brought these, she placed them into a basket and took them to the cremation ground. In the cremation ground she scattered them. All the Ammaṉ's demons (*pūtam* = *bhūta*) came down and picked them up. Ninety million Māyāśakti came and picked them up, and Vināyaka also felt a desire for the *kolukkaṭṭai* and he also picked them up. Ammaṉ kept throwing them. What did she throw? The turmeric and lime mixed with rice, that blood rice, she threw. And again all the spirits (*pey*, *picācu*, Skt *piśāca*) came and picked up the morsels.

Then the *kapālam* on Śiva's hand thought: "All these beings pick up these things, so let me also get down and take some to still my hunger." The *kapālam* left Śiva's hand and started to eat the food. As soon as the *kapālam* had left Śiva's hand, Śiva's head became clear again and he got back to his normal state. He said, "*Pĕṇṇe* ('woman'), Pārvatī," and he ran to her, making himself small. The Ammaṉ changed into her frightful (*akoram* = *aghora*) form, a huge form. Śiva ran behind her to hide, and she trampled the head. She, Īśvari, took the *aghora* form, the form of Kālī, of Aṅkāḷammaṉ, and she trampled the *kapālam*. Then the head of Brahmā (the *kapālam*) asked her: "Will you give me one hundred thousand lives a day?" The Ammaṉ replied, "Yes, I shall give them to you." He asked: "How will you give them to me?" She replied: "My people catch fish, they catch one hundred thousand fish and the lives of these they will offer to you." After she had granted this boon, she continued: "Since you made my lord suffer so much, there shall be no Brahmā temple anywhere in this and the two times seven worlds." Thus she cursed him.

Then the Ammaṉ "obtained" the left side of Śiva, and together they left for Kailāsa.

Thus the Ammaṉ came to settle in Malaiyaṉūr and took the Cempaṭavar as her slaves (devotees). . . . She releases people from their madness (*pittu*). She gives boons to people, and she gets *pūcai* (= *pūjā*) in return and eats.'[12]

By now, hunger—stubborn, nearly constant, relentlessly recurring—seems to lie at the very heart of reality. The skull suffers from it to the point that Śiva, attached almost as an excrescence to this grim, voracious being, is reduced to 'rolling around in the ashes of the cremation ground.' He, too, is hungry, and yet utterly unable to eat. The demons and ghouls,*pey*, in the village are ravenous creatures; Vināyaka, the guardian, must be fed if he is to remain on duty; and we can be sure that the fishermen are also in need of daily nourishment. Most striking of all, in a way, is the hunger of the great goddess herself; she releases people from madness, gives boons, is worshipped, and therefore eats. At no point can the business of feeding stop.[13] It is an ongoing compulsion, and there is madness, real or potential, momentarily blocked or newly re-emergent, at nearly every point.

Madness is intimately tied to emptiness—presumably the emptiness of solid forms. The text actually tells us, in so many words, how this works and what it means. The initial episode of mirroring, as in the previous version, lays down a basis for understanding. The problem

[12] Meyer 1984: 336–8. See Macilamani-Meyer's discussion of this text, *loc. cit.*, and further remarks in Shulman, in press (2).

[13] In this respect, the Tamil village is strikingly continuous with the ancient *Brāhmaṇa* texts that depict a world of eaters and the eaten, with (hopefully) regular transitions between them. See Malamoud 1989: 73.

clearly centres on the fifth, 'extra' head. This situation is not just a matter of replication and loss of distinction. Pārvatī mistakes five-headed Brahmā for her five-headed husband and bows to the former; Brahmā laughs in malicious glee. Listen to this laughter, which suggests an awareness far from free. The curse follows, as does Śiva's frustration, since every head he cuts off grows back immediately. It is not so easy to lose the fifth head. If we think back to the Bhairava text of the *Kanta-purāṇam*,[14] we may remember that the fifth head is the highest of the set. Think of it as something like a cork that blocks further expansion upwards. Heads in general, but certainly this fifth, dominating head, tend to get in the way. To grow, one needs to lose them, just as the *liṅga* at Nelveli, once decapitated, can now grow 'upon request.'[15] If you don't rid yourself of the upper head, all knowledge worth knowing will cease to exist within you.

Hence the deeper difficulty present in the act of mirroring. There is, throughout Indian sources and ritual praxis, a pervasive sense of the mirror as a non-linear well of being, or a space of potential emergence;[16] but here the reflection that Śiva sees only confirms the god's own potential blockage. He, too, has a head too many. In this condition, he cannot grow; at best, he can grow mad, begging, rolling on the earth, hungry, unfeedable, and unfed. Cutting off Brahmā's head is no help; the blockage simply transfers to this skull that eats up everything without allowing any nourishment to reach Śiva himself. Brahmā's head is starving Śiva, yet the food—real food, potentially nourishing—simply disappears into the bottomless void. The head has no body, so where could nourishment go? Disembodied heads, so prevalent in southern Śaiva contexts,[17] often seem to indicate a short-circuit in cosmic process; the site of generation, growth, or understanding becomes the most salient mark of blockage or, in our terms, of sorcery, the inability to *take away*. Brahmā's head takes in yet remains stuck, constricted, and isolated; Śiva attempts to take away yet remains empty. In this phase, all attempts to fill the deity from without are useless: we may try to feed him, to activate or exorcise him, but all our efforts only intensify the blockage working through the demonic head.

14 Above, pp. 52–6.
15 Above, p. 112.
16 See Shulman 2003.
17 Ibid.; below, n. 62.

Nothing moves through the god when he is in this state, and he can no longer move through himself; nothing fills him or refills him or lets him interact with others; the head takes all. He goes through the linear trajectory of the Beggar, pleading to be fed but actually pleading to feed the skull; if only it were satiated, he, too, might begin to extricate himself from the mad, bewitched state of perpetual hunger for existence. He is suffering from the mad horror of oneness—the inseparable extension of self as skull, sorcerer, and victim glued together as one—that is actually a movement toward insufferable two-ness, the direct consequence of the mirror image that first splits him, then rebounds to trap him. There is no middle ground for Śiva at this stage.

Oneness is mad. Two-ness is mad. Both are pathological inner states, heavy with rock-like obstruction, empty of breath and movement. This hungry Bhairava, writhing on the earth, has to be exorcised. It is up to the goddess to achieve this result, just as it is up to the devout worshipper of the *liṅga* to exorcise both god and self day after day.[18] Again like this ritual performer, Aṅkāḷammaṉ is herself in process, by no means static or at rest. In effect, she has absorbed Bhikṣâṭana's standard role as he moves toward his Naṭarāja persona. The goddess is not the same at the end as she was at the beginning. At first she, too, was confused, unable to see and know the god. She comes face to face with the two-ness that is generated by existence itself; she is unable to see the middleness out of which two-ness emerged.[19] If she could have seen it, she would have chosen Śiva; because of her failure, she, too, has to be filled, fed, recognized, known, and moved toward another existential pole. When the skull at last detaches itself from Śiva, he runs to her, calling her name, 'Pārvatī.' By now he is very small, while she swells into the huge *aghora-rūpa* that is identified as her 'true form' or 'true self.'[20] In this form she tramples on the skull, just as Naṭarāja dances upon Muyalakaṉ. She is moving, dancing, spinning herself into Śiva's left side.

[18] Above, p. 160. Thus temple ritual can be understood, in part, as the ongoing exorcism of the god, in the sense that the previous day has to be 'taken away' so that it will not block space for the coming day. Let us stress once more that quotidian ritual praxis and grand cosmic process reproduce one another continuously and systematically.

[19] Just as Śiva cannot distinguish one Nelveli from another when he reminisces on Kailāsa.

[20] For *aghora-rūpa* as 'self,' see Shulman, in press (2).

She has successfully exorcised him. Feeding the skull is like knowing the demon's name, so that this now identifiable entity can be reified at least enough to separate him from the possessed host. As soon as this point is reached, Śiva's head clears. Sanity is restored at least in the sense that awareness is no longer hopelessly bewitched. Instead, the two selves of god, female and male, are related, indeed interpenetrated—for to be related is to be inside one another to some degree. Or vice versa: innerness is actually relatedness. As Abhinavagupta says in an altogether different context that nonetheless articulates the same guiding principle: 'Multiplicity is external. However, unity through the reciprocal connection of forms is internal.'[21] It is striking to see the continuity stretching from Śaiva metaphysics to northern Tamil village rituals. What is not two and not one is deeply intermingled, like the eye that sees itself seeing. Precisely this far-reaching mutual interpenetration is the end-result of Aṅkāḷamman̲'s festival, when a vivified earth-and-ash figure—the goddess herself or a male figure drawn from her story (Mayān̲a-vīran̲, Dakṣa)—is trampled by the crowd as everyone vies for a piece to consume or to take home. This culminating moment is known as *mayān̲akkŏḷḷai*, the free-for-all in the cremation ground. It is sometimes preceded by yet another image that points in much the same direction: a man dressed as the goddess drapes himself in the intestines of a sacrificed goat and makes his way to the cremation ground, where he pulls the intestines out of this same clay figure and consumes them.[22] Who, now, is inside whom? Innerness, that is, issues from itself and re-enters itself, winding whatever is ostensibly outside into the inside.

To restate this principle in the abstract and deceptively sequential terms familiar from our earlier analyses: 'god' or 'goddess' is a process of coming—actually twisting or looping—to a surface, perceived from within as somehow outer or moving outwards; this movement is sorcery, integral to god, integral to self, especially insofar as he or she or we have a name, perhaps the wrong name, worst of all a singular one. On such a surface, relationship is blocked, and madness rules. God slows down, empties out. If enough resistance is generated, or under other favourable conditions connected to desire, he or she or we

[21] *Īśvara-pratyabhijñā-vimarśinī* 2.2.4, cited Lawrence 1992: 198.

[22] Meyer 1984: 111–112, 221, etc.; discussion in Shulman, in press (2). This latter component of the ritual is called *piḷḷaippāvu*.

may be exorcised, losing head, skull, self, and name, accelerating into the whorl of the dance, dissolving surface, boundary or edge into an active or, better, interactive middle. Yet this middle is perhaps mad in another way.

A Healthy Madness

Perhaps we use the term too loosely. Let us try to set out the major coordinates of the semantic field of madness in Tamil and Telugu, keeping in mind that Sanskrit lexemes (especially *unmāda* and its associated forms) are also present in the medieval south Indian texts,[23] including those relating to the Forest of Pines. In Tamil, a set of four primary terms structures this field: *vĕṟi*, attested in the earliest strata of the literature; *pittu* (also *pittam*, later *paittiyam*), by far the most common way to speak about madness; *māl*, which we have met as one of Viṣṇu's names;[24] and various derivatives of the roots *maya/mayaṅku/mayar*, all connected to notions of confusion, mixing, fusion, delusion, infatuation, and so on (thus we have the noun forms *mayakkam*, *maiyal*, *mayal*, *mayarvu*).[25] All four have Telugu cognates.[26] There is, not surprisingly, considerable overlap in usage. Let us look briefly at each of these domains, though a full semantic analysis cannot be attempted here.

Vĕṟi primarily suggests states of rage or fury, hence also intoxication, wildness, mental aberration, and what we call 'possession.' In Caṅkam-period texts, we find the 'dance of *vĕṟi*' (*vĕṟiyāṭal* or *vĕṟi ayartal*) performed by the priests of Murukaṉ for purposes of divination and of bringing the god into close proximity—in the body of the performer.[27] *Vĕṟi* is thus a matter of intensity, spill-over, and active divinity, tangibly

[23] On *unmattam/unmattaṉ*, also simply *mattam*, see Yocum 1983: 19–22 and n. 3.

[24] Thus already in *Mullaippāṭṭu* 3. The Dāruvana texts explicitly derive this name from *māl*, 'delusion,' though in older Tamil texts Viṣṇu is Māyoṉ, the 'dark god:' see discussion of the derivation in Hardy 1983, 153–67. And see *DED* 3950.

[25] See *DED* 3852.

[26] Thus *vĕṟi* is related to Telugu *vĕṟṟi*, the common term for madness and foolishness (see *DED* 4536); *pittu* is cognate with *picci* and, via Skt *pitta*, *paittyam*; *māl* is cognate with Te. *mālugu*, 'to be lazy;' *DED* 3852 leads us to Te. *maikamu*, 'intoxication, unconsciousness.'

[27] Discussion in Kailasapathy 1968: 63–4; Hart 1975: 28–9, citing the *vĕṟikkuravai* dance.

present, not easily controlled, affecting the senses and the mind.[28] Note the relation to the dance. When god fills a person, that person is given to non-normative states of intense *vĕr̲i*. The same term continues to apply to village goddesses like Aṅkāḷamman̲ when they see blood, for example, and become wild.[29]

Pittu or *piccu* has a humoral component: *pittu* is bile, related to Sanskrit *pitta*. An excess of *pittu* drives one into abnormal states of mind.[30] More generally, *pittu* is a matter of folly following upon a wide range of possible causes, from humoral imbalance to cognitive dissonance. Overtones of foolishness, silliness, and childishness are often present. One sign of *pittu* is a tendency to chatter incoherently: sober people go about their business with an awareness of impermanence, illness, old age, and death; in contrast, there are no greater idiots (*pittar*) than those who babble on (*pitar̲r̲u*) about grammar and astrology.[31] This root, *pitar̲r̲u*—to chatter, make meaningless sounds—is a steady companion to *pittu*; in devotional contexts, the lovers of the god are the crazy fools (*pittar*) who mumble and babble on like this.[32] So this sort of madness or silliness can easily become a virtue; we have already seen that Śiva himself is *pittan̲*, 'mad.' The *Tevāram* and *Tiruvācakam* frequently speak of him in precisely these terms.[33] Sometimes they 'explain' the aetiology of the god's craziness. He makes people free (*mutti-mul̲u-mutal*) by entering into their minds (*putti*) after taking the form of a *pittan̲* who is also a child (*piḷḷai*).[34] Notice how these two elements of childishness and mad folly blend together, reinforcing one another. Poets, especially god-intoxicated ones like Kampan̲, are particularly susceptible to such 'inspired' states.

But there may be a cognitive component to the transition into madness of this type. Thus Māṇikkavācakar cries out to Śiva as the madman (*pittan̲e*) who, 'becoming all living beings, remains the Trickster who

[28] See, e.g., Kampan̲, *Irāmâvatāram* 1.569 on the intoxicated and incoherent (*vĕriyān̲a milar̲r̲ukin̲r̲a*) women of Mithilā.

[29] Meyer 1984: 111–12.

[30] Thus in Āyurveda: Zimmerman 1982: 25, 112–15.

[31] *Nālaṭiyār* 52.

[32] Kampan̲ 1.1.8, combining *pittar*, *petaiyar* (fools), and *pattar* (devotees).

[33] Thus Appar 4.31.307: God is sweet as sugarcane to those who attach themselves to the *pittar* (*pittarkkup pattar āki*). See further examples in Yocum 1983: 25; also *Koyir̲-purāṇam* 2.56–7.

[34] *Tiruvācakam* 13.19.

grows and lives but is *not* all these beings' (*ĕllā uyirumāy taḻaittup piḻaitt' avai allaiyāy niṟkum ĕttaṉe*).[35] The poet is at home with the familiar paradox of existence as 'not one and not two.' Apparently, if you try to think, or rather feel, your way around this notion, you begin to see god as crazy in the very positive sense implied here; moreover, having reached this point, the poet can proudly proclaim that he has 'caught god' (*uṉṉaic cikk' ĕṉap piṭitteṉ*, the refrain of this entire decade). One catches him insofar as one holds fast to the paradox, just as Bhairava fiercely holds on to the voracious head of Brahmā, that was no doubt thinking too hard or too much. In an earlier verse from this decade (37.2), Māṇikkavācakar makes the same boast along with the strong adverbial phrase *iṭai viṭātu*—he has caught hold of god 'without leaving any space or crack in between.' Trapping Śiva in his hands, he is hardly one, but certainly no longer two; there is, indeed, no space for two-ness left in his world. Hence the preference for predicative negation, as we have seen.[36] Still, this neither-nor logic, like the poet's simultaneous affirmation and denial of god's identity with whatever lives, is readily classed as mad.

Such a stance in the face of the seemingly paradoxical, familiar also from the Mādhyamika dialecticians with their delight in exotic forms of negation,[37] recurs regularly throughout the literature of southern Śaivism as well as in sources from beyond its boundaries. Thus Annamayya, the fifteenth-century Telugu Vaiṣṇava poet at Tirupati, devotes a *padam*-poem to the god as possibly gripped by craziness (*vĕṟṟiva nīvu*).[38] Venkaṭeśvara-Viṣṇu acts in incomprehensible ways that, for this very reason, excite and attract:

You've taken thousands of names
so that people can choose what name they want.
Now you're Lord of the Hills.
Easy to reach.

[35] *Tiruvācakam* 37. 8. Note predicative negation (above, pp. 104–5) and the combination of 'becoming' with 'remaining.' One could also translate: 'who grows full but is not identified with their mistakes' (thus the modern commentator Navanīta Kiruṣṇa Pāratiyār, 1025, on *piḻaittu*). This commentator also suggests for *ĕttaṉe*, the 'trickster,' *ĕllāvuyirkaḷmaṭṭum kalantirukkum cūḻcciy uḷḷavaṉe*, 'who has a wily plan to mix with all that lives.'

[36] Above, p. 104.

[37] As in the tetralemma: see Ruegg 1977.

[38] *vĕnna muccilu nāṭi vĕṟṟiva nīvu*: *vĕṟṟi* is cognate with Tamil *vĕṟi* (above).

Are You Crazy?[39]

The god's very movement toward accessibility is enough to raise the ironic rhetorical question. If you think it through, it makes no sense; a certain lovable foolishness characterizes this deity's unmotivated, playful approach to human beings, especially insofar as this movement entails a thousandfold fragmentation in name (and presumably in form). Such acts of apparent madness are clearly superior to any norm-bound, easily intelligible roles.

Hence the Śaiva poets' fondness for *pittu*, which they see as Śiva's personal gift to them. On the one hand, they may complain of their mad life *before* the god's intervention: Manikkavacakar says he wandered as a *pittaṉ*, drowning in the ocean of women's lips, before Śiva gently embraced him.[40] In a word, he was a fool. On the other hand, the god gives *pittu/piccu* (*pĕrum piccut tarum pĕrumāṉe,* 24.3; the more common expression is *picc' eṟṟu*) at the time he cuts off the root of future births. Redeeming the poet from his former, stony state is a matter of several linked actions: first god makes him crazy (*picc' eṟṟi*), then he kneads or dissolves the rock (*kallaip picaintu*) and produces ripeness (*kaṉi ākki*), and finally he drowns him in compassion (*taṉ karuṇai vĕḷḷattu aḻutti*).[41] Here is the paradigm in its complete sequence. If melting and ripening are the immediate goals, then madness is the point of departure.

Vĕṟi and *pittu* are distinct yet related; both point to internal states of fullness or frenzy, often god-induced, though *vĕṟi* is by far the stronger term. *Pittu*, with a wider range, can include an element of cognitive or intellectual puzzlement that gives rise to an altered state of mind. Both terms suggest a process of transformation or psycho-physical transmutation not yet complete. The other two lexical fields take us in a somewhat different direction. *Māl* is in many ways the most straightforward term. It connotes delusion, sometimes as the result of sluggishness and mental torpor—something like the deceleration that, as we have seen, affects god and produces objectified, hence false, perception. Desire also induces *māl*.[42] But once again, this state, if

[39] We thank V. Narayana Rao. See Narayana Rao and Shulman, in press.

[40] *Tiruvācakam* 41.6. Cf. *Tirunĕlvelittalapurāṇam, tārukāvaṉaccarukkam* 185: the sages follow Mohinī like *pittar.*

[41] Ibid. 8.5.

[42] *Paripāṭal* 10.42: a male elephant, struck by *māl* at the sight of a female, is paralysed.

directed toward the god, becomes highly valued: the god is the one who brings up (*eṟṟu*) in the lover a state of delicious *māl* (*ānanta māl*), which no one *but* Śiva could remove.[43] The same rapture (*ānanda*) that belongs to the god's *tāṇḍava* dance is here part of the devotee's mad experience. Not surprisingly, then, the women in the forest also shift into this state, as we have seen in one of the *Kanta-purāṇam* verses already examined:

aṇaṅkiṉ nallavar aṇṇa' ṟaṉ koca' mel
[n]uṇaṅku māloṭu nokki ataṟku muṉ
vaṇaṅkum āṟ' ĕṉa maṟṟ' avar nāṇupu
kaṇaṅkaḷoṭu kaviḻntu cĕṉṟār cilar (77)

And there were some women—wild and good—who were scrutinizing his penis [kocam] *with a subtle intensity, as if they were devoting themselves to it, although they then bashfully rejoined the others, standing with bowed heads.*

The 'subtle[44] intensity' is *māl*, a passionate state far beyond normative self-awareness. These women have lost themselves in their desire, and loss of self to this degree is madness; small wonder they are described as 'wild' by means of the ancient word *aṇaṅku*, generally used in medieval Tamil to describe the fierce or raging goddess.[45] Here *māl* is thus not far removed from *vĕṟi*, frenzied possession.

The range of *mayaṅku* and its related notions has been studied by Trawick.[46] *Mayakkam*, the substantive, is by no means necessarily a state of 'madness.' It does frequently suggest mixing and fusing, hence also *confusing*, with common symptoms such as dizziness, stumbling, staring, mental wandering, and intoxication. Śiva himself is susceptible to such states as his internal composition shifts in relation to the cosmos: 'When god puts himself together, everything is fused and confused' (*it talaivaṉ muyakkañ cakala-mayakkan tāṉ ām*).[47] *Mayakkam* can thus be a clear sign of that full interweaving of presence that Śaiva ritual

[43] *Tiruvācakam* 47.2. See the further example noted by Yocum 1983: 21.

[44] Reading *nuṇaṅku*, with the commentator; alternatively, *uṇaṅku māl*, the 'tortuous passion.'

[45] The debate on *aṇaṅku* is ably summarized and analysed by Dubianski 2000: 6–19. Note Burrow's (1979: 283) definition of *aṇaṅku* as 'the possessing spirit' and 'the state of possession.' The wives of the sages would thus be hardly less bewitched than their husbands. Cf. *Tirunĕlvelittalapurāṇam*, *tārukāvaṉaccarukkam* 184 (*māl kŏṇṭa mātavar ĕllām*).

[46] Trawick 1990: 113–16, 257–8.

[47] *Koyiṟ-purāṇam* 3.52; above, p. 79.

strives to achieve; a sign, too, of love.[48] At times, this state or its analogues, marked by the various synonyms of *mayaṅku/mayakkam*, takes the person far beyond normative awareness to highly aberrant mental modes; bewilderment or confusion become ruinous disorder, stupor, sensual flooding, deadly lethargy, overwhelming disturbance. Demonic possession is of the same order: the poet Appar describes himself as the 'owl-like demon' (*pey ŏttuk kūkai*) whose mind is deranged (*maiyal kŏṇ ma<u>n</u>atta<u>n</u> āki*).[49] The sure indication of his condition is that he refuses to know what is false, seductive, or unreal (*māyam* < Skt *māyā*), though knowledge of this other realm is apparently available to him.[50] Such statements could easily be multiplied.

Note the semantic proximity of so many of these notions of madness, whether mild or intense, to active possession—Bhairava's wild and restless state in the village myths from Mel Malaiyanur. This contiguity is expressive of a profound affinity. Indeed, to formulate matters on a general and rather abstract level, it would seem that madness is an intimate potentiality alive in any self, including god's self or selves. A relatively slight shift in orientation, direction, or intensity may make all the difference between the intolerable madness of blockage and possession and the healthy madness of the middle space, where interaction and connection are realized in a fluid way. The former type follows upon severe disjunction, incapacitating the person and cutting him or her off from others as well as from the undefined inner domain of self-in-process; the paradigmatic recourse in such a case is to cut off the lunatic's head. Filling a human being with too much god can produce precisely this impossible state, just as filling up Śiva with too much self, or too many heads, can drive him into a Bhairava-style madness. In this mode, he faces outwards, as it were, in the object-ridden vector of blockage, isolation, and self-emptying. Lucid definition and sharp contours—our prerequisites for sanity or, at the very least, the lessening of anxiety—are, in this context, completely mad. Sorcery regularly aims at such effects. But the *pittu*-madness that melts and ripens is also an enduring divine potential: Śiva is the *pitta<u>n</u>* who un-defines, undermines, and sets in motion; who bubbles over into a space where one can move in any direction, where infinite possibilities exist for combination and re-combination, fusing and con-fusing. Here the madman's

[48] Trawick 1990: 13–14.
[49] Appar *Tevāram* 4.31.7.
[50] Ibid.: *māyattaiy a<u>r</u>iya māṭṭe<u>n</u>.*

mask faces inward and the eye sees itself seeing. It is a deeply inner gaze, flowing into what is seen—not a symbolic interaction or perception, in any sense, but a looking from within at or through the innerness of 'I.'

Once again we have to remember that Śiva's potential modes of existence emerge only in the interior, not in any conceivable exterior, at the moment of coming into subtle, and then less subtle, form, and that they have to be externalized, even for god, if they are to be taken away.

There is a language for just this process. We have been hearing its several tones and nuances in all the passages quoted in this section. 'Madness' is one possible translation, in the distinct patterns just discussed, including the critical distinction between healthy and unhealthy types. There is also the matter of differential intensities or, one might say, of different degrees of emptiness or fullness. Profound emptiness, as in sorcery-induced possession, is fully 'mad.' Overfullness, when the self spills outward and proliferates—like the insatiable growth of Brahmā's heads as Bhairava attacks him—may well be a precisely complementary state, and no more sane. But Śiva swelling into *pittu* together with the devotees who melt or ripen reveals a benign movement toward unconstricted play, seen as antithetical to normative perceptions. We have also seen the term *aghora-rūpa* turning up in the context of mad Bhairava's exorcism by the goddess. She assumes this huge, literally 'non-dreadful' or 'non-terrible' form in order to trample upon (or dance upon) the skull while Śiva, shrunken and terrified, hides behind her. As already stated, she is now reminiscent of the dancing Naṭarāja poised on Muyalakaṉ—she is, that is, in rapid movement, filling up with self. In this mode she can, of course, recognize her husband. But *aghora* is always a euphemism: a god or goddess in this form is 'non-dreadful' in the sense of being extremely dreadful.[51] In such cases, the privative particle *a* actually affirms the attribute it denies. It is, in fact, this culminating, terrifying stage in the intra-divine process that tends to be labelled mad. Even more to the point is the tendency to identify the *aghora-rūpa* of Śiva or the goddess with the *sva-rūpa*, their 'own form or self.'[52]

[51] Thus we find Śiva Aghora-mūrti, the violent 'Non-terrible' (Vīrabhadra), at Tiruvĕṇkāṭu, among many south Indian shrines.

[52] Meyer 221.

The Self Revealed at Lepaksi

A highly condensed but unusually interesting version of the Dāruvana story, from the same border region of Rayalasima that reaches down toward northern Tamil Nadu, explicitly shows us this process of producing the god's 'own self.' Lepaksi, in the south-western corner of Andhra Pradesh, is home to another violent and destructive form of Śiva—Vīrabhadra, the great hero who wrought havoc with the sacrificial rite of Dakṣa, Śiva's father-in-law.[53] Like the sages of the forest, Dakṣa left no room for Śiva in his worship; again like them, he was eventually forced to recognize god as god when Vīrabhadra emerged simultaneously to destroy and to complete the ritual. Implacable resistance once more brings Śiva to the surface and forces him into movement; ultimately Dakṣa, like Brahmā, both loses and regains a head.[54] Vīrabhadra has clear affinities with the no less violent Bhairava; both gods are wild, uncontrolled, 'mad' in the *vĕṟi* sense of blood-induced possession; in both cases, the progression conduces toward a new form of knowledge on the part of the resistant male, Dakṣa or Brahmā. Yet despite this strong emphasis on confrontation with the male and the central role of the male deity Vīrabhadra in the main shrine, Lepaksi is, to a large extent, a temple focused around the goddess in two main guises—the warrior Durgā, who inhabits a pillar as well as the deep space within an adjacent mirror,[55] and the nourishing and bountiful Annapūrṇā, 'Full of Food.' In both these forms, she, too, embodies a process of coming to see, recognize, and know.

Here is how the Lepaksi tradition tells us about this process:

> Satī/Dākṣāyaṇī, Śiva's wife and the daughter of the Prajāpati Dakṣa, died in her father's sacrificial fire after he had refused to invite Śiva to this rite. She was reborn as Pārvatī, daughter of Menā and the Himâlaya. Śiva knew this and wished to test her, so he took the form of a beggar (*bhikṣagāḍu*)—some say as a young child—and came to her house, calling *bhavati bhikṣāṃ dehi*, 'Please give me

[53] The present structure at Lepaksi was completed *c.* 1538, in the reign of Acyutadevarāya—but the temple clearly rests on much earlier cultic foundations. For discussion, see Kameswara Rao 1976; Pachner 1985; Gopala Rao 1969; Shulman, in press (2002).

[54] Dakṣa's new head is that of a goat.

[55] See discussion in Shulman 2003.

> alms.' Pārvatī was in the midst of her bath when she heard this call; she quickly drew a cloth around her body and ran to prepare a bowl full of rice, milk, and ghee. Śiva saw to it that the bowl was full, soaked through with the ghee and milk; at the same time, he made the cloth wrapped around her body slip down. Pārvatī remained entirely engrossed in offering the beggar-boy the food, and paid no heed to her disrobing.[56] Satisfied, Śiva appeared before her in his true form (*nija-svarūpamulo pratyakṣam ainādu*). (Some say he announced at that time: 'Pārvatī is my wife, born as Annapūrṇā—the goddess of food.')[57]

Satī, Śiva's first wife, goes into or through the sacrificial fire and is transformed, as we have seen;[58] she could be said to have crashed through the encrusted exterior of her father's world and to have emerged in the dimension of the middle where she can move freely, fill and become full, and reconnect with Śiva. But this potential of the reborn goddess requires testing. At the same time, her transformed state apparently offers an opportunity for Śiva to come into being, and to become visible, as his true self (*nija-svarūpam*). The two vectors, hers and his, converge in the revelation; neither is fully autonomous alone; god's selfhood is the work of mutuality under conditions of masking and unveiling. Hence the necessary presence of the Beggar, yet again. Hungry in himself, perhaps hungry *for* self, he nonetheless ensures the fullness of the bowl that can feed him. In this case, 'testing' is itself a manner of softening the initial contours enveloping the tested devotee, thus a property continuous with other aspects of the Beggar's role. The Beggar takes away, thereby opening up those parts of Pārvatī that he now takes into himself; his receptivity is the sign of her increasing openness and gentleness and of the intensifying connectedness between the two of them.

In marked contrast with the Tamil versions of the story studied earlier, here sexual hunger is completely displaced, replaced by oral needs and their cognitive or existential implications. Like the shrunken Bhairava

[56] Avvāri Nārāyaṇa adds: 'There was nothing obscene in this moment, only a total engagement in devotion.'

[57] This account follows the prose version of the pamphlet distributed by the temple: Avvāri Nārāyaṇa, no date. It has been supplemented by oral accounts collected at Lepaksi.

[58] Above, p. 95.

at Mel Malaiyanur, still possessed by Brahmā's unappeased skull, Śiva at Lepaksi shrinks into a child's tiny body. All now depends upon the goddess, on her single-mindedness in loving and feeding. Her clothes slip from her body, as in the case of her many analogues among the women of the forest, but she pays no heed; her surface is one with her depth, her nakedness thus in no sense seductive, not a mask—as Siva's nakedness tends to be[59]—but more an open face, fluid with feeling, or an eye seeing itself see.

She is, presumably, staring at the bowl, utterly absorbed in its fullness and intent upon not losing a single drop.[60] This is how she appears in the sixteenth-century painting of this scene above the entrance into the main sanctum (and again on a carved pillar in the magnificent pavilion leading to the sanctum). Beside her or before her, the god bends into the curved space from which he is emerging; even the trees that frame his apparition curve gently around him; his knees are bent, one foot forward, though his face is turned away from the woman (see Figures 3 and 4). As usual, the dwarf Kuṇḍodara carries the begging bowl on his head, and a deer rears up on the left in the hope the god will feed him a leaf.[61] She approaches, moving gently into the space that is already moving through her, her eyes fastened on the gift that will trigger change in god and accelerate *his* movement. Seeing, in this manner, is not a matter of detaching sight from what is seen but rather of curving and flowing into the latter, experiencing the eye as it, too, bends into the arc of acceleration: what we call reflexivity is not an act of splitting but rather a continuous curvature and at the same time a deep gaze inwards toward an emerging 'I.' As always, emergence is interaction. There is nothing symbolic in this scene.

The two parties are on the verge of flowing through one another, just as the rich, buttery milk soaks through the rice. The *nija-svarūpam*, god's own self, can mould itself into visibility only in this manner. At the moment of his complete appearance—full of food, full of her love—she, too, receives a name. Both are present. Śiva has been drawn to the surface in male and female forms. But notice the disparity in proportions as the process unfolds. The god is first a small child in relation

[59] Above, p. 146.

[60] As in the well-known Vedântic parable about Janaka, who was asked to carry a vessel full to the brim with oil around the walls of Ayodhyā without spilling a drop—in order to experience the kind of concentration that makes liberation possible.

[61] See Figure 1, p. 27.

to the full-grown goddess. As at Mel Malaiyanur, the instrumentality of the latter is crucial to the culminating revelation: the goddess feeds the god, fills him, recognizes him, brings him to life, forces him back to his true size. It seems that the worshipper, engaged essentially in exorcising the deity he worships, is initially huge in relation to this same deity. 'Giving' is large, the recipient small, needy, starving, perhaps even close to disappearing. This dynamic exactly replicates the daily task of the Śaiva who positions himself across from the *liṅga* and seeks to conjure up the ensorcelled god from within it in order to free him as well as himself from this unhappy state. As the two parties to this interaction 'take away' the obstacles and objects cluttering space—as they both 'take in' by breathing in, filling themselves and turning to movement in the middle—the god achieves his proper dimensions, the devotee his name.

Śiva's 'self' at Lepaksi thus has at least two related embodiments—the *svarūpa* made visible to himself and others by the gift of milk and rice, and the *aghora-rūpa* of Vīrabhadra, made visible to self and others by open conflict with Satī's father, Dakṣa.[62] If the latter embodiment is mad in the Bhairava mode, the former is probably so in the Bhikṣâṭana persona. These two forms belong to slightly different points in the sequence that takes this god from rather stark, indeed skeletal (and entirely masculine) states toward the spinning fullness and interweaving that we identify with his most active, most knowledgeable presence. It is well to remember that such a sequence must reflect, perhaps before all else, the sequential rituals of manifestation of which we have spoken. Śiva thus goes through sorcery to the integrated, dynamic, and spacious presence that is called *saṃnidhāna*—literally a putting together, the equivalent of Tamil *aruḷ*. Segmented linear narratives reproduce this movement within the deity, re-composing him by verbal means, though in a wider perspective this is always the result of cutting through, somewhat arbitrarily, some small strand of his loops and straightening it into intelligible sequence. It is not impossible to imagine the states of emptiness and fullness, for example, as occurring simultanecusly—the very breath that breathes out creating the space for breathing in. But driven as we are by the linear qualities of language, we can, perhaps, be forgiven for placing the Bhairava-Vīrabhadra moment at a point

[62] There are, of course, still more faces to the god at this shrine, including the *liṅga* known as Pāpa-nāśeśvara, 'the destroyer of evil.' Various disembodied heads, including Dakṣa's, litter the surface.

3. Bhikṣâṭana. Lepaksi, Nāṭya-maṇḍapa. Photograph: David Shulman

4. Pārvatī feeds the begging Śiva. Lepaksi, Nāṭya-maṇḍapa.
Photograph: David Shulman

slightly earlier than the Bhikṣâṭana phase in the continuum of the god's constant self-evolution and devolution. We have followed just such a logic at Cidambaram, and it is interesting to see it reappear, in muted form, at Lepaksi, some ways to the north.

Starvation, that is, is surface blocked from itself (as Brahmā's skull blocks Bhikṣâṭana's feeding), surface seen as external. On such a surface, the cosmos falters and loses its coherence. Sorcery starves selfness by blocking access, from within or without, to other selves. Exorcism unblocks. But we seem to have uncovered a deep complementarity built into the sequence itself. Bhairava takes away but then, as Bhikṣâṭana, is blocked by the sages, who are then taken away themselves, opening space for Naṭarāja. Both the Bhairava and Bhikṣâṭana 'faces' are necessary, and they are mutually dependent. Without blockage, there would be no taking away, and the cosmos would die. Without sorcery, Śiva would not come to be.

We could also state this relation in terms of a perhaps unexpected affinity between the starved and rather violent skeleton or Yogi—Bhairava, Kaṅkāla, Vīrabhadra—and the overfed, overfull Dancer who has reabsorbed the goddess and her liquids within himself, thereby momentarily attaining his 'own self' (*svarūpa*). Surprisingly, Lepaksi itself offers a striking example of this transformation. Adjacent to the carvings of Bhikṣâṭana and Pārvatī in the *nāṭya-maṇḍapa*, discussed above, we find the intriguing, familiar of Bhṛṅgin, usually the hypertrophied male witness to Śiva's dance and to the game of dice.[63] Bhṛṅgin is normally no more than a bag of withered bones, sometimes with a third leg to allow him balance enough to stand—for Bhṛṅgin refused to worship the female as part of Śiva and was therefore cursed by the goddess to lose all female components of his body, specifically his flesh and blood. But the Lepaksi tradition tells us that the third leg was a gift from Śiva, not from the goddess, in response to Bhṛṅgin's request that he be able to dance without pause 24 hours a day; he needed an extra leg so that one of the three, at least, could rest by turns. Thus we find him on the Lepaksi pillar as a soft, fleshy, rather feminine dancer, with pigtails and somewhat equine facial features (Figure 5). The transposition from rigid male to fluid female dancer is striking

[63] Bhṛṅgin is discussed at length in Handelman and Shulman 1997: 87–9, 113–14.

5. Dancing Bhṛṅgin. Lepaksi, Nāṭya-maṇḍapa.
Photograph: David Shulman

enough, and consistent with a more general pattern at Lepaksi; it also suggests two internally related poles of madness and a possible rhythm that connects them. Unbridled growth, or endless taking away—as when Bhairava repeatedly beheads Brahmā—may generate too deep a fullness, too much convexity in space; it literally feeds into the concave hunger of the Beggar. Bhairava gives rise to the bewitched Bhikṣâṭana who is no longer able to take away, since he is blocked by Brahmā's voracious skull. But by the same token, the black magic of the sages, meant to block and destroy Śiva, moves him directly to self-exorcism and the *tāṇḍava* dance.

The cosmos, that is, generates its own blockages through its normal operations, which include the sacrificial act of taking away and opening up space as well as the sorcery inherent in coming into being. The simultaneity and interdependence of these two poles are veiled in the telling of Śiva's stories, though they underlie each of the god's movements. We could now define unhealthy madness, on the basis of these stories, as alternating states of starvation and over-satiety, while healthy madness would be the malleability of play that takes place along the tensile stretch between the two extremes.

A classical statement of the Dāruvana story by Śrīnātha, the fifteenth-century Telugu poet, allows us to see this alternation with unusual clarity. This is the last of the south Indian Dāruvana texts we have to discuss, a lyrical and playful version that also constitutes a bridge to north Indian variants derived from the Sthāṇu pattern centered on the falling *liṅga*.[64]

Śrīnātha: *Hara-vilāsamu* 5.3-68[65]

The wedding[66] was over, and Love
brought back to life. The gods were sent off
to their homes. All Śiva's attendants
were serving him on the Himâlaya, where he

[64] Above, pp. 33–5.

[65] The translation is the work of Velcheru Narayana Rao and David Shulman. See Narayana Rao and Shulman 2002 (2). We omit verses 9, 20–7, 34, 50–1; and see note 86 below. Śrīnātha composed the *Hara-vilāsamu*, a compilation of Śaiva stories, under the patronage of Avaci Tippayya Sĕṭṭi, a wealthy merchant from Nelluru in southern Andhra. Some of the materials (for example, the Siriyāla story, set in Kancipuram) relate specifically to this border region of Telugu-Tamil speech.

[66] Of Śiva and Pārvatī, described in the preceding canto.

had accepted the joys of family life
and the burdens a new house entails.

Together with his Pramathas and the Seven Mothers and Nandikeśvara,
the lord of all three worlds was living in his father-in-law's house.[67]
He must really love his new wife!

He discarded his snakes and now wore golden threads.
He put off the elephant's raw skin in favour of fine silk clothes.
He stopped smearing himself with ashes, and took up sandal paste and musk.
He lost his taste for necklaces of bones, and instead covered himself with
strings of pearls.
He wore a fine headdress, the crescent moon fixed in the middle.
The Enemy of Desire was feasting, a new son-in-law in his wife's house.

Black-Neck rode galloping horses
through the streets of Oṣadhi-prasthā City,[68]
his hangers-on riding on either side.
His bull was left behind.

Fearless with harsh laughter, moon-sharp swords,
eyes red as burning coals, bold wide chests,
imposing forms, necks bright as conch,
and matted locks, Śiva's servants, firm as mountains,

had free run of the city, especially the streets of paid women.
Who was there to stop them?
They could face down Death himself.

They threw tiger-skins on the customers of Vidyādhara women
as they ran away. They pounded the lovers of Gandharva girls
with sticks and shamed them. They threw ash into the eyes
of men who came to sleep with an Apsaras
and whipped visitors to the Eagle Women
with their yogic straps. All the houses of heaven were boiling
with rage at these ruffians and hooligans and louts.

While these followers of the god were making such a nuisance of themselves in Oṣadhi-prasthā, Himavān[69] came to know. He consulted his wife Menakā, and they decided that they had had enough of Śiva. So he called his daughter and said:

[67] *illaṭamu*, modern Telugu *illarikamu*, living in the in-laws' home, is seen as a somewhat humiliating state for a new son-in-law.

[68] Oṣadhi-prasthā is the 'City of Herbs' on Mount Himâlaya.

[69] Himâlaya, Śiva's new father-in-law.

'My dear, your husband honours these rowdies,
the numberless Pramathas and ghouls and spirits.

Night and day, they are causing calamities
to people of all eighteen castes.

Thousands of times every day they get drunk on the honeyed liquor
they get from the wishing-trees. Then they start up with the gods' women.
Your husband has such awful friends—Jaṅgamas, Muṇḍas, Kāpālikas,
Kālāmukhas, and Vīra-Pāśupatas, with all their skulls and skins.

Can't Black-Neck put a stop to all this hooliganism,
this continuous insult to the good people in heaven and earth?

Herons honk as they hunt fish in the Ganges he carries in his hair.
The skulls he wears around his neck keep clattering and rattling against
one another.
The tail of the tiger skin rubs the back of the bull he rides, and makes him
bellow.
The snakes he wears as bracelets start hissing whenever ash from his pouch
spills into their eyes.
To the sounds of this chorus, he holds out Brahmā's skull
as he goes from street to street and demands in a ringing voice:
"Give me food." He prefers the food he begs for
to our palace delicacies.'

As he was talking, Śiva, lord of all the worlds,
knew how tired his father-in-law was, in his heart,
and also how much trouble lovers were having
because of his friends. So he thought of going
to the Forest of Pines.

He mounted his bull and, together with a few attendants, without taking leave of his father-in-law or saying anything to his wife, went through the sky to the Forest of Pines, which was in a corner of that mountain.

Lotuses with gold, diamonds in the centre,
bowers of wish-giving vines, pedestals studded
with all-giving stones, rivers that promise eternal youth,
brilliant women of the gods, whole herds of cows
that fulfil your want, strings of glowing herbs,
bright as lamps, with all seasons meeting in one place:
that was the Forest of Pines, where gods and sages worshipped,
on the slopes of the Snow Mountain.

The sages living there were each as handsome as the love-god,
and their wives more beautiful than the wives of the gods.

Fine golden silk set off the firmness of their breasts.
Beads of sweat at the edge of their curls smudged the musk-dot
on their foreheads. Their braids, slightly loosened,
were a deeper black than night itself. Earrings, golden
and studded with gems, reflected off their smooth cheeks.
As they fetched water from waterfalls in golden pots
and poured it over young vines, their bracelets chimed
through that peaceful place.

Fragrant smoke rising from the three sacred fires
used for Jyotiṣṭoma and other rites
drove evil from that region.

Cuckoos sang all the seven Sāman notes. Bees buzzed out
the mantra OM. Parrots and mynah birds recited the ritual texts.[70]
Peacocks gently discoursed on scientific disciplines.[71]

As for the sages, they kept Desire at a distance—along with
anger, pride, greed, jealousy, envy, excess, and conceit.
They were all descendants of noble families, of quiet minds,
subsisting on wild rice according to their vow.

From time to time, the sages' wives would rest from their household chores
by cooling moonstones in the shade of camphor-banana plants,[72]
their fragrance carried through the forest by a soft breeze.

Exhausted by housework, they would bathe their sweat-soaked bodies
in mountain streams, playing water-games with one another
in the early afternoons.

They bathe in turmeric in the limpid water of mountain streams,
peacock tails in their hair, and they dress themselves in peacock feathers,
beads and leaves on their breasts.[73]
The black dot on their forehead is made of rice-soot
mixed with oil. Red buds[74] swing from their ears, and pollen

[70] The Āgamas.

[71] Śāstras.

[72] *karpūra-rambha* is a species of banana (*karpūra-cakkara-keḷi*), unusually fragrant and delicious, local to the Godavari region of Andhra.

[73] Small beads of the *guruvinda* are black on the bottom, red on top.

[74] Of the *kaṅkeḷi* tree.

dusts their hair. The sages' daughters[75] play
at being wild Cěñcu women,[76] dressing up in their mothers' presence
when their fathers are away.

This is how these girls would spend their days:
playing in streams, watching peacocks dance, with spreading tails,
and the spectacular moonrise of full-moon nights, collecting flowers,
playing catch with bouquets, searching for fresh coral
on the sandy banks of mountain rivers, pretending to water the vines
with tiny golden pots carried in their dolls' tiny hands, and preparing
all that is needed to welcome a guest—water to sip, water to wash,
fruits and honey, puffed rice, *darbha* grass, coral, sandal paste, flowers,
yellow rice, and all the rest.

The Forest of Pines was home to fourteen dynasties of celestial pleasure-women, who came there to break the discipline of the sages. Each clan of women had its own quarter, marked by a decorated flag that proclaimed their source and tale of origin, as follows: Solar Sphere, Lightning Bolts, Gaping Mouth of Death, Nārāyaṇa's Thigh, Vedic Chants, Flames of Fire, Bow of Desire, Burning Eye of Śiva, the Two Gandharva Families, and so on. Every house had its walls painted with exciting stories, each stimulating a special mood, so you could see Manmatha, the god of desire, resting his head on Rati's round breasts while straightening out his flower-arrows, his eyes squinting as he worked; or Parāśara's rising passion, as he stared openly, in broad daylight in the middle of the river, at Yojanagandhā's big breasts;[77] or the Moon gently flirting with Tārā, the wife of his guru, Bṛhaspati;[78] or Viśvāmitra drunk with love, kissing the gods' whore[79] in the privacy of a *guruvinda* bush on the sandy banks of the Mālinī river; or Ṛṣyaśṛṅga overcome by love for many women—the ultimate triumph of Desire;[80] or Kṛṣṇa's display of adulterous love with

[75] Note this unusual reference to the presence of young girls in the Dāruvana.

[76] Cěñcu are tribals living in Andhra. (Śiva at Srisailam is married to Cěñcu-Nāyakī, a tribal woman, as his second bride.)

[77] The sage Parāśara fell in love with the daughter of the fisherman as she ferried him in a boat across the river; as a result of their union, Vyāsa was born.

[78] Candra, the Moon, fell in love with Tārā, and she with him, and they consummated their passion during Bṛhaspati's absence; the child born of this union was Budha. Eventually, Bṛhaspati won his wife back from Candra with the help of the gods' army (the so-called *Tārakā-maya* war).

[79] Menakā, sent by Indra to seduce the sage from his discipline.

[80] Ṛṣyaśṛṅga grew up in isolation, in the forest, and never saw a woman until King Daśaratha sent a group of courtesans to seduce him, as the necessary precondition for performing the sacrifice out of which Rāma would be born. At first Ṛṣyaśṛṅga mistook the women for an odd variety of deer, with horns on their chests, but soon he was overtaken by desire.

the cowherdesses of Vraj; or Brahmā losing his mind and running after his own daughter; or Indra seducing Ahalyā under cover.[81] In these houses lived, one by one, Tilottamā, the most beautiful of all celestial women; Pramlocā, who keeps the God of Desire under her control; Rambhā, her breasts proudly bearing the scratches and love-marks of her lover, Nalakūbara; Sukeśī, truly outstanding; Mañjughoṣā, of the seductive voice; Urvaśī, liquid with love; and Menakā, in whom all feminine beauty has come to rest. These remarkable women held sway over all three worlds by their captivating looks, the way they would glide through the streets, playfully exposing their lithe waists, their golden anklets chiming, and by the luminous smiles that stole across their faces and their delicious murmuring tones.

Śiva came, hungry for women,[82] to that Forest of Pines.
He sent Nandikeśvara to graze in some grassy spot.
He asked the Pramathas to worship the *liṅga* beside a lake.
He left the ghouls and spirits to wander as they will on a sandy beach.
He ordered the Seven Mothers to rest in a cave.
With a golden bowl, a green staff, yogi's band and pouch,
kohl in his eye, a delicate dot on his forehead, and a garland of crystals,
beautifully dressed, he went begging for alms in the courtesans' streets.

Pramlocā offered him alms: rice and cakes,
banana and ghee. She served him with her own hands,
the precious stones in her rings casting light and colour
where she touched.

Rambhā fed him—the enemy of Love—
on more bananas, and mangoes too. It was a splendid feast
he ate, staring at the nailmarks left on her breasts
by her heavenly lover, Kubera's son.[83]

Toe-rings and anklets chiming together,
flashing finger-rings reflected in her nails,
pearl necklaces tracing the line of her breasts,
dangling earrings dancing doubled on her glossy cheeks,
Mañjughoṣā came toward him, Desire's Foe,
with a golden pot overflowing with butter, honey,
sugar, fruits, rice, and a milky pudding.

[81] Indra disguised himself as Gautama, Ahalyā's husband, in order to make love to Ahalyā.

[82] *miṇḍa-jaṅgama*, a playboy Śaiva mendicant.

[83] Nalakūbara, Rambhā's usual lover. In serving Śiva, she presumably bent over him, exposing her breasts.

Now it was Hariṇī's turn:
milk and sugar, ghee, and honey,
grapes, pomegranates, and mangoes, all given as alms
with love unfolding in her eyes.

Gracious and elegant, Urvaśī brought Himâlaya's son-in-law,
Pinākin the elephant-killer,[84] white rice, ghee from cow's milk,
jaggery, soft pulp of coconut meat, and ripe fruit, served
with longing.

Tilottamā gave him
the woman's gift
with candied jaggery and ghee
in a golden bowl, the sash of her sari
slipping slightly from her shoulders
as she bent and his three eyes feasted
on the contours of her breasts.

Sahajanyā spread a banquet before him,
her breasts, pressing against her arms,
bursting from her sari:
this was the offering proper to the moment.

So these divine women—Vidyullekhā, Viśvāsī, Citrarekhā, and others—skilled as actresses on stage, gave him alms with greedy glances from the corner of the eye. And he, who killed Desire, was honoured at every door with sandal and flowers and incense and lights. Still unsated by the alms he received in the courtesans' streets, the skull of Brahmā in his hand still only half full, he took himself, magic sandals tapping, to the quarter where the sages lived. He stood in front of their houses and called with the deep tones of a thundercloud, '*Bhavati bhikṣāṃ dehi*: Lady, I beg food of you.' He winked at the housewives and flashed a smile, for his main goal now was to undo the chastity of the sages' wives. And he strolled around, exposing his desire with double meanings, whenever the opportunity arose.

With gentle smiles, his eyebrows dancing,
jokes and knowing, greedy glances,
the Great Lord stole the hearts of the sages' wives
as he went playing, wildly, through the Forest of Pines.

With the moon in his hair, he inspired sexual longing
in all those married women, some with children and grandchildren,
chaste, entirely devoted to their husbands, and pure,
from all the well-known, ancient Brahmin lineages.[85]

[84] Śiva as slayer of Gajâsura, the elephant demon.

[85] A long list is given of the famous Brahmin sages, from prestigious families, whose wives are involved.

He went from house to house, begging for food, intent on the business of secret sexual delight, as desire demanded, and on deceiving their husbands. He waited for the moment when the men were away—twilight and dawn, when they would leave home to gather firewood, darbha grass, and fruit, to perform the rituals. Then he would give the wives the ultimate ecstasy of love—biting their lips with a vengeance, but holding back the heavy breathing, talking very little, quickly bringing them to orgasm, all in the fear of being discovered. They would send him love-letters and seductive messengers, setting up rendezvous in the bushy bowers, and he would respond with winks and lewd looks from the corners of his eyes and quivering smiles. Still, he was not tired in the least.

He kept on begging, standing in the middle of the main street,
holding his axe, with a soft tiger's skin of three colors tied
to his waist and the serpent Karkoṭaka as his turban,
and other smooth little snakes hanging from his long ears,
his body smeared with the ashes of Desire, and the baby moon
with its cool light held on his head, and a fawn poised
on two fingernails, the elephant's freshly flayed skin
draped around him, a staff with bells jingling in his hand
as he held out the skull of Brahmā, a bowl plated with gold.

In this way the god who killed Desire, now blind himself with passion and out of control, ruined the fidelity of the sages' wives. The sages came to know of this, hearing it from one another, and they were buzzing with it, but unable to expose the scandal to view; they held it in, until it was simply no longer possible to hide what was happening in every home. Ganging up, they surrounded him, in order to catch hold of him.

He, the killer of Desire, was smiling slightly,
pleased with himself, standing where everyone could see him,
as the sages struggled to grab him.[86]

Now, while eight-formed Śiva was playing these rowdy games, the heads of houses were manhandling him; so he threw off his loincloth and made his *liṅga*—long as the trunk of Airāvata, Indra's elephant—stand up erect, and with that powerful weapon he hit those Brahmins on the head, nape, earlobes, faces, noses, bruising them. He struck them with it on the back, made their teeth fall out, rubbed against their chests, poked up their anuses, attacked their shanks, and smashed against their knees, paralysing them, chasing after them, yelling loudly. He extended his *liṅga* up to the sky, as if it were a golden handle for the canopy of heaven, studded with pearl-like stars. And he bathed it in

[86] The passage breaks off at this point (the Vavilla edition prints dotted lines); at least one verse is missing. What follows is taken from other manuscript versions of the text (printed as an appendix in the modern editions); we see no reason to doubt Śrīnātha's authorship of it.

the water of the heavenly Ganges descending, step by step, through the worlds of sun and moon. He pressed it against the very zenith of the egg-shaped cosmos.

The gods, Garuḍas, flying Vidyādharas, Kinnaras,
Siddhas, Sādhyas, and anti-gods
bowed to this long, erect *liṅga*
with suitable devotion

and began to praise it. Brahmā watered it from his water-pot with a thousand streams as it reached up to his world, and worshipped it with sandal paste, flowers, incense, lights, food offerings, and betel. He prostrated full length before it and sang:

'All praise to Śiva's *liṅga*,
the shining *liṅga*,
the *liṅga* that emerged erect,
the *liṅga* of the three Vedas,
the unmarked,[87]
the touchable *liṅga*,
the forgiving *liṅga*,
the *liṅga* of good thought,
the only natural *liṅga* . . .
undifferentiated in time or space,
the self-born *liṅga*, the *liṅga* of the underworld,
the *liṅga* of action,
the *liṅga* of five syllables,[88]
the *liṅga* of five modes,
the *liṅga* that stands in Varanasi, Gaya, the two Rudra shrines, in Srisaila, Sonacala,[89] Tiger-Town,[90] and all the rest,
the unmeasurable *liṅga*,
the *liṅga* of knowledge,
the *liṅga* of the six schools,
the *liṅga* of the ritual texts,
the securely established,
housed in the triangle,[91]
the *liṅga* of ecstasy flowing with thick ambrosia from the opening at the top of one's head,[92] reached by connective lightning that flashes deep inside the six lotus-ponds of intuitive insight,[93]

[87] *Liṅga* means 'a mark.'
[88] *namaḥ śivāya,* 'homage to Śiva'—the Śaiva mantra.
[89] Arunacalam/Tiruvannamalai, in northern Tamil Nadu.
[90] Cidambaram.
[91] Presumably, the *yoni*.
[92] The *brahma-randhra*, an invisible aperture through which the Yogi aspires to elevate his inner energies.
[93] The six *cakras*?

the *liṅga* known to have no beginning, no middle, no end,
the staff *liṅga*,
the snake *liṅga*,
the *liṅga* of the heavenly river,
the *liṅga* of the antelope,
the *liṅga* of the self-born,
the *aim-liṅga*, *im-liṅga*, *om-liṅga*,
the *liṅga* that sprinkles divine syllables,
the *liṅga* of Virūpâkṣa, "Three-Eyes."'

Brahmā and Sarasvatī worshipped this weapon of Black Neck with golden lotuses, and Brahmā said, hands folded in devotion:

'Withdraw it before the cosmos cracks.
Relax it, before the path of stars is disturbed.
Make it soft, lest the Seven Winds are blocked.
Let go of your power, lest the ends of space crumble.
Pull it back, stop this defiance, let it become supple,
leave it, your ever-so-lovable *liṅga*.'

Śiva listened well, laughed a wild laugh, and said,
so that all the world could hear:
'You sages, gods, demons,
my incomparable *liṅga* is worthy of worship
from now on.

I will happily bring into my company
whoever worships the *liṅga*
with a good heart. . . .'[94]

Śiva froze his big *liṅga* in that erect form that had swallowed the whole universe like a glutton. Then the householders living in the Forest of Pines folded their hands in worship and gave up the flaw of jealousy. They devoted themselves to the god draped with serpents and achieved pleasure and release.

Anyone who writes down this story of the games of the Forest of Pines, or who recites it, or hears it, or talks of it, or appreciates it, will achieve whatever he or she desires.

Liṅga as Curve

More than any other version we have studied, Śrīnātha's Telugu masterpiece of Śaiva mythology takes the god through strongly contrasting states and displays the radically distinct, context-sensitive textures of

[94] This verse is incomplete.

his inner experience. The profound seriousness and intensity of playfulness—*vilāsa*, as the title of the work states—is apparent throughout. The game moves Śiva from an initial condition of severe depletion and division to a fullness so abundant that it overflows and nearly drowns him, leaving him dwarfed by the seemingly autonomous *liṅga* generated or set free by the whole series of events. Ironic touches abound, beginning with the surprising portrait of the newly-married god as largely exhausted, hemmed in, unhappy, perhaps even lacking in erotic interest.

Marriage, it seems, constricts and empties Śiva. He truly loves his wife, and for this reason he is prepared to put up with the humiliating status of the new son-in-law in his father-in-law's home. But in this oddly domesticated mode, Śiva has become deeply impoverished. His salient attributes have been discarded—no more snakes, no elephant skin, no ashes or necklaces of bones. He has lost aspects of himself in the process of settling down on the Himâlaya. Moreover, these outward signs of the god are not merely external realities. As we know from other versions of the Dāruvana story, it is Śiva's bizarre appearance, complete with snakes, ash, skulls, and so on, that makes him so irresistibly attractive. These attributes are never incidental to his nature. The ash he smears over his body is the product of his inner fire—that is, his inner liquidity and continuous movement. This fire now appears to have gone out. The silken clothes and golden ornaments he wears at home are not blackened or burnt.

Śiva as newly-wed is thus emptied and diminished, very much as in the game of dice that he plays with Pārvatī.[95] He has, in a sense, transferred these pieces of himself to her, or sacrificed them for her sake. The story of the Dāruvana, here as in other versions we have examined, is, on one level, that of the god's reclaiming his lost components or integral parts. Denuded by virtue of the ebbing and flow of his own internal processes, in this case his love for Pārvatī and attack upon Desire, Śiva waits, rather helpless, for some way to escape the golden cage.

Even in this occluded and limited state, he naturally and unconsciously drifts into the Beggar's role, as if this were the latent, primary persona always seeking to come to the surface. We see this in the culminating passage of his father-in-law's complaint:

[95] See Handelman and Shulman 1997.

'Herons honk as they hunt fish in the Ganges he carries in his hair.
The skulls he wears around his neck keep clattering and rattling against
one another.
The tail of the tiger skin rubs the back of the bull he rides, and makes him
bellow.
The snakes he wears as bracelets start hissing whenever ash from his pouch
spills into their eyes.
To the sounds of this chorus, he holds out Brahmā's skull
as he goes from street to street and demands in a ringing voice:
"Give me food." He prefers the food he begs for
to our palace delicacies.'

The rich food at the family table clearly cannot fill the god's true emptiness or satisfy his hunger. Only alms that he begs taste real. The cacophony aroused by his more familiar attributes, beautifully imitated in the Telugu by an onomatopoeic series, suggests the living, discordant presence veiled by the bourgeois guise. This presence is, of course, just what disturbs his new relatives. No one wants to live too close to god.

There is another sign of Śiva's distress on the mountain—the wild fury of his *gaṇa* retainers, who are clearly living out, in a split-off manner, the furious and unconfined aspect of their master. If he has become strangely passive and detached, they, for their part, are actively aggressive, noisy, annoying. Among other things, they attack lovers who are visiting the celestial courtesans—a strong anti-erotic trend that seems to resonate with Śiva's own largely extinguished state. Passion, connection, physical and emotional fusion—all 'middle' states or themes—are temporarily abrogated in the vicinity of this overly domesticated, docile god and his uncontrolled retainers. Manmatha, Love, is being destroyed again.

Perhaps most striking in all this is the sense that Śiva seems not to be aware of what his own *gaṇa*s are doing. He learns about it by eavesdropping on his father-in-law's conversation with Pārvatī. Śiva is out of touch with his split and polarized selves. He has, to begin with, split into a formal, ritually reinforced Śiva-Pārvatī existence, clearly circumscribed by domesticity (and very similar to the split that allows him to enter into the dice-game with his separate female persona, to whom he habitually loses). Then there is the additional split into god vs. *gaṇa*s, one as against many, a further externalization and emptying of his integral being. 'Normal' living induces fragmentation in this refractory deity as it does in all of us. Sorcery—the bewildering blockage and opacity that affect, to greater or lesser degree, all ongoing social life, interpersonal and kinship relations, and individual awareness—is a dynamic of cosmos, no different for god than for human beings. Thus Śiva's life on Himâlaya is a series of variations on the theme of 'otherness,' that is, two-ness, an unacceptable eventuality for such a god. Suddenly, he is surrounded by tangible others, by autonomized pieces of himself that have truly detached themselves from him, and that he barely recognizes as his. At best, he can overhear one of these other beings telling the truth about his state. Passivity, epistemic failure, unappeased hunger, and a certain static helplessness are all diagnostic signs of his illness.

None of this is unfamiliar after our extrapolations from the Tamil versions of the story, but the extremity of Śiva's distress is nonetheless very impressive. Once again, as at Nelveli, he has devolved toward a kind of edge of limit, where existential otherness has become a real possibility within god's range. He can become so empty that he utterly fails to know himself for who he is. Trapped, limited, and occluded, he is in danger of falling into far-reaching forgetfulness, as if the demon Apasmāra-Muyalakaṉ actually constituted his own horizon, as if this demon were momentarily Śiva's own external face. For Śrīnātha, as for the authors of the Tamil Dāruvana texts, the Dāruvana exists in order to heal the god of his disorder—to re-compose him, fill him, and re-activate him from the outside. That Śiva can devolve to this degree suggests that his calibration within the cosmic system is far from stable. Śiva, like other living beings, can never be certain that he will not lose his innerness, that the process of creation and self-definition will not destroy that which makes him unalterably him to himself—his density, the dense interconnectedness of knowledge and feeling that might be called 'self.'[96]

A certain empathy allows the first suggestion of movement. 'Śiva, lord of the worlds, knew how tired his father-in-law was, in his heart.' He is also aware of how much trouble lovers are experiencing. Saying nothing to anyone, not even to his new bride, without taking leave of his father-in-law—as a proper son-in-law should—he simply leaves

[96] See Dasgupta 1969: 25 on the distinctiveness of 'self;' below, 'Conclusion'.

for the Forest of Pines, which turns out to be in another corner of this same mountain. Perhaps this location, too, should not surprise us. Unlike some visions of the Dāruvana, Śrīnātha's portrait of this critical site of transformation suggests a powerful continuity with the god's point of departure. Here the Dāruvana is at once radiantly beautiful, indeed paradisiac, and eerily static and empty. Śiva chooses a site that is all too like the celestial city he has left behind. In effect, he wanders into a frozen, externalized landscape made up of his own detached and crystallized fragments. He is re-entering his externalized self.

There is no doubt that the forest is a rather charming place. Flowers and vines are studded with diamonds and gold. Various rivers and cows supply any wish. Birds recite the Vedas and other texts from wherever they have perched (can they still fly?). You can smell the sweet fragrance of smoke rising from the sages' rituals. Not much effort is required in any domain, though housewives like to rest from their chores in the early afternoon. Women and young girls, who can be found there in profusion, have time for swimming, ball games, and moonrise picnics. The sages themselves are pacific creatures, noble-minded, free of anger, desire, greed. In short, the Dāruvana is perfect for a short vacation. The depleted Śiva has chosen well.

The trouble is that nothing ever happens there. Indeed, time itself has stopped: all the seasons are bunched up and superimposed in a single atemporal, unchanging moment. Herbs glow like lamps (there is apparently no shade, no contrast). A certain deadly perfection reigns supreme. The forest reveals a world of extreme order, with everything in its proper place. All that breathes is drawn into the timeless cycles of ritual and recitation. Even the courtesans who live there—each in her proper house in the quarter allocated to her clan, with the flag and title and wall-painting appropriate to her station—are somehow static and subdued. They came there 'to break the discipline of the sages,' and clearly they have failed. For the moment, they are simply waiting.

This forest is a rather empty setting. The sages have emptied themselves of all emotion and are busy only with rituals, probably performed mechanically. These rituals seem to bear no fruit. Everything goes on in its given rhythm, never accelerating or breaking through to something new. Indeed, novelty has no place in this utopia. Neither does evil or, to use a milder term, the possibility of making a mistake. Any real connection between living beings may also be ruled out: the husbands subsist on wild rice; apparently their wives do not cook for them; indeed, there seems to be no relationship at all between males and females. They live utterly separate lives. The anti-erotic stance of the *gaṇa*s on Himâlaya, which resonates with Śiva's own frozen state, is further solidified and intensified in the forest. The only hints of movement or action come from the women, who can play with one another, pretend to be someone else (wild Cĕñcu women), enjoy the landscapes, especially the local bodies of water.

In no other text we have seen is the setting of Śiva's adventure so uniform or perfect. The Dāruvana is frozen in a mode of apparent oneness, lacking contrast, lacking shadows, with little space for movement of any kind. Not by chance, there are only daughters here, probably generated asexually; the sexual production of male offspring, always rife with paradox and tension in relation to the father, is too violent to contemplate. The very beauty of the forest precludes longing and frustration. What is there to long for? What is there to feel? Still, in relation to Śiva, the forest is separate or cut off—this is a two-ness experienced from within as oneness—and we should remember that the sages themselves fail to feel how frozen they are, and how remote from god. They are fragments utterly unaware of their own fragmentation. In this respect, there is already an incipient contrast with Śiva's evolving state.

Into this relatively inert domain, Śiva abruptly enters in the mode of apparent two-ness. He is divided in self, diminished, disintegrated, and moving toward the linear sequence of the Beggar. His appearance in this state—alone, 'hungry for women,' his *gaṇa*s and other retainers left behind—will crack the forest open. No sooner does he arrive than he starts begging for alms.

Two separate phases ensue. First he is fed milky, soft foods by the seductive courtesans, who perhaps begin to arouse him without actually entering into overt sexual acts, without even articulating such desires (in contrast to the brazen women of the *Kanta-purāṇam*). Their task is to begin to fill him. They soften his hardness, start to heal his loneliness and isolation; they are, of course, all curves and flow, or overflow, and he takes their curvature into himself, thereby melting or bending the harsh linearity that has propelled him toward this meeting. Slowly, he swells and grows. Then, still 'unsated' (*tanivi sanaka*), he moves on into the streets where the sages' wives live. Begging for food, he plays with them, exposing his desire, inflaming theirs. His main goal is now 'to undo the chastity of the sages' wives.' Unlike the courtesans in relation to the sages, Śiva enjoys astonishing success. Śrīnātha revels in the details of the amorous trysts, the love-letters, flirtations, the furtive joys quickly satisfied. This is nothing like a trial or masquerade, no mock seduction by a false libertine, but the manifold enactment of Śiva's 'own desire' (*nijâbhilāṣambu*, 52), openly revealed. He is 'intent on the business of secret sexual delight' (*cora-rata-vyāpāra-pārāyaṇuṇḍai*, 55). The secret is integral to the playfulness. This god is heating up, filling himself with the women's love, accelerating, moving internally, tasting passion, losing control.

And still he remains the Beggar:

> He kept on begging, standing in the middle of the main street,
> holding his axe, with a soft tiger's skin of three colours tied
> to his waist and the serpent Karkoṭaka as his turban,
> and other smooth little snakes hanging from his long ears,
> his body smeared with the ashes of Desire, and the baby moon
> with its cool light held on his head, and a fawn poised
> on two fingernails, the elephant's freshly flayed skin
> draped around him, a staff with bells jingling in his hand
> as he held out the skull of Brahmā, a bowl plated with gold. [56]

At last, Śiva looks like himself again. Not only are his parts and attributes in place, but he is also acting like himself—wild, discordant, seductive, scandalous, disorderly. Everything that was lost in his father-in-law's household has come back to him. A rich liquidity bathes both this god and his illicit lovers; as they fill him and flow into him, he fills them with their own, no longer modulated feeling. Śiva has recovered a female persona by activating the femininity of these ignored and pious wives. The interaction itself is generative. For the first time in the frozen forest, someone wants to take from them that which they have always wanted to give—food, sexual aliveness, feeling. The forest itself begins to thaw. Somehow, Śiva has moved into a dimension of abundance. This, incidentally, is the last we hear of Brahmā's ravenous skull.

If we focus only on the god's progress, we observe something like maturation. It is almost as if he were evolving from child to mature male—sucking up milk, learning to walk, finding his balance, positioning himself vis-à-vis others, collecting pieces of himself from the outside and putting them back into play. The courtesans welcome him like a god (with sandal, flowers, incense, lights) and offer him food fit for a god. Through their offerings, he begins to know that he is, indeed, the being they think he is. They bring him to the surface and make him present by replenishing his desiccated interior.[97] He has, we may assume, forgotten that he is Śiva. Feeding him, they remind him. More precisely, they bring him into being. For Śiva does not exist as Śiva in the Forest of Pines until he arrives there in a desperate state. The forest is empty of Śiva before he comes, as he is himself empty of awareness, empty in self. He is, we might say, the sorcerer ensorcelled. Stasis usually reflects just such an occlusion of knowledge or awareness: something is missing, connections are attenuated or torn apart, movement dies away. In this sense, the courtesans could be said to begin the work of exorcism on this god, who emerges into tenuous selfhood under their ministrations, much as the god repeatedly undergoes a process of exorcism with the help of his worshippers in the morning *liṅga*-worship, day after day. The courtesans, by feeding, giving out, position Śiva in the mode of taking in, which is also a taking away, hence an opening up of middle space, ripe with mutuality. Note this relation: *giving out* to *taking in* or *taking away*. All social experience may finally be modelled after these terms, as we shall see. In any case, the densely interconnected being who knows himself as Śiva is a creation of his experience in this episode, first with the two classes of women, then with the enraged husbands.

This latter element takes a new form in Śrīnātha's text, almost as if one narrative plot (the Tamil Dāruvana) slips unconsciously into another (the classical northern one).[98] Of course, the sages must attack the god, though not, in this case, by a rite of black magic. In keeping with the tangible physicality of this entire version, they grab at him with their hands, poking and mauling him. He fights back—or perhaps it is his *liṅga* that fights back, at first under his intention and guidance, but very soon as an autonomous force. This vast *liṅga* swallows up the god and then threatens to swallow up the rest of his cosmos. Like the *tāṇḍava* dance as it attains its rapid rhythm, the *liṅga* could suck

[97] Just as Gaṅgamma at Tirupati, who is lost in the recesses of her self, comes to know herself as a goddess by the way her devotees welcome her into their houses: Handelman 1995: 325–6.

[98] See Appendix (*Kūrma-purāṇa* 2. 37).

everything back into itself, filling itself with whatever was once outside the god.

His state, obviously, has radically changed. Interweaving himself with the sages' wives, enhanced and inflated with their love, he is 'blind with passion and out of control' (*madanonmādambunan gannu gānaka . . . viccalaviḍi jariyimpa*, 57). We could also translate these phrases into a condition of madness (*unmāda*) and uninhibited freedom to act (*viccalavidi*).[99] Spinning at high speed, Śiva has moved from hollowness and dependence to complete independence, the primary indication of his godly nature at its fullest realization.[100] He is free and, being free, he takes away.[101] Full and unconfined, he is free to become 'Śiva'—for the first time in this version. His *liṅga* takes in the cosmos, taking the cosmos away from within itself, subsuming all space by sucking or breathing it into himself—up to the point where the god, acceding to Brahmā's prayer, freezes it, 'lest the ends of space crumble.' By taking space away, Śiva effectively holds the cosmos together through its interior, thereby, however, threatening all visible, surface objects with extinction. Beginning as a sort of mobile extension of Śiva, a weapon he can use to poke and pound and batter the sages, the *liṅga* grows and expands beyond god himself. Yet this *liṅga* that has 'swallowed the whole universe like a glutton' still somehow belongs properly and uniquely to Śiva (*nikhila-brahmâṇḍa-sambhāra-kukṣimbhariy agu nija-mahāliṅga-stambhambu*, 68): it is his own (*nija*) great *liṅga*, that he can still, at the last moment before the cosmos crumbles, fix in place.

In the northern *purāṇic* versions of the Dāruvana, Śiva allows his *liṅga* to fall to earth in response to the sages' curse.[102] Often this moment is accompanied by cataclysmic violence, until the *liṅga* is stabilized in its ritual setting and held in place by the *yoni*. In this standard image, it could be said to emerge continuously outward from the *yoni* into the world and to allow for the ritual activization of Śiva's presence in this form. In another sense, the *liṅga-yoni* unit are an ongoing process of male-female exchange and fluid transformation,

[99] *viccalaviḍi* = *svātantryamu*, 'independence' or *svecchā-pravṛtti*, 'acting at will,' according to the *Sūryarāyândhra nighaṇṭuvu*, s.v.

[100] See pp. 56–61 on Śiva as *svatantra*. Cf. *Ānanda-sāgara-stava* of Nīlakaṇṭha Dīkṣita 3 (the goddess as the being most free, *svatantra*, in the cosmos).

[101] Above, p. 59, for this linkage; *Śiva-jñāna-bodha*, *sūtra*s 1 and 2.

[102] See pp. 33–6.

each element generating and flowing into the other, becoming the other, moving through the other, driving god further through his coils and turns. In the always ambiguous transition from god to phenomenal world, the *yoni* is the membrane through which god exhales himself into the world, while the *liṅga* is a form of innerness creating its own, non-external surface. But in Śrīnātha's powerful description, the *liṅga* itself is strangely aggressive, openly sexual, hungry, and destructive, and there seems to be no *yoni* present (outside of Brahmā's mention of the 'triangle,' *koṇa-trayī-geha*). The wildness of god leaves no room in the world for anything other than itself. And yet this deep core of Śiva as motion into and beyond the world, into and beyond a full self, apparently undergoes a change at the end of its manifestation. The sheer, erect verticality of this *liṅga* begins to soften and curve. This is just what Brahmā pleads for: 'make it soft,' 'let it become supple.' He uses the imperatives *muḍupumu*, 'make it bend,' and *vālpu*, 'make it slant, slope, incline.' Again we see the *liṅga* replicate the sequence of Śiva's dance.[103]

There is something moving about this entire evolution. The discrete and isolated come together, the empty becomes full. God can truly be healed if he is capable of feeling his own desire. The Śaiva Siddhântins are very insistent about this point: whatever else may be said about the cosmic process, it makes no sense at all without god's *icchā*—usually translated as 'will,' but more properly 'want.' Of course, Śiva, by definition, is always satisfied (*nitya-tṛpta*).[104] How, then, can he want? But satisfaction at this level is an achievement even—especially—for god. We can see from the Telugu text how Śiva reaches this fulfilment of his own nature, not without outside help; we can see, that is, how he becomes Śiva. Intentionality exists, if at all, on a barely conscious plane. Trapped in a crystallized two-ness in the home of his new bride, Śiva has diminished, lost autonomy, turned empty, split into disconnected components. A thought occurs to him, as if without reason, as in play. He will go somewhere else—to the Forest of Pines—where he can beg to his heart's content. He leaves behind him the external personae of his household (Pārvatī and his in-laws) and his followers (the rowdy *gaṇa*s). But he is heading in a still more outward direction,

[103] See pp. 83–5, and Śiva's statement to Ananta at Cidambaram: 'Meditate on our delightful dance as if it were the *śiva-liṅga*.'

[104] Sivaraman 1973: 138.

toward a space frozen into oneness, without love. Śiva is now at the limits of his external being, having exhausted whatever knowledge he may once have possessed.

Here he meets a set of courtesans rather different from those higher up the mountain. Rambhā, Urvaśī, Tilottamā, and the others, having failed at their more usual task, are simply waiting to feed him. In his father-in-law's city, Śiva's *gaṇa*s had disrupted all erotic relationships; in the forest, the isolated and lonely god allows himself to be melted, nourished, made liquid, curved by these somewhat isolated and exiled women. A far more effective and fruitful eroticism begins in the flow of milk. But the women also seem to recognize him, and the magical effect of their welcome is an immediate ontic increment in this god who will have to want if he is to grow to his full stature. The epistemic, heretofore impoverished, recovers its inherent ontic energies. There is hope that Śiva will now need, find, or create, a self.

Disarticulated fragments begin to come together, acquiring momentum and direction. Quite soon the god will enter into play. At its height, he will draw all remaining outer beings back into himself. Between the two-ness of Himâlaya and the superficial oneness of the forest, Śiva, at last replenished, almost swallowed up by his own *liṅga*, once again bends into an arc. He is on the edge of disappearing when fullness turns back on itself, as fullness must. Such is the course of active desire as it touches the infinite, or of the infinite as it evolves through its own desire. Infinity, in such a system, like fullness, is never static but is rather flowing, coming into being or presence, surprising itself by the (often crazy) forms it assumes. It—'he'—wants this process to continue and offers companionship (*sāṅgatyamu*, 67) to anyone with a heart good enough to help.

Conclusion

> Don't look at what is before you.
> Look at looking.[1]

Recall the facts. God wanders into a forest of Himalayan pines. Human beings who inhabit this forest encounter him; the meeting changes both parties. The males begin to experience, through hate, something that could be called love, perhaps for the first time. The females, freed from shame or restraint, turn fertile. God becomes more alive, more full of self, more fluid, more present, in deeper and more rapid movement. He starts to dance on one foot, bending the other that remains poised in open space. Forgetting is forgotten, literally trampled under god's foot. The eye sees itself seeing. This movement within god and cosmos is also an exorcism, unlocking pieces of the self, setting both parties free.

But is he not always free, axiomatically, in this particular Śaiva cosmos? Yes. It is the nature of Śiva to be alive (*ajaḍa*), aware (*jñātṛ*), non-other (*ananya*), continuous (*anusyūta*), unchanging (*avikārin*), autonomous (*svatantra*), unstained or unencrusted (*amala*), unmarked (*aliṅga*), pervasive (*vyāpaka*), subtle (*sūkṣma*), full (*paripūrṇa*), beyond measure or knowledge (*aprameya*), free to move in any direction, and so on. For all that, though omniscient, there are many things he does not know—everything that has to do with non-sentient phenomena, for example.[2] In fact, most of the attributes just listed, all of them salient

[1] *Tiruvaruṭpayaṉ* 6. 8.

[2] *Civa-ñāṉa-potam* 7; see Śivâgrayogin ad *Śiva-jñāna-bodha* 6; *Tiruvaruṭpayaṉ* 2.7; Surendranath Dasgupta 5: 25: 'The *acit* or unconscious material passes before Śiva, but does not affect it, so that Śiva is quite unconscious of the world appearance.' See also Schomerus 1912: 318–19, on the complementary inadequacy of *pāśa-jñāna* in relation to Śiva.

in the south Indian Śaiva sources,[3] turn out, upon closer examination, either to contain or to issue into their opposites. So pronounced is this feature that one might take it as a basic law of operation within the conceptual system as a whole. Sometimes the result looks like a bona fide paradox: Śiva is both invisible and visible (unknowable and knowable).[4] He is also, as we have seen, not one and not two (more than one). But perhaps the latter statement is not paradoxical after all. What is not one and not two is probably not somewhere *between* one and two but is rather engaged in a deep and ongoing process of mutual interweaving. In other cases, too, apparent paradox is capable of resolution by restricting the field or level of application of superficially contradictory attributes. It is important to distinguish these two processes, especially since the Śaiva theologians always claim to adhere strongly to the rules of logical argument.

On the whole, they are right. Our failure to understand this conceptual world derives mostly from a rigid, overly static, strangely idealistic reading of its stated premises. Nothing could be further from its intuitions than to absolutize a set of given, deliberately defined features applying to god. If we think, even for a moment, in terms of bounded states rather than evolving processes, all is lost.

Thus Śiva is the god who takes away. He has to do this all the time. The cosmos—his cosmos—constantly becomes cluttered, yet this clutter is *not* not-god. If negation can affirm, a double negative affirms doubly.[5] The god who breathes in is the same god who breathes out—also the same great Yogi who holds his breath in a moment outside time. He is never not in process. Even the timeless moment of holding the breath is a kind of time. Taking away, Śiva comes into being and becomes free. He always has the potential to become free, aware, spacious, and so on; in some sense he *is* this potential, but never only that. For the process sub-sumed under the name Hara, the emblem of 'taking away,' brings him repeatedly to a surface where he is at least partially, on some level, impeded, occluded, discontinuous, unaware, marked (*liṅgin*—he has a *liṅga*), empty, encrusted, and dependent (*paratantra*). In fact, it is in these forms that we habitually encounter him, as the sages see him in the forest.

[3] See for example Śivâgrayogin, *loc. cit.*

[4] *Civa-ñāṉa-potam* 6.

[5] See discussion in Ruegg 1977.

You could class many of these limitations and tensions under a single heading of otherness, the alienating of parts of god from god. Śiva, that is, is not always Śiva, if by this name one means the axiomatic series with which we began. Stated positively, Śiva is sometimes not-Śiva. We have seen him reach states of such severe alienation and depletion that his very aliveness is called into question. The Dāruvana story is largely about such states. Better, it is largely about how one can heal such states in god—how, that is, we can re-compose this deity from his dispersed segments; how we can put him back together after his dissolution and petrification, as Vedic ritual sought to restore the fragmented and exhausted creator, Prajāpati (by building an altar of bricks, for example). In the south Indian Śaiva case, god's inevitable and continuous self-devolution, self-loss, and segmentation can be addressed in terms of filling, liquefaction, and, above all, putting into motion. All of these acts are also elements in an ongoing process of exorcism, and all make sense only in terms of Śiva's potential aliveness, his coming into being—never simply being. Being god, he cannot simply be.

The Dāruvana story is the great Śaiva essay on healing, paradigmatic for all other instances. It shows how god can emerge as god from out of a prior state of profound brokenness or emptiness or absence. Passive, distant, blocked, unmoving, he is drawn forth interactively into his axiomatic fullness and freedom. He cannot do it alone. He is only rarely able to fill himself up from within—or rather, since surface is not truly external, he could be said to struggle repeatedly with a certain potential nothingness of being or self, where cosmos falters and loses itself, its own coherence, and becomes thin or hard. Topologically, Śiva probably meets surface as inner hardening and blocking that temporarily halt or constrict expansion, growth, and depth. To be infinite (*ananta*)—another necessary and salient attribute—he has to be moved away from the edge or edges (*anta*) of such emptiness in the direction of the middle, where such edges cannot persist. In other words, he becomes infinite insofar as he becomes god. He is not alone in undergoing this sequence. For that matter, Śiva could, once again, be said to *be* this sequence.

Stated differently, but again in the hope of eluding apparent paradox, Śiva is a god in need of constant calibration in relation to his own inner composition and to the workings of his cosmos.[6] He naturally twists and turns and bends as he breathes out and in, and in this sense he can be said to be self-calibrating and self-regulating; he takes away from himself, cleansing and purifying himself in the process even as he purifies and liberates parts of cosmos through becoming present in a mode of fullness. But there are also specific modalities or momentary configurations in which his calibration is our responsibility. We have pointed to several of these, including the mode of resistance that is powerful enough to drive him to the surface, and also the dense mutual interpenetration, not easily achieved, that allows him to reach toward self-knowledge. Remembering him can also help.

Clearly, such a cosmos cannot be hierarchically organized in any straightforward way. We will simply have to give up, if we have not yet done so, the theory of an encompassing, higher-level whole integrating, in regular transitions, all possible diminished transforms and allowing itself to be reconstructed from within any given part. Maybe there are contexts in South Asia where such a principle would have explanatory power. It will not work for southern Śaivism. Apparently, there are moments or universes in which Śiva can empty himself to the point where he freezes over and can only be thawed out and filled up again from outside. In such moments, the self, even god's self, is so attenuated that it loses all distinctiveness, and can no longer change.[7]

Such attenuation has a name: *abhicāra* (or its equivalents),[8] which we have glossed as sorcery. Here, too, we may be in danger of overly rigid categorization. Becoming 'ensorcelled' is a slow process of accumulating blockages in relationships, devolving toward an alien 'otherness;' like many other illnesses, it is, however, usually recognized by sudden onset in a moment of crisis, in this case by the suffocation or paralysis that results from the complete loss of inner spaciousness and autonomy. Sorcery produces the emptiness that is static solidity,

[6] What we are calling 'calibration,' obviously our own, somewhat exotic term, is sometimes implied by terms such as *anusyūtatva*—literally, 'being sewn together,' that is, unevenly continuous over phases of transformation. See, e.g., Śivâgrayogin *ad Śiva-jñāna-bodha* 3 and 4.

[7] We would argue that even extreme hierarchical positions such as we find in the Śankara Advaita still fail to escape the constraints of a cosmos in process, hence fail also to conform to the Dumontian principle of encompassment.

[8] Tam. *pillicūṉiyam.* See Türstig 1985.

cutting off the self from other selves and simultaneously making the self alien to itself. Sorcery thus blocks the self's capacity to become aware, self-to-self, as well as the capacity to relate to those pieces of itself that have been made other, alien, and threatening. All forms of objectification contribute to this process. Its antidote lies in sacrifice, the generalized mode of taking away—in effect, a kind of exorcism. Sacrifice, no less than sorcery, is an ongoing occurrence, consistently removing blockages and opening up middle space. Sacrifice enables the cosmos to turn freely through itself, feeding itself, knowing itself, healing itself, taking itself away.

European languages tend to separate these two semantic fields—sorcery and sacrifice—but in India they are usually contiguous or partially overlapping.[9] They have a high degree of connectivity and are, seen abstractly, complementary. As the devotee comes close to Śiva, he should 'stand still and do nothing, until the quality of possession by a demon (*pey*) is born.'[10] (This verse closely follows Umāpati's definition of the connection as not-one and not-two.) Being filled with god looks and feels like possession. Sorcery and sacrifice describe together different segments of the same trajectories that enable god to curve, to move outward, to encounter or generate resistance, to come into being, to know, and to return. The cosmos generates its own barriers and edges through its normal operations, just as it continuously erases the borders and surfaces it has evolved. When you take away the surface, as god does by breathing in or dancing or knowing, you are left with only an interior: there is no moment in the time-driven cosmos when this reversion inwards is not taking place, as there is no moment when it is not itself being reversed. Hence the insistence on repetition as a law of experience. Śiva cannot exist, just as none of us can exist, without breathing out borders and emerging onto a surface. Even for god, potentialities must be defined if they are to be taken away.

A true paradox presents itself at this point. Stated simply, resuming an earlier discussion: the more surface, the more self. Take away the surface, or turn the surface into depth—this being a primary goal of much Śaiva ritual and cognitive activity—and 'self' disappears, even Śiva's self. So does nearly all that is known or can be known. Lines

[9] Think of the sages' *apicāra-vomam*, a sacrifice that is sorcery.
[10] *Tiruvaruṭpayaṉ* 8.7.

become curves. The paradox now shifts and can be reformulated. Under 'innerness' conditions, the curve may come to know itself as curve.[11] We have even argued that such a perception or understanding is, in a certain sense, the point of the entire process and one possible rationale, so to speak, for Śiva's entering into it. But such knowing seems superfluous, for it is in the nature of the curve to curve, and knowing this is no different than the supple movement of the curving line itself. To know—consequential knowledge—*is* to curve.

Still, this experience is in no way foreign to us. We are all capable of seeing ourselves seeing, which amounts to much the same thing as the curve's self-knowledge. You move through the same space that is moving through you, and you see yourself seeing not by detaching yourself from this movement but by remaining or becoming entirely continuous with it, curving into the seeing. Reflexivity of this sort can never be schizoid or alienating. Rather, it suggests a very powerful interpenetration. Whatever is inner is a matter of links and relations, as we have said;[12] being related is being inside one another to some degree.

So there is seeing and seeing. Any given form, visible on the surface, apparently diminishes the eye's ability to see itself see. Indeed, seeing such objects is itself a projection of sight outwards—the eye emitting a subtle extension that folds itself around the object's contours and replicates them internally.[13] Such vision is always a displacement. But what of the eye within the eye that sees the eye? How does it feel to know yourself as Śiva knowing himself *through* you? Imagine seeing the world with the god's eyes that are staring through you. It is no longer you who see, and the visible surface vanishes before your—his—eyes. What remains visible is only an inside that is in restless movement, the depth that is yourself known as Śiva's knowing. This is the eye inside the eye looking deeply into you. Under the full force of such a gaze, the synthesizing mind swirls into madness, accelerating with the spinning god, hiding itself in his luminosity, knowing itself in this

[11] Once again, we wish to stress that the language of curving, bending, inclining, folding, and spinning is integral to these Śaiva texts, which use Skt *kuñcita*, Tamil *tiri*, *kūṉ*, *kuṉi*, *maṭi*, Telugu *muḍucu*, *vālucu*, etc. in contexts studied above.

[12] Above, p. 174, citing Abhinavagupta. On this mode of reflexivity and its linguistic aspect, see also Shulman, in press (1).

[13] On sense perception in this domain, see Devasahayam (on Śaṅkara).

hidden form.[14] Umāpati bluntly orders his listeners to adopt this practice: 'Don't think. Don't contemplate anything.[15] Don't look at what is before you. Look at looking.'[16]

The Śaiva Siddhânta correctly posits a distinction between such states and the conceptual option of unmitigated unity. Were the relationship of god to living beings one, there would be no difference between these categories, and cosmos as we know it—constituted through difference—would cease to exist, along with all living selves. This is unacceptable. 'Don't contemplate what is one.' Were the relationship definable as two beings relating to each other, there would be radical existential difference, perhaps precluding relation of the sort just described. Cosmos would utterly congeal, encrust, and crack apart. Both two-ness and oneness exist as theoretical possibilities in the cosmic process, but both are rejected in all versions of the story we have been studying. Śiva goes to the Dāruvana in order to intervene before two-ness comes fully into being, in order to curve the cosmos back into himself and to reopen the depths of middleness, so that movement in any direction becomes possible again. He does this naturally as part of the weaving and unfolding in and beyond surface that define him; there are always segments or trajectories of Śiva that straighten themselves out of their own accord but that are then released from their stiffness by Śiva's acts of taking away. But there is also want, desire, or need implicit in this process within Śiva, to the point that ritual action on the part of human beings will always be in order if Śiva is to revert to being free.

Note that a certain, somewhat unexpected form of mutuality underlies this system. Śiva's relations with other beings consistently replicate a dynamic of *bringing forth* and *taking away*. Each side of the relation enters into these inherently interpenetrating processes. The women of the Dāruvana are eager to give, bringing forth (love, fullness, children) vis-à-vis the god; he, for his part, is ready to take away from them, unblocking stoppage, creating liquid movement. At other moments he is the prime giver, extending parts of himself into the cosmos, only to have these parts taken away (perhaps with the help of other beings).

[14] *Tiruvaruṭpayaṉ* 6.9.

[15] Or: 'don't contemplate what is *one*' (*ŏṉṟaiyu' muṟṟ' uṉṉāte*).

[16] Ibid., 6.8. Nirampav aḻakiya Tecikar: *uṉṉaik kaṇṭa ñāṉattiṉaik kāṇpāyāka*, 'look at the knowledge that looks at you.'

It is likely that this template characterizes *all* relationships between beings in the Śaiva cosmos. People give forth and take away necessarily; relating to any other involves this exchange, in which each gives forth to the other, who in turn takes this in, takes this away. This process is the very stuff of cosmos and the medium of all connectivity. Giving out and taking in become a foundational logic for the existence of the social, moral/cosmic ordering of existence. Such exchanges are routine throughout cosmos. Within this context we can understand sorcery, more profoundly, as the blocking of just this mode of exchange, isolating and enclosing selfness within itself. We can begin to see why sorcery constitutes a threat on the scale implied by our texts—why god himself is in constant danger of being caught up in its constricting and alienating action. We can see why sorcery serves as a dominant theme in all the southern Dāruvana materials, which study Śiva in his most extreme transformations, at the farthest edge of self or selves. The beauty of the episode of the sages' sorcery lies in its stark, ironic juxtaposition of the two vectors present in exchange and the existential consequences of their interaction: the sages give out (resistance) through sorcery, and Śiva takes in whatever they emit, thereby exorcising himself. They touch him, he takes away. Their blocking is his unblocking.

That god should live out such processes is, in itself, only natural. Śiva is far more than a paradigm or exemplar: he enacts cosmos as precisely these ongoing currents of bringing forth and taking in. They define, create, and decompose his world. But what becomes clear from such a description is the utter inadequacy of the classical Maussian notion of exchange and reciprocity, which has been applied, rather unconvincingly, to India.[17] It is not giving and taking, with consequent tension and interdependence, that are crucial but rather giving out and taking away—quite different processes at base. Every exchange, that is, involves both 'inner' and 'outer' selfness, not without distinction, but always continuous with one another. More deeply, the connections among beings (between god and people, or among living selves) are always active only through the inside; finally nothing and no one can be truly said to go *out*, to break through and away from the organic interior whole. What is external is at most the thinning and slowing of reality to the point of temporary encrustration, again from within

[17] Mauss 1950; Heesterman 1985.

(and knowable only from within). This understanding stands in absolute contradistinction to most Western notions of self. There is nothing here like the Maussian balance of reciprocity, only an ongoing imbalance of bringing forth and taking away by reaching into and touching one another in a volatile middle space, exhaling and inhaling through and for the other. Social life, ritual praxis, and mythic logic reinforce and reproduce this primary pattern; what transpires between god and other beings is in no way different from what individual or collective social entities do continually with one another, taking in what is being given forth, reaching inwards in order to be taken away. Think of this process as the interchange of substance, if substance is movement in between.

There are other ways to articulate this scheme in more traditional philosophical language. Not-one-ness, we are told, emerges through processes of cosmic evolution from the passive oneness or inertness of Śiva in his depletion. This aspect of evolution is usually referred to as the extrusion and activation of Śiva's Śakti, the female drive that externalizes the thirty-six *tattva*s or elements as well as all conceivable categories of difference and relatedness. As a result, Śiva will always be less than his imagination of himself and possibly less than his devotee's imagination of him. The sages of the forest suffer from just this bewildering experience when Śiva manifests himself before their eyes. How, they wonder, can god be less than god? It never occurs to them that they have a role in enhancing, inflating, and exorcising him, and that it is precisely through this mutual interaction that he comes to be present, in his fullest reality, as god, or more than god. Not-twoness comes into existence as god's presence among living beings acts to curve cosmos away from further evolution, differentiation, and difference, all of which rupture the relationship between god and human beings; were these processes to continue unchecked, they would ultimately cause the destruction of cosmos. A similar result would become possible if Śiva's involution were to fuse god and living beings to the point of final oneness.

If the cosmos is to continue to exist, as it seems empirically to do, and as the scriptures tell us it will, in its rhythmic phases, and if god is to be present within it, then a middle space-time between not-one and not-two must potentially exist and occasionally come fully into being. This middleness is dependably linked to Tamil *aruḷ*, a loving, intensifying presence. *Aruḷ* integrates—as the etymology of its Sanskrit gloss, *saṃnidhāna*, suggests—but only from within. *Aruḷ* ties living beings together or weaves or folds them into one another, allowing them to move rapidly through one another. When the fullness of Śiva's *aruḷ* is actualized, all possibilities exist, and movement is possible in any direction—but ultimately only in loops and curves, even if temporary segments of the movement may appear flat or straight. Think, again, of Naṭarāja's flowing, bending, curving lines within the rounded flame of burning lights. *Aruḷ*, like middleness, is counter-evolutionary for cosmos. It always has an aspect of god's involution, a turning inwards or a breathing in. Just as it links beings to one another, it ties god into himself by swirling his parts together in the dance, creating self as axis—so that the *tāṇḍava* dancer is situated between Śiva and Śiva, in the middle space, just as any selfness comes into being somewhere between self and self. To internalize this notion fully is to touch the intuitive core of southern Śaiva metaphysics: the language of self, applied to god, and perhaps not only to god, implies a movement among, through, or beyond any crystallized face, mask, surface, story, name. Coming into being is always its own displacement. What comes to the surface can be, at best, a part-self in danger of rapidly becoming non-self, thus awaiting transformation back into depth. God comes alive for living beings by moving or being moved into such a deepening mode, that is necessarily in-between.

He is a tensile god, stretched between not-one and not-two—tensile, labile, and evolving. He has a generative, processual module, the *liṅga-yoni*, active within him, moving him through the transforms we experience in and as his world. A deep tension connected to knowing pervades his somewhat tenuous selfness, which is *not*, it must be stressed, equivalent to consciousness. *Cit*, awareness, is clearly differentiated from *ātman*, 'self.'[18] *Cit*, we have seen, is not and cannot be aware of its opposite, *a-cit* (or *a-sat*, 'non-being'). God's self, if he 'has' one, can be located right here, in this very lack of awareness and in the astonishing, far-reaching changes it consistently generates, including

[18] *Śiva-jñāna-bodha* 3–4. 'Consciousness' (*citta*) is also, of course, distinct from 'mind' (*manas*), as Kapferer (2002) shows in his explication of Sinhala exorcism. In his reading, 'intense consciousness of self is indicative of a . . . collapse in consciousness,' as we might expect from our materials as well. Yet there seems to be a contrast with the southern Śaiva sense of reflexive knowing—the eye that sees itself seeing in the middle space—and its existential consequences: see above, p. 107.

the resistance and opposition that we, for our part, can contribute to the process. If we persist to the end, thereby 'reaching' him, he gives us joy; but, since his body is itself a dense mass of joyfulness (*iṉpa-kaṉam*), he cannot actually experience what we can.[19] In fact, as Nirampav aḻakiya Tecikar says with startling and moving simplicity, he cannot experience (literally, taste) himself at all (*tāṉ taṉṉai nukarvat' illai*).[20]

It is up to us to help him taste. It is our task, or promise, to feed him and fill him. In fulfilling it, we spin into him as he whirls through us. Both parties come to be and to know in this way, though never in a stable or harmonious manner. There is nothing static about tasting. It requires not-one-ness but cannot survive two-ness. Freedom (*svātantrya*) is its condition—an elusive one. Not even the sages' wives can achieve it for long, though Śiva's presence turns them fertile. In at least one text, Śrīnātha's, both they and the god are satisfied by the intensity of secret loving; but in most cases, he takes himself away from them too soon. His habit is to slip away. It is extremely difficult to maintain even a modicum of mutuality between this emergent god and other beings. Even though we have always been connected to him (*iyaintu*), so far, to this very day (*iṟṟai varai*), we have had very little practice (*paḻakkam*) in this regard. Being empty ourselves, freedom (*vīṭu*) is too much for us, a remnant (*mikai*) left over from our being as we wander through the liquid field of his compassion.[21]

They say, as we have seen, that infinity somehow characterizes this deity. Ananta, literally the 'infinite,' is the great spectator of the dance at Cidambaram; he is also the serpent Ādiśeṣa, the 'residue' left behind. What turns infinity into a left-over? And why should something be left over anyway? Is infinity sacrificed—taken away—in order to produce this remnant? As something comes into self-consciousness, something else is being lost. An edge (*anta*) is produced—this is always repetition, there is no first time[22]—but then edgelessness is what is left over as all that is and is not, all that might be and all that will never be, all

[19] *Tiruvaruṭpayaṉ* 8.3.

[20] Nirampav aḻakiya Tecikar on this verse.

[21] *Tiruvaruṭpayaṉ* 4.10: *iṟṟai varaiy iyaintum etum paḻakkam ilā/vĕṟṟ' uyirkku vīṭu mikai*. Ibid., 10. 10: *taṅ karuṇai vĕḷḷatt' alaivar mika.*

[22] The self stands, by Śiva's command, at edge after edge (*tad-anteṣu sthitvā sthitvā*), like a comet waiting to traverse the universe: *Śaivâgama-paribhāṣā-mañjari* 5. 89.

that vanishes as it emerges. Freedom is another such remnant, or perhaps only another term for it. Infinity, in this case, is an uneven flow, not a quiescent end to a regular series; whatever comes into being from this infinite reservoir is its own displacement, as any numeral divides and displaces the potential fullness of zero (*śūnya*).[23] Śiva is always on the edge of disappearance; hence he mostly 'hides his real beauty.'[24] By the same token, this beauty is never far from our eyes, could we but use them to see.

[23] See Arunacalam (1984), citing *Mallana gaṇitamu*.

[24] *Tirunĕlvelittalapurāṇam*, *Tārukāvaṉaccarukkam* 187 (*tulaṅk' ĕḻil karantu*: above, p. 130).

Appendix

Kūrma-purāṇa 2.37.1-164[1]

The sages said:

> Tell us, please, storyteller, how god came to the Forest of Pines and deluded the Brahmins there.

The storyteller said:

Long ago there were sages, by the thousand, intent on *tapas* together with their sons and wives in the delightful Forest of Pines, where gods and various perfected beings (*siddha*) also used to live. They were engaged in scrupulous performance of rituals (*karma*) of various kinds, including many types of sacrifices; and they were continually heating themselves up in this regimen. Śiva, Trident-Bearer, went to the Forest of Pines, since he was, as ever, eager to reveal to those whose heart is set on action (*pravṛtti*) just where they were making their mistake. We are talking about Śaṅkara, god himself: and I can tell you that he took Viṣṇu, the universal teacher, along with him when he went there, to create an awareness of what disengagement (*nivṛtti*) means.[2] Moreover, he assumed a very significant guise (*veṣa*) for this purpose: he was beautiful, languid, playful, just a little plump, with bright eyes and strong shoulders, like a nineteen-year-old man. His whole body glowed with golden light, his face was brilliant, his gait graceful as that of an elephant in heat (nothing more graceful than that!), and he was stark naked. I want to remind you that he is god, the lord of the universe. He was smiling, too, as he moved along, wearing a garland of pure gold studded with jewels. Viṣṇu, the unbending Male who is also the

[1] Edited Anand Swarup Gupta (Varanasi: All-India Kashiraj Trust, 1972).
[2] Reading *nivṛtti-vijñāna-sthāpanârtham.*

Vulva of all the worlds, assumed a female guise (*veṣa*) and followed Śiva. He—or rather she, Viṣṇu—was also smiling, full of charm, her face luminous as moonlight, her breasts taut and full, her anklets chiming; her dark body was clothed in yellow, her eyes glistened as she glided along like the noble and graceful goose—all in all, a captivating sight.

That is how god arrived in the Forest of Pines, together with Viṣṇu: it was enough to make everyone a little crazy. And in fact the women there were entirely bewildered, infatuated by this vision (*māyā*) of the great Śiva, and shamelessly they ran after him, throwing off their clothes and their ornaments. They—even the most faithful among them, fully committed to their husbands—just wanted to be with him, to play with him, in all the pain of love. Meanwhile, the sons of the sages, those who had come of age, were no less infatuated with Viṣṇu, whom they followed in hopeless passion.

So the women were singing and dancing and flirting with god, their one and only lover, though they saw him there together with his wife. They loved him, they wanted him, and they kept trying to embrace him. Their sons were flashing smiles and singing seductively to Viṣṇu, the first god, who had stolen into their hearts—theirs, and the women's too—and was arousing them all with great precision, until they were tingling with tactile pleasure, experiencing the play (*māyā*) in all its fullness. The god of gods, Śiva, surrounded by the women, including Viṣṇu,[3] was fully engaged in this moment, this plan, now coming to fruition with the help of his female persona (*śakti*): he was dancing and thus emerging, once again, into his ultimate form of being—and Viṣṇu, too, was achieving the fullness of *his* nature along with Śiva.

But the sages saw it all, saw Śiva beguiling the women and Viṣṇu bewitching their sons, and they were very angry. They hurled harsh words at Śiva and cursed him in many ways, for they were deluded by his play. All their heated energies, however, were lost in Śiva, as the stars fade away in the light of the midday sun. They insulted him: 'Who are you, anyway?' As I have told you, they were totally deluded. And he replied: 'Just someone who has come here with my wife, to discipline myself together with you.'

'In that case,' said Bhṛgu and the others, 'assuming it is *tapas* you are after, first put on some clothes, and then get rid of that wife of

[3] Reading *mādhava-strī*.

yours.' Now Śiva laughed (all blue and red), and looking straight at Viṣṇu, the Vulva of the universe, who was right there beside him, declared: 'You think you know dharma quite well, don't you, with your minds and hearts at peace. Still, you are eager to keep your own wives—and yet you insist that I have to abandon mine!'

'Of course,' said the sages; 'a husband should always abandon a wife who is lewd and wrong-headed. And we would certainly get rid of this one of yours, lovely as she is.'

Śiva: 'My friends, she has never, even in thought, wanted anyone but me, and I will never desert her.'

The sages: 'We have seen what was going on here, you lout, you lowly male. Now you are lying to us: get out of here fast!'

'No,' said the god, 'I spoke the truth. She merely seems like that to you.' And he moved on—to the ashrama of the great sage Vasiṣṭha, where, together with Viṣṇu, he begged for alms. Arundhatī, Vasiṣṭha's beloved wife, saw him begging at her door; she welcomed him and bowed to him with love. She washed his feet, seated him comfortably and, noticing that his body had grown weak as a result of the Brahmins' attack upon him, she—a good woman, but with sadness showing on her face—put him back together, healing him with medicines. Then she asked him, as she honoured him: 'Who are you, Sir? Where are you coming from? What practice have you been pursuing?'

Said Śiva, 'I am the very best of all perfect beings (*siddha*). This pure and luminous universe, truly divine, is the god I worship—and I am the one who keeps it going.' And off he went again, taking leave of that devoted wife.

Now the Brahmins saw him moving along, naked, a bizarre apparition, and first they lashed out at him with sticks and canes[4] and their bare fists, and then they spoke to him, insulting him: 'Tear off that *liṅga* of yours, won't you?' Śiva, the great Yogi, agreed at once: 'I will do just that, if you feel some dislike for this *liṅga* of mine.' So god, who had once before blinded Bhaga, now tore off his *liṅga*. At that moment they could no longer see him, or Viṣṇu, or the *liṅga*. But various terrifying shocks were felt throughout all the worlds: the sun no longer shone; the earth shook; the planets went black, and the ocean shuddered.

[4] v.l. *loṣṭibhir*, clods of earth.

Meanwhile, Anasūyā, the wife of Atri, had a dream which she reported, in her fear, to the Brahmins: 'Śiva has been seen, begging for alms, in our homes. Viṣṇu was with him, and he was so bright that the whole world was full of light.' Anxious at this statement, the sages went to find Brahmā, the great Yogi who is the source of everything. They found him seated on a brilliantly illuminated throne, a throne of Knowledge and Power, together with his wife Sāvitrī and the four Vedas in visible form; Yogis who knew about god were singing his praises, and he was smiling, serenely illuminating the world with his beauty and the light from his eyes. He had four heads, and he was composed entirely of Vedic words. They bowed to him, touching the earth with their heads, and he asked them—from his four mouths and fourfold body—why they had come. So they told him the whole story:

'Some remarkably handsome male came to our so-very-auspicious Forest of Pines, together with his stunning wife. He was totally naked, and he drove all the women crazy, including the young girls, while his wife ruined all our sons. We tried all kinds of curses on him, but they were all deflected back, so then we hit him hard, and we made his *liṅga* fall off. At that point he simply disappeared, together with his wife and his *liṅga*, and a whole series of terrifying calamities took place. Now we're scared, and we want to know who that man was. That is why we have come to you—the Supreme Male, who never falls or moves. You know everything that goes on in this world, so kindly take care of us.'

Brahmā meditated on god, the Trident-Bearer, before replying:

'You're really in trouble, all of you. You've lost your one chance. So much for the forest life, and for your discipline (*tapaś-caryā*)—for you, it was all for nothing. You had right there, in your hands, the one treasure everyone wants, the best of all, and, in your confusion and frivolity, you didn't even notice. The one priceless treasure for which Yogis hunger and determined people give up the world came to you of itself, and you didn't even notice. The one imperishable god who gives the other gods their power came straight to you, and you didn't even notice. By constantly meditating on that god I achieve *my* universal power: but you looked right at him and ignored him, you unlucky fools. He is the treasure that concentrates all that is divinity in itself, that never dies—and you wasted it! He is god himself, knowable as such; there is nothing higher.

He is one who becomes Death to all living beings—gods, sages, ancestors—by reabsorbing them and bringing them to completion at the end of thousands of eons. He is also the one who externalizes them again from out of his own radiance. He is the great king who carries the discus and who bears the Śrīvatsa mark.[5] In the Kṛta Age he is a Yogi; in the Tretā Age he is the Sacrifice; in the Dvāpara Age he is Death; and now, in the Kali Age, he bears the banner of Dharma. There are three congealed forms of Rudra, out of which everything here is woven and strung—in black darkness (*tamas*) he is Fire, in red passion (*rajas*) he is Brahmā, in pure reality (*sattva*) he is Viṣṇu. And there is yet one more congealed form—naked, gentle (*śiva*), and constant: that is where the godhead itself is situated, held in place by yoga. As to the woman you said followed at his side, that is Nārāyaṇa, the eternal deity of ultimate innerness (*paramâtman*). Everything is born out of him, and everything is reabsorbed into him; he bewilders the whole universe, and he is its final recourse. He, Hari-Viṣṇu, is the Male with a thousand heads, a thousand eyes, and a thousand feet;[6] he has a single horn, and an inner core of being that never dies. The Supreme Lord, Śiva, has forms: he is the four Vedas, and the twisted triple cord of qualities (*guṇa*s); Nārāyaṇa-Viṣṇu has a single form and infinity within him.

The Brahmins who hunger for Release say that the latter, Viṣṇu, is the fluid womb for the former, Śiva. After Puruṣottama, the Ultimate Male, reabsorbs all living beings at the end of time, he drinks the elixir of Yoga and falls asleep in the last domain, the world of Viṣṇu. He is never born himself, nor does he die or undergo growth. He sees all there is to see, and he is the latent foundation of all manifest being, as Vedic Brahmins like to say. And when that dark night turns to dawn, and god wishes to externalize a world again, he pours out his seed in the navel of unborn Brahmā—that is to say, into *me*, the same god talking to you now, the Male who is the watery womb that faces in all directions. But you, deluded as you are by his play (*māyā*), simply cannot know god, in all his creativity, when you see him. That was he, Śiva himself, god without beginning: he is yoked to Viṣṇu; that is how he acts and trans-acts, though there is nothing he *has* to do, and nothing beyond him. He is the one who, in his body of yogic artifice,

[5] i.e., Viṣṇu.

[6] Quoting *Ṛg Veda* 10.90.1

gave me the Vedas long ago. He is a tricky one, doing and undoing all that is; to know him is your only hope of escape.'

The sages, from Marīci on, bowed to Brahmā and asked him: 'Is there any way we can see this Śiva again? You are the only one who can help us.'

Brahmā said: 'Make a *liṅga* just like the one you saw fall to the earth, the sign of that god who is modelled like that sign,[7] and worship it together with your wives and sons, with all the proper Vedic rules, in sexual abstinence. Set it in place with Śiva's mantras from the Ṛg Veda, the Yajur Veda, and the Sāma Veda; then hold fast to your discipline (*tapas*), as you sing the Śatarudriya hymn. Worship, with children and relatives, in a state of deep meditation, concentrating totally on Śiva—and then you will see him. He is not visible to those who have not prepared themselves in this way; but when one sees him, all ignorance and badness disappear.'

With this advice from Brahmā, the sages returned to the Forest of Pines, where they at once embarked on the worship of Śiva, as advised; although they still knew nothing about ultimate reality, at least they were now free from envy and passion. On the open ground, or in mountain caverns, or on the deserted, sandy banks of rivers, they performed their meditation: some eating only moss, others lying in water or standing, naked to the sky, on their tiptoes; some using their teeth as mortars to grind unhusked grain, others stooping to using stones; some subsisting on vegetables and leaves, others on sunlight; some given to constant ablutions, living at the foot of a tree or on some rock or other. This was how they passed their time, heating themselves in relation to Śiva.

After a while, Śiva turned his mind to them, to awaken them and bring them clarity—for god always cares for those who come to him, doesn't he? He was pleased and clear in himself when he went to the Forest of Pines on the slopes of the Himâlaya—and now it was the Kṛta Age, this age, the best. His whole body was white with ash and he was naked, of course, and looked bizarre; he held burning coals in his hand, and his eyes were reddish-yellow. He was laughing, guffawing really, unpredictably, and singing and dancing in his amazement. Over and over again he would start roaring and yelling as he wandered through the ashram, begging alms. He was, you know, very beautiful,

[7] *tal-liṅgânukṛtīśa.*

in that body that he assumed for the forest—a truly glorious disguise (*māyā*). And, as before, he took Pārvatī, the Mountain's daughter, along with him.

And they saw him—god with his long, matted hair, together with the goddess. He had come to their forest, and they bowed to him, touching their heads to the ground, blessing him with Vedic mantras and hymns of praise, from the Atharvaśiras Upaniṣad and other Śaiva texts:

'We bow to you: God of gods, greatest god, Tryambaka, Trident-Bearer, the naked, disfigured Pinākin, the Unbowed who becomes a body for all who bow, Killer of Andhaka, Killer of all, the Dancer, Bhairava, the Androgyne, the Yogi, the Guru, Śiva the Serene, the Disciplined, the Gruesome Rudra, draped in antelope skins, Black Neck with the tongue that licks all, Vāmadeva, whose form is both Unhorrible and Horrible, garlanded in gold, Lover to the goddess, Śambhu, Supreme Lord, with the Ganges in his hair, Master of Yoga and of Goblins, the Breath of Life itself, Fire shrouded in ash, the Fanged, the Fiery Seed, Black Time who beheaded Brahmā—we know nothing of your comings and goings, whoever you may be. Generous lord of the Pramatha Ghouls, with the skull in your hands,[8] the most deeply loved of all—we bow to you, to the golden *liṅga*, the *liṅga* of water, the *liṅga* of fire and sun, the *liṅga* of wisdom, decked in serpents, decked in Karṇikāra flowers, with crown and earrings, Death to Death himself. O three-eyed god, Vāmadeva, forgive whatever we have done, in our confusion; you are our hope. No-one, not even Brahmā, can know you very well. You act in ways that are remarkable, mysterious, profound. Whatever a human being does, whether out of wisdom or out of ignorance, is really an act of god through the play of his Yoga (*yoga-māyā*).'

Then, entirely focused inward, they asked him: 'Let us see you as you were before.' So he showed them himself, his ultimate form, and, standing there as before, they saw him together with the goddess, and they were happy.

There were many great sages there—Bhṛgu, Aṅgiras, Vasiṣṭha, Viśvāmitra, Gautama, Atri, Sukeśa, Pulastya, Pulaha, Kratu, Marīci, Kaśyapa, Saṃvartta, and others—and, bowing to him, they asked: 'How should we worship you, great god—through the Yoga of action, or through wisdom, or through Yoga itself? Which way is best? Tell us how to proceed, and what not to do.'

[8] *v.l. kalāpa*, 'quiver.'

Śiva said: 'I will tell you: it is a profound secret, the ultimate mystery. Brahmā spoke of it long ago. Sāṅkhya and Yoga divide into two paths—for Sāṅkhya, coupled with Yoga, brings release to Puruṣas. The Supreme Male (*puruṣa*) cannot be seen through Yoga alone—one needs wisdom, too, to find release. You were working hard at Yoga, to achieve freedom, but you had neglected pure Sāṅkhya. That is why I came here—to teach men obsessed with ritual the true origin of confusion. It is critical that you know, and hear, and see, through your own efforts, this wisdom that brings freedom. The *ātman* is one, pervasive, alone, the mother of awareness, pure, joyful, and eternal: that is what Sāṅkhya teaches. This is the ultimate knowledge known as Release, the state of freedom and total being. It is by achieving that state, in all intentness, that one can see me. This wisdom is supreme, a delight in Being. As for me, I am the god who can be known, and this is my congealed, auspicious form (*mama mūrttir iyaṃ śivā*).

There are many ways that produce results, but my form of knowledge is the best. Those devotees of mine who are at peace, happy in the Yoga of wisdom, trusting in me, meditating on me in their hearts, their bodies smeared with ash—they are devoid of evil, and I immediately destroy the cycle of their suffering. I invented, long ago, the Pāśupata way, the final secret, the true core of the Vedas, to produce freedom: this is the path one should take, controlling the mind, covering oneself in ash, remaining chaste and naked. Or you can cover yourself with a single cloth, a loincloth, while meditating on Śiva as Paśupati, lord of creatures. The Veda itself says that anyone seeking release should adopt this Pāśupata Yoga, abandon desire, and smear himself with ash. Many have attained my state of being through this Yoga, relying on me, becoming me, released from passion, fear, and anger.

I have filled this world with many other kinds of texts meant to confuse people, texts contrary to the Vedas. There are the Vāma, Pāśupata, Soma, Lākula, and Bhairava texts—all said to be outside the Veda, and therefore to be shunned. I am the real form of the Veda, and this form of mine cannot be known by those who follow other texts. Establish this path, worship god, and knowledge will quickly arise. You should have intense devotion (*bhakti*) for me; if you simply meditate on me, I will bring you close.'

Then Śiva disappeared, though they went on worshipping him there, in the Forest of Pines. Chaste, serene, intent on Sāṅkhya and Yoga, these metaphysically-minded sages debated various doctrines among themselves, relying on their self-knowledge. 'What is the root of this world?' they asked, and the answer was: 'Our own innerness.' 'What is the cause of all states of existence?' 'God, and god alone.' And so on—until the goddess Pārvatī appeared to them in the midst of their meditation, like a million sunrises, so the heavens were filled with light. They stared at her, held within this overwhelming brilliance, and knew her to be Śiva's wife and seed. They were happy, for they saw themselves and everything else in her—god's wife and inner being, whose name is 'Sky,' who is the true way. She, for her part, saw them too, and at that very in-between moment they saw Śiva, the universal cause, the poet and ruler, Rudra, the ancient Male. As they looked at the goddess and the god, joy flooded them, and wisdom, the kind that does away with the cycle of birth, became manifest through the god's compassion:

'This goddess, this Śakti, is the Vulva of the Universe, the one inner being within all, controlling all, timelessly accessible, shining in heaven, bearing the name "Sky." Śiva, the one god, Rudra, who is beyond her, created everything in her, in play (*māyā*), dependent upon her (*para-śakti-niṣṭham*). He, Rudra, alone is hidden in all living things. He is playful, fragmented, and whole. He is also the goddess, an undivided being. To know this is to be immortal.'

And Śiva disappeared again with the goddess while they kept on serving him in the forest.

So now I have told you everything—all that the god did long ago in the Forest of Pines, just as I have it in the *purāṇa*. Whoever recites this story or listens to it is freed from evil of any kind, and whoever tells it to peaceful Brahmins goes the highest way.

Bibliography

Texts

Ānanda-sāgara-stava of Nīlakaṇṭha Dīkṣita. Edited with commentary by H.V. Nagaraja Rao. Mysore: Sudharma Prakashana, 1999.

Brahmâṇḍa-purāṇa. Edited by Jagadīśa Śāstri. Delhi: Motilal Banarsidass, 1973.

Brahma-sūtra-bhāṣya of Śaṅkara. Edited by Mahādeva Śāstri Bakre. Bombay: Nirnaya Sagar Press, 1934.

Cidambara-māhātmya. Edited Somaśekhara Dīkshitar. Kadavasal: Sree Minakshi Press, 1971.

Cilappatikāram of Iḷaṅkovaṭikaḷ. Edited U. Ve. Cāminātaiyar. Madras: Dr. U. Ve. Cāminātaiyar Library, 1978.

Civañāṉacittiyār (*cupakkam*) of Aruḷnanti. Tarumapuram: Tarumaiyātīṉam, 1962.

Civa-ñāṉa-potam. See *Mĕykaṇṭa cāttiram patiṉāṅku*.

Cūrṇi-kŏttu. See *Mĕykaṇṭa cāttiram patiṉāṅku*.

Hara-vilāsamu of Śrīnātha. Madras: Vavilla Ramasvamisastrulu and Sons, 1966.

Irāmâvatāram of Kampaṉ. Tiruvāṉmiyūr: U.V. Cāminātaiyar Library, 1967–72.

Jaiminīya Brāhmaṇa. Edited by Raghu Vira and Lokesh Chandra. Delhi: Motilal Banarsidass, 1986.

Kāmikâgama, *pūrva-bhaga*. Madras: South Indian Archakas Association, 1975.

Kāñcippurāṇam of Civañāṉacuvāmikaḷ. With commentary by Pŏn. Caṇmukaṉār. C. Kancipuram: Muttamiḻ accakam, 1964.

Kanta-purāṇam of Kacciyappa civâcāriyar. Takṣakāṇṭam. With commentary by C. Kaṇapatip Piḷḷai. Perātaṉai: Ilaṅkai Palkalaikkaḻakam, 1967.

Kāśī-khaṇḍa [*Skanda-purāṇa* 4]. Calcutta: Manasukharaya Mor, 1961.

Kauṣītaki-brāhmaṇa. Edited by E.R. Sreekrishna Sarma. Wiesbaden: Franz Steiner, 1968.

Koyir-purāṇam of Umāpati civâcāriyar. With commentary by Nallūr Āṟumuka Nāvalar. Madras: Vittiyânupālaṉa yantiracālai. 3rd edition, 1862.

Kūrma-purāṇa, Varanasi: All-India Kashi Raj Trust, 1972.

Liṅga-purāṇa. Bombay: Venkatesvara Steam Press, 1906.

Mahābhārata. Southern Recension. Edited by P.P.S. Sastri. Madras: V. Ramaswamy Sastrulu and Sons, 1931–6.

Mĕykaṇṭa cāttiram patiṉāṅku. Edited by Kȧ. Cuppiramaṇiya Piḷḷai. Tirunelveli: South Indian Saiva Siddhanta Works Publishing Society, 1972.

Mudrā-rākṣasa of Viśākhadatta. Delhi: Motilal Banarsidass, 1991.

Naḷa-vĕṇpā of Pukaḻentippulavar. Edited by L. Śrīnivāsa Aiyar. Madras: U. Ve. Cāminātaiyar Library, 1960.

Nālaṭiyār. Madras: South India Saiva Siddhanta Works Publishing Society, 1958.

Pāratam of Villiputtūrār. Madras: Vai. Mu. Kopālakiruṣṇamācāriyar Kampeni, 1966–70.

Paripāṭal. Introduction, traduction et notes par François Gros. Pondicherry: Institut Français d'Indologie, 1968.

Raghu-vaṃśa of Kālidāsa. Edited by Gopal Raghunath Nandargikar. Delhi: Motilal Banarsidass, 1972.

Śaivâgama-paribhāṣā-mañjari of Veda-jñāna (*Le florilège de la doctrine śivaïte*). Edited by Bruno Dagens. Pondichéry: Institut Français d'Indologie, 1979.

Śivâdvaita-nirṇaya of Appaya Dīkṣita. Edited by S.S. Suryanarayana Sastri. Madras: University of Madras, 1974.

Śivâgra-bhāṣya on *Śiva-jñāna-bodha*, by Śivâgrayogin. Madras: Sastra Sanjeevinee Press, 1920.

Śiva-jñāna-bodha, with *Laghu-ṭīkā* of Śivâgrayogin. Kashi: 1908.

Śiva-purāṇa. Bombay: Venkatesvara Steam Press, 1953.

Somaśambhupaddhati. Edited H. Brunner. Volumes I-III. Pondicherry: Institut Français d'Indologie, 1963–77.

Takṣa-kāṇṭam of *Kanta-purāṇam* by Kacciyappa civâcāriyar. See *Kanta-purāṇam*.

Tevāram of Cuntaramūrttināyaṉār. Tarumapuram: Tarumaiyātīṉam, 1964.

Tevāram of Tiruñāṉacampantar. Tarumapuram: Tarumaiyātīṉam, 1953–5.

Tevāram of Tirunāvukk'aracu cuvāmikaḷ. Tarumapuram: Tarumaiyātīṉam, 1957–63.

Tirunĕlvelittalapurāṇam of Nĕllaiyappap Piḷḷai. Edited by Cālivaṭīcura Otuvamūrttikaḷ. Tirunelveli: Muttamiḻākaram Press, 1869.

Tiruvācakam of Māṇikkavācakar. With commentary of Ka. Cu. Navanīta

Kiruṣṇa Pāratiyār. Māviṭṭapuram-Tĕllippaḻai, Ilankai: Patmā patippakam, 1954.

Tiruvāppaṉūrppurāṇam of Tiruvāppaṉūr Kantacāmippulavar. With commentary by Pa. Vācavaliṅka Paurāṇikar. Maturai, 1909.

Tiruvaruṭpayaṉ of Umāpati civâcāriyar. With the commentary of Nirampav aḻakiya Tecikar. Tarumapuram: Tarumapura ātīṉam, 1957–8.

Tiruvātavūraṭikaḷ purāṇam of Kaṭavuḷmāmuṉivar. Edited by Pu. Ci. Puṉṉaivaṉanāta Mutaliyār. Madras: South Indian Saiva Siddhanta Works Publishing Society, 1967.

Tiruvuntiyār of Uyyavanta Tevanāyaṉār, with the commentary of Civappirakācar. Edited by Pŏṉ. A. Kaṉakacapai. Yāḻppāṇam: Yāḻppāṇam kūṭṭuṟavut tamiḻnūṟ patippu viṟpaṉaik kaḻakam, 1970.

Tŏlkāppiyam. Cŏllatikāram. Madras: South India Saiva Siddhanta Works Publishing Society, 1955.

Viṣṇu-māyā-vilāsamu of Rosanūri Veṅkaṭapati-kavi. Madras: 1899.

Other Sources

Adiceam, Marguerite E. 'Les images de Śiva dans l'Inde du Sud: II Bhairava,' *Arts Asiatiques* 11 (1965), 23–44; 'III. Bhiksatana, IV. Kankala Murti,' *Arts Asiatiques* 12 (1965), 83–112.

Āṟumuka Nāvalar. *Pirapantattiraṭṭu*. Edited by T. Kailācapiḷḷai. Madras: Āṟumukanāvalār vittiyânupālaṉa accakam, 1954.

Arunachalam, P.V. 'Pavuluri Ganitamu,' in *Proceedings of the Andhra Pradesh Oriental Conference*, Third Session, 13–15 June 1981 (1984), 76–82.

Balasubrahmanyam, S.R. *Middle Chola Temples: Rajaraja I to Kulottunga I (A.D. 985-1070)*. Faridabad: Thomson Press, 1975.

Becker, A.L. *Beyond Translation: Essays toward a Modern Philology*. Ann Arbor: University of Michigan Press, 1995.

Biardeau, Madeleine. 'Études de mythologie hindoue (III).' *Bulletin de l'École Française d'Extrême-Orient* 58 (1972), 17–89.

Brunner, Hélène. 'Les membres de Śiva.' *Asiatische Studien/ Études Asiatiques* 40 (1986), 89–132.

———. 'Toujours le niṣkala-liṅga.' *Journal Asiatique* 256 (1968), 445–7.

———. See *Somaśambhupaddhati*.

Burrow, Thomas. Review of George L. Hart, III, 'The relation between Tamil and classical Sanskrit literature'. *Indo-Iranian Journal* 21 (1979), 283.

Burrow, Thomas and M. B. Emeneau, *Dravidian Etymological Dictionary*. Oxford: Clarendon Press, 1961.

Chevillard, Jean-Luc. *Le commentaire de Cēṉāvaraiyar sur le Collatikāram du Tolkāppiyam*. Vol. 1. Pondichéry: Institut Français de Pondichery, 1996.

Coomaraswamy, A.K. *The Dance of Śiva*. New York: The Noonday Press, 1957.

Curtis, J.W.V. 'Space concepts and worship environment in Śaiva Siddhânta: An interpretation of the use of ritual space in Śaiva architecture and symbolism,' in Fred W. Clothey and J. Bruce Long (eds), *Experiencing Śiva: Encounters with a Hindu Deity*. New Delhi: Manohar, 1983.

Daniel, Valentine. *Fluid Signs: Being a Person the Tamil Way*. Berkeley: University of California Press, 1984.

Danielou, A. *The Ragas of Northern Indian Music*. Delhi: Munshiram Manoharlal, 1980.

Dasgupta, Surendranath. *A History of Indian Philosophy*, Vol. 5. *The Southern Schools of Śaivism*. Cambridge: Cambridge University Press, 1969.

Davis, Richard H. *Ritual in an Oscillating Universe: Worshipping Śiva in Medieval India*. Princeton: Princeton University Press, 1991.

Devaraja, N.K. *An Introduction to Śaṅkara's Theory of Knowledge*. Delhi: Motilal Banarsidass, 1962.

Devasenapathi, V.A. *Śaiva Siddhānta as expounded in the Śivajñāna-Siddhiyār and its Six Commentaries*. Madras: University of Madras, 1974.

Dhavamony, Mariasusai. *Love of God according to Śaiva Siddhānta: A Study in the Mysticism and Theology of Śaivism*. Oxford: Clarendon Press, 1971.

Doniger, Wendy. See O'Flaherty, Wendy Doniger.

Dorai Rangaswamy, M.A. *The Religion and Philosophy of Tēvāram*. Madras: University of Madras, 1958.

Dubianski, Alexander M. *Ritual and Mythological Sources of the Early Tamil Poetry*. Groningen: Egbert Forsten, 2000.

Gaston, Anne-Marie. *Śiva in Dance, Myth, and Iconography*. Delhi: Oxford University Press, 1982.

Gengnagel, Jörg. *Māyā, Puruṣa und Śiva. Die Dualistische Tradition des Śivaismus nach Aghoraśivācāryas Tattvaprakāśavṛtti*. Wiesbaden: Harrassowitz, 1996.

Gopala Rao, Amancharla. *Lepakshi*. Hyderabad: Government of Andhra Pradesh, Archaeological Series no. 37, 1969.

Graefe, W. 'Legends as milestones in the history of Tamil literature,' in H.K. Hariyappa and M.M. Patikar, eds, *P.K. Gode Commemoration Volume*, Poona, 1960, 129–46.

Grinshpon, Yohanan. 'Inference and self: A note on Śaṅkara's cogito,' in press.

Guy, John. 'The Nataraja Murti and Chidambaram—Genesis of a cult image,' *Marg*, in press.

Halbfass, Wilhelm. *On Being and What there Is: Classical Vaiśeṣika and the History of Indian Ontology*. Albany: SUNY Press, 1992.

Handelman, Don. *Models and Mirrors: Towards an Anthropology of Public Events*. Cambridge: Cambridge University Press, 1990. 2nd edition: Berghahn, 1998.

———. 'The guises of the goddess and the transformation of the male: Gangamma's visit to Tirupati and the continuum of gender,' in D. Shulman, ed., *Syllables of Sky: Studies in South Indian Civilization in honour of Velcheru Narayana Rao*. Delhi: Oxford University Press, 1995.

Handelman, Don, 'Towards a braiding of frame,' in D. Shulman and D. Thiagarajan (eds), *Behind the Mask* (forthcoming).

Handelman, Don and David Shulman. *God Inside Out: Śiva's Game of Dice*, New York: Oxford University Press, 1997.

Hardy, Friedhelm. *Viraha-bhakti. The Early History of Kṛṣṇa Devotion in South India*. New Delhi: Oxford University Press, 1983.

Härtel, Herbert et al. *Die Meisterwerke aus dem Museum für Indische Kunst Berlin*. Stuttgart and Zurich: Belser Verlag, 1980.

Hart, George L., III. *The Poems of Ancient Tamil, their Milieu, and their Sanskrit Counterparts*. Berkeley: University of California Press, 1975.

Heesterman, Jan C. *The Inner Conflict of Tradition: Essays in Indian Ritual, Kinship, and Society*. Chicago and London: University of Chicago Press, 1985.

Hiltebeitel, Alf. *The Cult of Draupadī*. I. *Mythologies: From Gingee to Kurukṣetra*. Chicago: University of Chicago Press, 1988.

———. *Rethinking India's Oral and Classical Epics: Draupadī among Rajputs, Muslims, and Dalits*. Chicago: University of Chicago Press, 1999.

Irācamāṇikkaṉār, Ma. *Caiva camaya vaḷarcci*. Madras: Auvai nūlakam, 1958.

Jahn, Wilhelm. 'Die legende vom Devadāruvana.' *Zeitschrift der Deutschen Morgenländischen Gesellschaft* 69 (1915), 529–57; 70 (1916), 301–20; 71 (1917), 167–208.

Kailasapathy, K. *Tamil Heroic Poetry*. Oxford: Clarendon Press, 1968.

Kaimal, Padma. 'Shiva Nataraja: Shifting means of an icon.' *Art Bulletin* 81, no. 3 (1999), 390–419.

Kameswara Rao, V. *Select Vijayanagara Temples of Rayalaseema*. Hyderabad: Government of Andhra Pradesh, Archaeological Series no. 47, 1976.

Kapferer, Bruce. *The Feast of the Sorcerer. Practices of Consciousness and Power*. Chicago: University of Chicago Press, 1997.

———. 'The sorcery of consciousness,' *Social Analysis* (2002).

Kramrisch, Stella. *The Presence of Śiva*, Princeton: Princeton University Press, 1981.

Kulke, Hermann. *Cidambaramāhātmya. Eine Untersuchung der religionsgeschichtlichen und historischen Hintergrunde für die Entstehung der Tradition einer südindischen Tempelstadt*. Wiesbaden: Otto Harrassowitz, 1970.

Lawrence, David Peter. 'Argument and the recognition of Śiva: The philosophical theology of Utpaladeva and Abhinavagupta,' Ph.D. dissertation, University of Chicago, 1992.

Madras Tamil Lexicon. Madras: University of Madras, 1936.

Malamoud, Charles. *Cuire le monde. Rite et penśee dans l'Inde ancienne*. Paris: Editions La Decouverte, 1989.

———. 'A body made of words and poetic meters,' in D. Shulman and G.G. Stroumsa, eds, *Self and Self-Transformation in the History of Religion*, New York: Oxford University Press, 2002, 19–28.

Marriott, McKim. 'Hindu transactions: Diversity without dualism.' In B. Kapferer (ed.), *Transaction and Meaning: Directions in the Anthropology of Exchange and Symbolic Behavior*. Philadelphia: ISHI , 1976, 109–42.

———. 'Constructing an Indian ethnosociology,' *Contributions to Indian Sociology* (n.s.) 23 (1989), 1–39.

Masilamani, Eveline. See Meyer, Eveline.

Matilal, Bimal Krishna. *Perception: An Essay on Classical Indian Theories of Knowledge*. Oxford: Oxford University Press, 1986.

Mauss, M. 'Essai sur le don,' in *Sociologie et Anthropologie*. Paris: Presses Universitaires de France, 1950, 144–279.

Meyer, Eveline. *Aṅkāḷaparamecuvari*. Ph.D. dissertation, University of Heidelberg, 1984.

———. *Aṅkāḷaparamecuvari: A Goddess of Tamilnadu, her Myths and Cult*, Wiesbaden: Franz Steiner Verlag, 1986.

Mimica, Jadran. *Intimations of Infinity: The Cultural Meanings of the Iqwaye Counting System and Number*, Oxford/New York/Hamburg: Berg, 1988.

Mitchell, Stephen. *The Selected Poetry of Rainer Maria Rilke*, New York: Vintage Books, 1984.

Nabokov, Isabelle. *Religion against the Self: An Ethnography of Tamil Rituals*. New York: Oxford University Press, 2000.

Nārāyaṇa, Avvāri. *Lepâkṣi devâlaya caritra*. Bukkarāya samudramu, Anantapuram District, no date.

Narayana Ayyar, C.V. *Origin and Early History of Śaivism in South India*, Madras: University of Madras, 1974.

Narayana Rao, Velcheru and D. Shulman. *The Sound of the Kiss, or the Story that Must Never be Told: Piṅgaḷi Sūrana's Kaḷāpūrṇodayamu*, New York: Columbia University Press, 2002.

———. *God on the Hill: Temple Poems from Tirupati*, in press.

———. *Classical Telugu Poetry: An Anthology*, Delhi: Oxford University Press. 2002 (2).

Natarajan, B. *Tillai and Nataraja*. Madras: Mudgala Trust, 1994.

O'Flaherty, Wendy Doniger. *Asceticism and Eroticism in the Mythology of Śiva*, London: Oxford University Press, 1973.

———. *Women, Androgynes, and Other Mythical Beasts*, Chicago: University of Chicago Press, 1980.

Olivelle, Patrick. *Upaniṣads*, Oxford and New York: Oxford University Press, 1996.

Pachner, Regine. 'Paintings in the temple of Vīrabhadra at Lepakshi,' in Anna Libera Dallapiccola, with Stephanie Zingel-Avé Lallemant (eds), *Vijayanagara—City and Empire: New Currents of Research*, Wiesbaden: Franz Steiner Verlag, 1985, 1:326–43.

Padoux, Andre. *Vāc. The Concept of the Word in Selected Hindu Tantras*. Albany: State University of New York Press, 1990.

Pāskarat Tŏṇṭaimāṉ, To. Mu. *Veṅkaṭam mutal kumari varai. Pŏrunait tuṟaiyile*. Tirunelveli: Es. Ar. Cuppiramaṇiya Piḷḷai, 1967, reprinted 1971.

Piatigorski, A. *Materiali po istorii indiskoi filosofii*. Moscow: Izdatel'stvo vostochnoi literaturi, 1962.

Puṉṉaivaṉanāta Mutaliyār, Pu. Ci. *Cuvāmi nĕllaiyappar tiru kāntimati ampāḷ tevastāna varalāṟu*, Tirunelveli: Published by the Devasthanam, 1966.

Rajam, V.S. 'The duration of an action—Real or aspectual?,' *Journal of the American Oriental Society* 105 (1985), 277–91.

Ramanujan, A.K. *The Collected Essays of A.K. Ramanujan*. Edited by Vinay Dharwadker, Delhi: Oxford University Press, 2000.

———. 'Why an Allama Poem is not a riddle: An anthological essay,' in Galit Hasan-Rokem and D. Shulman (eds), *Untying the Knot: On*

Riddles and Other Enigmatic Modes, New York: Oxford University Press, 1996, 179–90.

———. 'The ring of memory: Remembering and forgetting in Indian literature,' Unpublished manuscript, 1993.

Reich, Tamar. 'Dāruvana,' Ms, Jerusalem, 1987.

Ruegg, D. Seyfort. 'The uses of the four positions of the *catuṣkoṭi* and the problem of the description of reality in Mahāyāna Buddhism,' *Journal of Indian Philosophy* 5 (1977), 1–71.

Sanderson, Alexis. 'Śaivism and the Tantric traditions.' In Friedhelm Hardy, ed., *The Religions of Asia*. London: Routledge, 1988, 128–72.

Schomerus, H.W. *Der Çaiva-Siddhānta, eine Mystik Indiens nach den tamulischen Quellen bearbeitet und dargestellt*. Leipzig: J.C. Hinrichs'sche Buchhandlung, 1912.

Shulman, David. 'On the prehistory of Tyagaraja-Siva at Tiruvarur,' *Art and Archaeology Research Papers* 13 (1978), 55–8.

———. *Tamil Temple Myths: Sacrifice and Divine Marriage in the South Indian Śaiva Tradition*. Princeton: Princeton University Press, 1980.

———. 'Terror of symbols and symbols of terror: Notes on the myth of Śiva as Sthāṇu,' *History of Religions* 26 (1986), 101–24.

———. *Songs of the Harsh Devotee: The Tēvāram of Cuntaramūrttināyaṉār*. Philadelphia: Department of South Asia Regional Studies, University of Pennsylvania, 1990.

———. *The Wisdom of Poets: Studies in Tamil, Telugu, and Sanskrit*, Delhi: Oxford University Press, 2001.

———. 'Concave and full: Masking the mirrored deity at Lepaksi.' To appear in Aditya Malik, Anne Feldhaus, and Heidrun Bruckner (eds), *In the Company of Gods: Günther-Dietz Sontheimer Memorial Volume*, Delhi: Manohar Publishers/IGNCA, 2003.

———. 'Axial Grammar.' To be published in a volume on Axial Age Civilizations, edited by Johann Arnason and Björn Wittrock (Leiden: E.J. Brill), in press (1).

———. 'Toward a new theory of masks,' in D. Shulman and Deborah Thiagarajan (eds), *Behind the Mask*, in press (2).

Shulman, David, and Deborah Thiagarajan (eds). *Behind the Mask*. Center for South and Southeast Asian Studies, University of Michigan, forthcoming.

Sivaramamurti, C. *Royal Conquests and Cultural Migrations in South India and the Deccan*. Calcutta, 1955.

———. *Nataraja in Art, Thought, and Literature*, New Delhi, 1974.

Sivaraman, K. *Śaivism in Philosophical Perspective: A Study of the Formative Concepts, Problems and Methods of Śaiva Siddhānta*, Delhi: Motilal Banarsidass, 1973.

Smith, David. *The Dance of Śiva: Religion, Art and Poetry in South India*. Cambridge: Cambridge University Press, 1996.

Sontheimer, Günther-Dietz. *Pastoral Deities in Western India*. Translated by Anne Feldhaus. New York: Oxford University Press, 1989.

———. 'Between ghost and god: A folk deity of the Deccan,' in Alf Hiltebeitel (ed.), *Criminal Gods and Demon Devotees: Essays on the Guardians of Popular Hinduism,* Albany: SUNY Press, 1989, 299–337 (1989a).

Stephen, Michele. 'The Mekeo "Man of sorrow": Sorcery and the individuation of the self,' *American Ethnologist* 23 (1996), 83–101.

Sūryarāyândhra nighaṇṭuvu. Hyderabad: Andhra Pradesh Sahitya Akademi, 1979.

Trawick, Margaret. *Notes on Love in a Tamil Family*, Berkeley: University of California Press, 1990.

Türstig, Hans-Georg. 'The Indian sorcery called *Abhicāra*.' *Wiener Zeitschrift für die Kunde Südasiens und Archiv für Indische Philosophie* 29 (1985), 69–118.

Umāmakecuvari, Pu. Pa. *Nĕllaiyappar koyil*, Tirunelveli: South Indian Saiva Siddhanta Works Publishing Society, 1990.

Vajracharya, Gautama V. 'The adaptation of monsoonal culture by Ṛgvedic Āryas: A further study of the Frog Hymn,' *Electronic Journal of Vedic Studies* 3 (1997), Issue 2.

van Buitenen, J.A.B. *Studies in Indian Literature and Philosophy*. Delhi: Motilal Banarsidass and American Institute of Indian Studies, 1988.

von Stietencron, H. 'Bhairava.' *Zeitschrift der Deutschen Morgenländischen Gesellschaft* 1969, supplement 1, Vorträge, Teil 3, 863–71.

Yocum, Glenn E. ' "Madness" and Devotion in Māṇikkavācakar's *Tiruvācakam*,' in Fred. W. Clothey and J. Bruce Long (eds), *Experiencing Śiva: Encounters with a Hindu Deity*. New Delhi: Manohar, 1983.

Zimmer, Heinrich. *Myths and Symbols in Indian Art and Civilization*, Princeton: Princeton University Press, 1972.

Zimmerman, Francis. *The Jungle and the Aroma of Meats: An Ecological Theme in Hindu Medicine*. Berkeley: University of California Press, 1982.

Zvelebil, K.V. *The Smile of Murugan: On Tamil Literature of South India*. Leiden: E.J. Brill, 1973.

———. *Tamil Literature*, Leiden: Handbuch der Orientalistik, 1975.

Index